HYPER-SOCIALISED

Hyper-Socialised explores the challenges of late capitalist times for education systems, schools and teachers. It looks at how trends of accountability, 'teaching to the test', using pupil voice and reliance on network technologies are all connected to powerful social and economic forces, shaping the curriculum as it is taught in classrooms. Such forces threaten to overwhelm teachers but, in the right hands, they can also be harnessed to create, influence and teach a truly powerful curriculum for their students.

Presenting a historical view of curriculum change, the book examines how society, curriculum and teachers are linked. Using geography as an illustrative subject, the chapters investigate what influences teachers, to what extent they are in control of the curriculum, and what else is shaping it. Divided into two parts, it offers:

- An in-depth exploration of the relationship between society, teachers and the curriculum, including that *what* and *how* to teach remain wide open to debate
- Evidence-based research into the significance and implications of 'hyper-socialised' curriculum enactment for teachers and teacher education
- Four case study 'portraits' of geography departments and personal curriculum stories of each Head of Department
- Insights into the nature of teaching as a profession and how a crisis of teacher recruitment and retention may be addressed.

Written in clear and accessible terms, this book is an essential resource for teacher educators, subject teachers, headteachers and educational researchers who want to understand how and why schools and teaching are changing – and what this means for them.

David Mitchell is a lecturer in education at UCL Institute of Education (IOE). He taught geography in secondary schools and colleges before becoming a teacher educator. His current role is researching Geography education and leading the Geography Postgraduate Certificate in Education (PGCE) course at UCL-IOE. Prior to that, he led the Secondary PGCE programme at UCL-IOE (a programme which each year prepares up to 700 new High School teachers in 18 different subjects). He is interested in the influences over the school curriculum, teachers' roles as 'curriculum makers' and how teacher education can support curriculum leadership in schools.

HYPER-SOCIALISED

How Teachers Enact the Geography Curriculum in Late Capitalism

David Mitchell

LONDON AND NEW YORK

First published 2020
by Routledge
2 Park Square, Milton Park, Abingdon, Oxon OX14 4RN

and by Routledge
52 Vanderbilt Avenue, New York, NY 10017

Routledge is an imprint of the Taylor & Francis Group, an informa business

British Library Cataloguing-in-Publication Data
A catalogue record for this book is available from the British Library

Library of Congress Cataloging-in-Publication Data
Names: Mitchell, David, 1968- author.
Title: Hyper-socialised : how teachers enact the geography curriculum in late capitalism / David Mitchell.
Description: Abingdon, Oxon ; New York, NY : Routledge, 2020. | Includes bibliographical references and index.
Identifiers: LCCN 2019025370 (print) | LCCN 2019025371 (ebook) | ISBN 9781138339095 (hardback) | ISBN 9781138339101 (paperback) | ISBN 9780429441295 (ebook)
Subjects: LCSH: Geography--Study and teaching. | Curriculum change--Social aspects. | Teaching, Freedom of. | Capitalism and education.
Classification: LCC GF73 .M57 2020 (print) | LCC GF73 (ebook) | DDC 910.71--dc23
LC record available at https://lccn.loc.gov/2019025370
LC ebook record available at https://lccn.loc.gov/2019025371

ISBN: 978-1-138-33909-5 (hbk)
ISBN: 978-1-138-33910-1 (pbk)
ISBN: 978-0-429-44129-5 (ebk)

Typeset in Bembo
by Taylor & Francis Books

CONTENTS

FIGURES

TABLES

ACKNOWLEDGEMENTS

I am deeply grateful to the geography teachers who welcomed me into their schools, giving their time for me to interview them, attend meetings, access documents and observe lessons. My sincere thanks also to colleagues (and former colleagues) at UCL Institute of Education (IOE) for their support, guidance and interest in my work, particularly Clare Brooks, David Lambert, John Morgan and Jane Perryman. I am also very grateful to colleagues in the wider community of geography educators, in particular Eleanor Rawling and Graham Butt, who have given feedback, advice and encouragement to me over a number of years. Thank you all.

PART I

The origins of 'curriculum making' – why changing times matter

Introduction – Teaching in changed times

This book is about education in the current times – late capitalist times, and the challenges they present for education systems, schools and teachers. More than ever we need to ask: In this day and age, *what* shall we teach our young people? And then we have to ask: *How* can we make this teaching happen? These are *curriculum* questions and by curriculum, I mean the content, which is actually taught or 'enacted' by a teacher (rather than as outlined in a national curriculum, an examination specification, or in a textbook for example). Teachers therefore have a weighty responsibility to take frequent and significant decisions about what to teach – to 'make' the curriculum taught in their classrooms. This is both challenging and exciting. I believe there is an opportunity, and a necessity in changing times, for teachers to embrace a leadership role for the curriculum they offer to their students.

I am exploring the relationship between the curriculum and the teacher, because it is only the teacher who can *enact* the curriculum. This is true for the time being at least – computer algorithms cannot (yet) take the place of human beings in making the morally careful curriculum decisions on which education depends. However, it is less certain that subject teachers are 'making' a curriculum for their pupils, by which I mean that they are making careful, informed and balanced decisions about what to teach young people in a certain time and place. This distinction between *enacting* and *making* a curriculum is an important one, to which I return. My aim in this book is to shed light on *how* subject teachers are enacting the curriculum in the changed times in which we all live, work or go to school. Looking at geography, I want to understand what influences teachers, how far they are in control of the curriculum they teach and what else is shaping the curriculum. By deeper understanding of this, often overlooked, aspect of teaching, we can better support subject teachers to become the curriculum leaders (and 'curriculum makers') we need.

I have studied and researched *how* geography teachers are enacting their curricula. This book draws on my findings to describe in detail how teachers enact the geography curriculum in four case study geography departments. I present what is influencing their work and how they navigate through challenges and pressures of changing times. But perhaps more importantly, my overall analysis of curriculum (at the level of classrooms and school geography departments) shows that current global scale social-economic structures are shaping curriculum enactment significantly. I argue that there is a distinctive process happening, which I call 'hyper-socialisation'. In this introduction and through this book I hope to make clear what I mean by this and the implications of 'hyper-socialised' curriculum enactment for schools, teachers and teacher education. To help explain and illustrate my argument, I will begin with a vignette of a geography lesson I observed during my research, and an interpretation of what the lesson reveals.

Sian's lesson – an illustrative example

It is 10am on a Friday morning in May at a High School in London, England. The school has had its challenges in recent years with difficult behaviour, struggling to achieve consistently above national average results and the 'good' or 'outstanding' inspection grades (which will make it more attractive to parents choosing between local schools), and quite a high turnover of teachers. It has well over a thousand pupils and a comprehensive intake serving the local community (non-selective). We could call it a fairly 'typical' London school of its time – to the extent that such a thing exists.

A class of thirteen year olds have just begun a geography lesson. Ms Hall (Sian) is their teacher. She is also the Head of Geography at the school. She's an experienced teacher and dedicated to helping her students. She's kind but firm, conscientious and very hard working. She is enthusiastic about geography and a team player – she's very aware of school policies and she respects them. Like all teachers at the school, Sian is regularly visited by members of the senior management team or 'SMT' who take 'learning walks' around the school. On these walks the managers pause at classrooms, observing through the large windows – making classrooms visible from the corridors (which have become commonplace in modern school buildings) – to check that policy is being followed, for example, that the teacher is not talking for too much of the lesson and the children are learning 'actively'.

As the children enter Sian's classroom, the lesson objectives – the 'LOs' – are already on the classroom screen (an interactive whiteboard). The lesson title is 'What can we do to develop sustainability?'. Sian settles her class and explains that it is their final lesson in a unit called 'wild weather' and involves investigation and evaluation (words in the LOs). Throughout the lesson there is much attention to language and the learning skills or conceptual tools of learning, such as 'how to evaluate'.

A PowerPoint slide shows pictures to prompt the students' task of working in groups to come up with examples of (or ideas for) what can be done to improve environmental sustainability. The students are engaged and 'on task'. Sian is attentive to them, using skilful classroom technique to encourage, give support and manage behaviour. The students discuss ideas in groups for the national scale (fewer wars, setting rules and limits) and for the individual scale (less electricity use, ride bicycles, walk to school, use renewable energy sources). They have less to say about the global scale. Sian brings the class to her attention and debriefs the activity. She gives much attention to helping the students think about the way they are learning. She asks, 'How did you find this task? Easy? Hard?' Then the class discuss how they might limit their own contribution to global warming.

The lesson proceeds to a card sort task in which statements are to be sorted into a category of responsibility (see Figure 1).

This leads to discussion on tables. Sian debriefs the activity asking, 'Who had the most responsibility for reducing global warming?'. And she probes further as students offer responses, to reach conclusions that some actions must be enforced by governments, but that individuals can take actions (she uses the example that she cycles to work herself). A new slide defines sustainable development and this is discussed in relation to the previous activity.

The lesson moves on to an activity in which students must leave their seats to gather information from sheets that have been stuck up around the walls of the room. Their task is to investigate what is happening in some different countries to reduce global warming. Each sheet gives the detail of a scheme, with photographs or diagrams. Students have a 'data recording sheet' in the form of a map with boxes to write in, summarising each scheme in their own words. There are seven schemes in all, from five continents. They include, for example, using bio-ethanol in cars in Brazil, solar power to dry crops in Uganda, and locally made wind turbines for power in Tamil Nadu. The task takes about ten minutes and the students appear very engaged by it, with a sense of purpose and urgency as they gather the information.

Sian then leads questioning and probes students' answers to help them to evaluate the schemes. She asks which of the governments are the most sustainable and doing the best job and which the worst? This leads to more whole class discussion, with Sian carefully involving a wide range of children in her questioning. The concept of cost-benefit is applied to reducing greenhouse gas emissions (such as

Individual	National	International
provide renewable energy resources	cycle lanes	high taxes
raise petrol prices	use public transport	build energy efficient
homes	buy locally sourced food	wash clothes at lower temp
	pledge to cut carbon emissions	

FIGURE 1 Card sort activity

through changes to transport and lighting). The problem of secondary, knock-on effects, which are not as sustainable as first seems, is discussed. Finally, the students are asked to evaluate by justifying what they see to be the most and least sustainable of the examples. Individuals are warmly praised and the lesson ends.

In many ways this is a good geography lesson and is even exemplary for the teachers' classroom management, pace and structure and high levels of engagement (at least at surface level). But I am interested in the *subject curriculum* here – that is to say, *what geography* is being offered – and what is influencing that curriculum enactment. This is just one lesson of many I observed in my research, a snapshot of one group of children's geography curriculum, but nonetheless it illustrates some common themes I found across the geography departments I researched. Some questions helpful to consider here are: *What geography are the children learning? Where have these ideas come from?* and *What structures are influencing the curriculum as enacted?*

The geographical concepts in the lesson are: people/nature interaction (including sustainability), scale (local, national and global scales of human action in relation to environmental change), space and place (world maps and case studies are used to locate and contrast a range of human development projects with human and environmental impacts). There is also a focus in the lesson, which is not on the school subject, but is about the children 'learning to learn' – in the emphasis on generic skills (such as evaluation and investigation) and what Sian calls 'basic skills' of listening, following instructions and co-operating in a group. It is also striking how 'active' this lesson is – broken into a number of short tasks, which involve the students talking in groups and even physically moving in the room. What is also striking is the 'drift' in the geography curriculum as planned (intended) and as enacted. The unit is the last of a weather and climate unit, but there is not much about weather and climate in the lesson. The focus has shifted to sustainability, including the relationship of governance and individual behaviour. It is a good and successful geography lesson in many ways – it engages children in thinking about environmental responsibility (and I think geography lessons should fully explore the people-nature relationship) but has it drifted away from the intended geography curriculum of understanding weather and climate? We may ask, what is influencing the curriculum here? And, how far is the teacher in control of what gets taught?

A closer look shows that the ideas (for this part of a geography curriculum) came *through* Sian. When asked later about the lesson, she explains she found it ready-packaged on the Royal Geographical Society (RGS) schools' website. From the way Sian taught the lesson so assuredly, it appeared that she had designed it herself, but in fact, another teacher (or teachers) had designed this for sharing, online, among the geography teaching community. The geographical data in the lesson (the case studies of sustainable development projects) comes from a development-focused non-governmental organisation (NGO), which in turn sourced some material from the World Bank. A brief examination therefore reveals how the internet allows the rapid sharing of curriculum materials and plays a key role in determining what gets taught. The internet plays a role in: where and from whom geographical data comes; how (and how far) geographical knowledge is re-contextualised by the teacher; and how lessons and teaching ideas are shared and recycled.

When I interviewed Sian, she talked about her ideas about education, particularly the importance of keeping the subject 'relevant' to the children. This seemed to be a stronger personal driver than the geographical concepts and contexts from her academic background. Her degree was a joint honours course, which included geography. Sian was enthusiastic about how geography constantly changes and she had a vision of taking these children 'out of their London bubble' to broaden their horizons, but she did not talk about her academic background as a strong influence on her school teaching and curriculum thinking. Sian may be applying some personal agency to achieve her vision for the curriculum, but this lesson also reveals wider structural influences shaping the curriculum as enacted for these young people.

Structures influencing the enacted curriculum

To consider the wider influences (the structures) operating here it is helpful to focus on *how* the lesson (this piece of curriculum) is enacted. Sian's lesson is illustrative, but these are common themes across the departments I observed in my research, so here I will begin to generalise across those observations. Lessons use Microsoft PowerPoint as a convenient way to plan, store and share the lesson between teachers, as well as the mode of presenting the lesson and resources to the class. Teachers 'pull off' the PowerPoint lesson from 'the system' (the shared network drive). PowerPoint serves not only to 'deliver' the lesson, but to plan, store and share it with the other teachers of geography in the school (not all of them geographers) so the busy teachers can 'deliver' each lesson with minimal preparation from one year to the next. The internet is significant. Lessons are often sourced from websites and online support communities so we can rarely trace the original lesson author.

Lessons pay attention to generic skills with 'learning to learn' challenging subject knowledge for priority. Schools emphasise 'learning skills' in the early stages of High School so that students can be well placed to succeed in their examination courses that run from 14 to 16 years old. Regardless of the subject content, learning is typically very 'active' and broken into a variety of task styles, materials and mix of whole class, individual and group work. This gives (as in Sian's lesson) an apparent energy and vitality to the room. When interviewed, Sian talked about 'nice lessons' as ones in which students spend time on a variety of activities. This was an example of such a lesson, which the senior management team would undoubtedly support. But there is a sense that much of the vitality in the room comes from the nature of the activity itself, which risks sidelining the intellectual vitality of developing subject (geographical) knowledge, which is less easy for a passing observer (such as a manager, a non-subject specialist) to appreciate.

Teachers are taking care to make the geography 'relevant' to the young people's lives and engaging for them. To use Sian's lesson, the sustainable projects explored in different countries are related back to what the children think about their own actions and values around sustainable behaviour. Much of the content in the lesson is co-constructed between the teacher and learners, and on the face of it this is a skilful teacher at work. But this 'relevance' – which extends into a focus on the immediate enjoyment of curriculum content – can be distracting. Note that there is a difference between immediate 'relevance' and the deeper notion of educational 'significance' for young people's futures. Using Sian's lesson to illustrate, here is a unit of geographical content one would imagine is intended for children to understand weather and climate as deeply as possible given limited curriculum space (for most this is the only time they will learn about weather and climate in their formal education). An imperative for engagement and 'relevance' is influencing or even leading the curriculum thinking here. The subject (in this case geographical) curriculum thinking by the teacher seems to be under constant threat of being squeezed out by other prerogatives.

We might hope that subject teachers are in control of the detailed decisions of what and how they will teach sequences of lessons (within certain constraints such as national curriculum coverage). But there are forces at work that are outside the teacher's control. There is an accountability pressure and school policy, which the teacher is obliged to follow. Taking Sian as an example, she had been too preoccupied with pushing her exam classes to perform, to devote the time she would like to curriculum planning for the younger age groups. There is challenging behaviour in the school and a worry that if lessons are not fun and 'relevant' to the young people then they will disengage. And there is technology (and the internet) influencing curriculum content as well as the way lessons are structured and presented to children. And Sian is frustrated that her geography team have so many other school responsibilities such that they can rarely meet. They rely instead on technology to share curriculum resources and plans on 'the system'.

Sian's lesson could, of course, be portrayed in different ways and you may be minded to think too much is being read into one lesson here. But the analysis on which this book is based is not about just one lesson. Data and analysis from four schools – lessons observed, interviews recorded, department meetings attended and curriculum plans collected – reinforce these themes. Something significant is going on. Influences beyond the classroom, in wider society, are playing out in school classrooms and affecting (even controlling) the teacher's choices about what and how she teaches.

Wider (global) forces

The influences or 'forces' at work here are within contemporary society and they are pervasive and global in reach. This book takes a lens of social theory and a long historical view to analyse the influences and controls over teachers. In particular, the notion that we are in late capitalism is central to the book's analysis of curriculum enactment. 'Late capitalism' is explored in more detail later in the book, but key is the notion that in late capitalism life is accelerated, more fluid, networked and highly financialised. Very significantly for teachers, late capitalism brings a somewhat schizophrenic conceptualisation of the individual. On the one hand, the post-Fordist economic world is driving a technical and competitive individualism, in which there is pressure to make a highly skilled and effective workforce. On the other, postmodern culture encourages a 'self-centred and narcissistic individualism' in which the person is a consumer (Hartley 1997: 3). The authority of subject-based knowledge is weakened in late capitalism and teachers must navigate the dual individual conception as they enact the curriculum in changing times.

My argument is that late capitalist society has a tendency to distort the teacher's curriculum enactment in what I describe as 'hyper-socialised' education (see Mitchell 2016 and 2017). Teachers are making curriculum decisions under excessive pressures and controls flowing from changes in wider society. Lambert argues that teachers cannot 'sub-contract' curriculum making (2018: 367). I agree, but there is a subtle distinction between curriculum *making* (led by the teacher's careful handling of subject, child and teaching), and curriculum *enactment* (what actually happens, that may or may not be within the control of the teacher). The latter, I argue, is often being 'contracted out' in the sense of sub-contracting the thinking behind 'what to teach' as a way to cope with the pressures of the times. These include increased accountability, rigid assessment processes, focus on 'effective' pedagogy, stronger 'pupil voice', and reliance on the internet as a support 'community'. Such conditions have been documented – but this book distinctively brings a social-economic lens to *explain* these conditions. It can be summarised in this way:

> Hyper-Socialisation describes the intensification of teachers' curriculum work and how teachers cope (when the demands exceed their personal curriculum making resources) by 'contracting out' curriculum making to others, particularly through internet reliance. This intensification is driven by a late capitalist society, which tries to hold a contradiction of seeing the individual (including the student) simultaneously as narcissistic consumer and competitive producer.

The teacher's agency

The hyper-socialised picture is not all negative and part of my aim for this book is to offer a way forward for subject-teacher development in late capitalism. Technology (globalisation of communication and the internet) is an opportunity as much as threat, for supporting teacher collaboration and curriculum development. However, and more importantly, it is only the *teacher* who can *enact* the curriculum (at least so long as physical schools and classrooms remain the main way that children are educated). Teachers do still have some agency to be 'curriculum makers' and this potential – a key professional role – must be not be downplayed. Among the pressure and controls over teachers found in my research, there is a story of 'resistance' as some teachers turn to their *subject* teacher identity to be 'curriculum makers'. Such teachers are beacons of hope for a high-quality education. This book makes a case for preparing and supporting subject teachers to take on a curriculum leadership role. Such teachers will create a more powerful subject-based curriculum for their learners (and be more likely to have fulfilling professional lives as a consequence). In England and many other countries there is a crisis not only of recruiting teachers, but retaining them in the profession. Hyper-socialised education helps to explain this. This book therefore speaks to anyone with an interest in training, developing and retaining teachers in an enhanced teaching profession where the curriculum question: 'What to teach?' is taken seriously.

Geography – an illuminative example

Geography is used as an illustrative subject throughout the book. However, the arguments presented can be applied to other subjects and I hope that both geographers and those interested in a different subject will find this book equally useful. Nonetheless, geography is significant as a subject choice to illustrate the relationship between the curriculum and the teacher. There are two main reasons for this and it is useful to explain these here, both for the interest of the geographers and for the benefit of other subject specialists, in relating the case of geography presented here, to your own subject.

First, there is a long tradition of geography teachers taking responsibility for the curriculum, and of geography educators advocating teacher-led 'curriculum development' notably in the Schools' Council curriculum development projects before the arrival of a statutory National Curriculum for England and Wales and the idea that teaching should be an 'activist' profession rather than a passive one (see Sachs 2003). Also teacher-led 'curriculum planning' models in geography education were emphasised in geography education (see Marsden 1976 and Graves 1979). In both these traditions of curriculum development and planning in geography, teachers are viewed as critically engaged in decisions over *what to teach* (often working in groups or as a community). Norman Graves' model exemplifies this tradition, placing the responsibility for the 'curriculum problem' squarely with the teacher.

> Essentially a teacher's curriculum problem should be that of deciding what he is going to try to get his students to learn.
>
> *(Graves 1979: 1).*

As the vignette at the beginning of this introduction illustrates, the current times are threatening to undermine the tradition of the geography teacher as critically engaged in curriculum matters. This is explored in Chapter 2 in a historical examination of how changing times have affected schooling and teachers. But it is sufficient to note here that 'curriculum making' can be read as a geography education response to a crisis of teacher professionalism, and a call for a renewed teacher professionalism as curriculum leadership.

The second significance of geography is that the *geography* curriculum has been particularly contested and is open to more change and variability than most other school subjects. This happens both between schools and over time. Roberts (1996) found that, even when a national curriculum is firmly prescribed, the geography curriculum can be different between schools depending on their 'philosophies of knowledge'. So, for example, one department may think of geography curriculum as a more open process of the child enquiring into an aspect of the world using geographical concepts, while another may see the curriculum as a closed set of facts that can be listed, taught and checked off. This leads to a very different enacted curriculum between one department and another.

Some other school subjects are similarly open to teacher interpretation, but Geography is distinctive in spanning the physical and social sciences giving a unique breadth of content. Furthermore, there has been much specialisation and fragmentation of the university discipline, such that one geography graduate can have a very different knowledge base to another. The school subject remains somewhat loosely coupled to the university discipline and weight given to aspects of geography wax and wane in the school curriculum over time. There is considerable inertia in the *school* geography curriculum despite the dynamism of the *university* discipline. Nonetheless, in the post war period, school geography has changed emphasis from regional study and landscape description to a systems and positivist approach with the 'new geography' of the 1970s, humanist and radical geographies of the 1980s, and ecological modernisation, postmodern geographies and geographic information system (GIS) since the 1990s. The geography national curriculum has been revised substantially several times and each version has been controversial and contested (see Lambert and Hopkin 2014). Thus, the teacher *needing to be* an active 'curriculum maker' is of profound importance to the quality of a child's geographical education (and, I suggest this is so to some degree for all other school subjects).

The notion of curriculum making originates from geography education – and I do not think this is coincidental. Lambert and Morgan argue that geography is distinctive as a 'curriculum resource' (2010: 46) in school because the discipline evolves in ways that other disciplines do not. The phrase 'curriculum making' became widely known in the geography education community following the publication of the Geographical Association (GA)'s manifesto for geography education in 2009 entitled 'a different view'. However, the notion of curriculum making was emerging before the manifesto 'launched' the idea widely to geography teachers and educators (or at least to those engaged with the GA) in 2009. In their book, which laid the ground for curriculum making, Morgan and Lambert (2005) argue that the geography curriculum is *produced* through the subject, the classroom (with students) and the teacher. The combination of these three concerns is needed for 'curriculum–thinking' (2005: 58). Other geography educators have also contributed to the idea of curriculum making. Brooks (2006) links the term to the Department for Education and Skills (DfES) geography focus group, which referred to 'curriculum making' as 'the curriculum which is experienced by students and made by teachers in school' (DFES 2005, quoted in Brooks 2006: 77).

And so, 'curriculum making' although originating as a geography educational idea, has value as a model for teachers and teacher educators of all school subjects. Every subject has (to a greater or lesser extent) a dynamic and evolving disciplinary base. Every subject teacher must ask the same questions of: 'Who am I teaching?', 'What content should I teach? (Why does it matter?)' and 'How shall I teach this?'

The 'research problem' – where is the geography?

My argument that education and curriculum enactment has become 'hyper-socialised' is based on research I conducted in 2012 to 2017. I am a geography teacher educator (a former High School geography teacher) and the starting point for my research was my concern that geography teachers, under ever greater pressure in school, have become distracted from thinking about the geography content of their lessons. I am not alone in this concern. In 1997 Marsden warned that state intervention in curriculum and league tables of performance were exacerbating the problem of 'taking the geography out of geography education' (1997: 241). Ofsted (2004, 2011) and Roberts (2010) found that many school geography lessons lack challenge for pupils, despite the potential of the subject's conceptual framework.

Curriculum making offers a model for teachers to begin to tackle the problem of 'taking the geography out of geography education'. Lambert and Morgan (2010) argue that 'curriculum making' can re-balance teachers' attention to the subject (as well as the student's needs and teacher choices) and therefore strengthen the knowledge component of their education. The argument for curriculum making is supported by theoretical work to explain how school subjects offer 'powerful knowledge' or more precisely 'powerful disciplinary knowledge' (PDK) (Young and Muller 2010), which students may gain through education. 'Subject knowledge' holds very different meanings to different people and has been appropriated by different groups for different purposes. For example, from cultural restorationists, who see subject knowledge as fixed and backward looking, to radical educators, who see subject knowledge as a critical lens to interrogate from and for whom controlling knowledge is being projected (this is explored more in Chapter 2). PDK is also a nuanced concept and as it has become more commonly used and referred to as 'powerful knowledge', the term risks being similarly appropriated. But PDK is a significant concept and a necessary component of the notion of curriculum making. This is explained further in Chapter 2.

I am sure it is now apparent that I think curriculum making is a good idea! The big problem that this book explores is that curriculum making does not necessarily happen. However good their intentions to help young people, however skilful in the technical craft of the classroom, and even if they begin with a strong personal subject disciplinary knowledge base and get good examination results for their pupils, we cannot assume that teachers are curriculum makers. Put another way, we cannot assume that curriculum making is an inevitable part of the process of teaching a subject.

Teachers are not fully autonomous curriculum makers because they work in a system of curriculum controls including examination and accountability arrangements, financial constraints, inspections and so forth (see Oates 2011) and they have limited agency over a curriculum, which is always linked to the society of the time (see Bourdieu and Passeron 1977, Huckle 1985 and Morgan 2002). I am particularly concerned with the influence of wider society. My research explores geography teachers' agency to 'make' the curriculum in times when the teacher's responsibility has moved away from curriculum thinker toward teaching and learning 'technician' (see Moore 2004, Weber 2007, Connell 2009, Goepel 2013, Mitchell and Lambert 2015). My research asks: *'what is the relationship between recent times and curriculum making?'*

The relationship between the current times and curriculum making cannot be easily tested, measured or proven because both are complex, nuanced and open to interpretation. However, the relationship can be explored by producing detailed case study descriptions of curriculum making and interpreting these descriptions through the lens of society-economy (in particular, schooling in late capitalism) to draw conclusions about how curriculum making is influenced by the times. My research produced case studies (of four geography departments) and the personal curriculum making stories of each Head of Department. The themes were constructed by a combination of induction, allowing the description to be built up from the data itself, and by analysing literature in the field of geography education and curriculum studies with the lens of social and economic change over time.

The meanings of 'current times' and 'curriculum making' are examined in more depth in Chapters 2 and 3; however, they can be briefly outlined here. Lambert and Morgan (2010) describe curriculum making as the 'in between work' of the longer term 'curriculum planning' and 'curriculum development' and the shorter term 'lesson planning' (2010: 50). Curriculum making is best understood as a diagram (2010: 50) showing three 'pillars' of the teacher's concern. These are geography (the subject), student experiences and teacher choices. In 2012 the diagram was adapted by the Geographical Association to show the teacher acting within an overarching concern for the discipline of Geography (see Figure 2).

The 'current times' cannot be defined by measured time alone (for example, 'twenty-first century') as this is inadequate to capture a distinct phase of social-economic life. Some notable critical accounts of curriculum in recent times, refer to the society and economy of the times as 'neoliberal' (for example Apple 2004, Kelly 2008, Fielding and Moss 2011, and Pring 2013) others refer to the times as 'late capitalist' (including Hartley 1997 and Morgan 2011). My research uses the lens of late capitalism to examine curriculum making. The terms neoliberal and late capitalism are linked, and within the main lens of late capitalism used in my research, there is scope to draw on a neoliberal analysis at times (as is the case in some literature, including Hartley 1997).

Connecting the immediate challenges and concerns of teachers 'on the ground' to a bigger picture of societal change is not an obvious priority for educational researchers concerned with teachers and teaching. This is particularly true for those concerned with school effectiveness and improvement – a government priority in England in recent years (although, in a welcome recent development, Amanda Spielman, Head of the school inspectorate of England and Wales, has called for more attention on curriculum). But raising the gaze outside schooling and education is important to understand how the curriculum is enacted.

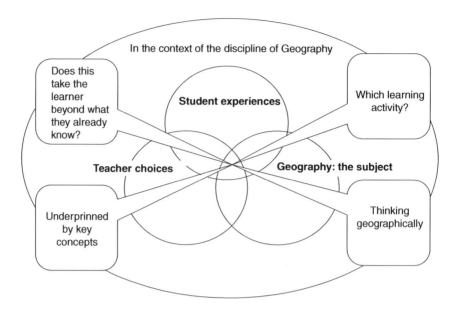

FIGURE 2 'Curriculum making'
Source: based on the description in the Geographical Association's manifesto (Geographical Association 2009) and discussed by Lambert and Morgan (2010)

A social-economic lens

A social-economic analysis of my research problem is important because curriculum making cannot happen unless two conditions are fulfilled. These two conditions become more difficult to achieve as late capitalism extends. The conditions are, first, the teacher must adopt a *professional self-image* as 'curriculum maker', taking responsibility for knowledge in the curriculum and engaging with their subject discipline (Mitchell and Lambert 2015, Firth 2013). Such a professional self-image will require a change from a model of teacher professionalism as 'learning technician', which has become embedded in many schools in response to accountability driven by the marketisation of schools (see Connell 2009, Goepel 2013, Mitchell and Lambert 2015). This marketisation of schooling is deepening in late capitalism. And secondly, the teacher needs *sufficient freedom* to make meaningful curriculum decisions. In late capitalism 'performativity' increases with consequent managerial control over teachers (see Hartley 1997 and McCullough, Helsby, and Knight 2000) and bureaucratic controls over teachers extend, for example, to the statutory National Curriculum, accountability arrangements and teacher training.

Society and economy have power over curriculum, which limits the potential of teacher agency in late capitalism and indeed in any given historical period (Bourdieu and Passeron 1977, Huckle 1985, Morgan 2002) so that even if the teacher can negotiate relative freedom to make a curriculum at the local level, wider society will always be an influence. Even the nature of their subject and how the student and 'good teaching' is conceived (the three pillars of curriculum making according to Lambert and Morgan, 2010) are in part a function of society at that time. Late capitalism permeates all aspects of society including these three 'pillars' of curriculum making. But on a more positive note, we must recognise, that society and curriculum are in a *dialectical* relationship (each constitutes and reinforces the other – see Bourdieu and Passeron 1977). This means that if teachers and an educational community can assert agency over curriculum, potentially we can change society for the better. Put another way, the society-curriculum dialectic offers hope that teachers and educators are not powerless to effect change in the globalised world of late capitalism.

Curriculum making offers a model of the teacher's curriculum role and responsibility, which Lambert and Young (2014) argue could revitalise education by placing 'powerful knowledge' at the heart of schooling (see also Firth 2011a, 2011b). However, we need to recognise that curriculum making is an idealised situation, subject to caveats and controls, which are connected to the late capitalist times. To move toward a better understanding of curriculum making in practice and how it can flourish, there is a need to know what is influencing teachers and how they are responding to the pressures of the times as they make the curriculum. This book contributes an original analysis of 'hyper-socialised' curriculum enactment in late capitalism.

The research basis of the book

I collected data from four London schools from teacher interviews, lesson observations, department meetings and curriculum plans. These were analysed by applying the curriculum making model and four case studies were constructed as 'portraits' of curriculum enactment in the contrasting geography departments. Common themes were identified inductively across the case studies and interpreted through the theories of curriculum making (ibid) and social theory (notably that of schooling in late-capitalist society, Hartley 1997) to draw conclusions about how curriculum making can be influenced by the changing times. The in-depth interviews gave insight into the human 'stories' behind the ideal of curriculum making. These stories tap into the distinctive power of narrative research – which is to better understand 'big' theories like late capitalism and curriculum by exploring the lived experience of teachers. The result, presented in this book, is both rich 'real life' accounts of teachers as curriculum enactors, showing that the teacher (still) matters (teacher agency over the curriculum exists and this can be nurtured) and to argue that there is a common phenomenon revealed – of hyper-socialisation.

How the book is structured

The book is structured in two parts. Part 1 explains the notion of curriculum making and its origins. A historical view of curriculum change shows how society, curriculum and teachers are linked. Then the current times are examined and I draw on a range of contemporary social theories to describe life in late capitalism and particularly what this means for teachers, students and education, with a focus on the teacher's curriculum enactment.

Part 2 provides the research basis for the hyper-socialisation, presenting four case study 'portraits' of geography departments in England and teachers' curriculum making 'stories'. The book concludes with the significance and implications of 'hyper-socialised' curriculum enactment for teachers and for teacher education.

The overall message I hope this book sends, is one of concern about the threat of 'hyper-socialisation' to the enactment of a 'quality' subject curriculum, but I also hope the reader is left with some sense of optimism and a way forward. The evidence I present shows the importance of teachers self-identifying as 'curriculum maker'. Curriculum leadership flourishes through good communication within a department, in a critical and open culture when there is a shared commitment to curriculum making. In both their initial training and ongoing professional development, teachers can reflect critically on the influences over their own curriculum enactment to develop attitudes, values and beliefs that support them becoming curriculum makers and curriculum leaders.

1

TEACHERS AND CURRICULUM AGENCY

The geography teacher's first concerns should be about curriculum – what to teach these young people and how this can be made to happen. In the introduction, I referred to the idea that the geography teacher is best placed for careful, informed and balanced attention to these concerns, resulting in the construction or 'making' of a geography curriculum, rather than a more passive 'delivery' of a given curriculum. The implicit message here is that 'curriculum making' (a process led and engaged with by the subject specialist teacher) will provide a 'better' education for the child. But what is a 'better' education, and who has authority to say what counts in that? The answers of course, are that it depends what you believe, what you value and on who has the power to decide. We cannot proceed far in any exploration of curriculum (including the teacher's role) without considering how different philosophies, traditions and ideologies affect the way education is conceived and therefore how curriculum fits in that big picture of how we imagine the educated person to be.

So, questions about what the teacher's professional role should be, are located in a wider debate about what it means to be 'educated'. 'The curriculum' is therefore always open to question and ultimately dependent on values held. This chapter argues that a 'social-efficiency' curriculum ideology dominates at present, which threatens to undermine the subject teacher's curriculum making. There is a tension between 'curriculum making' (an idealised model) and the curriculum as it is actually enacted in schools. Curriculum making requires teacher agency but society exerts a controlling influence over school, teachers and curriculum. In this book, I take a liberal-humanist philosophy of education. Such a position is consistent with recent arguments in subject education communities, for 'powerful', curriculum knowledge (see Young and Muller 2010) but is somewhat in tension with the dominance of testing, skills and 'learnification' (Biesta 1995) in the present schooling landscape. Put simply, in this chapter, I am exploring the question – does the teacher really have curriculum choices (agency to 'make' the curriculum)? To answer this it is important to first clarify my meanings of some key, contested concepts, in particular 'curriculum', 'curriculum making', educational (and curriculum) 'ideologies' and 'society' itself.

What is 'curriculum' and why are there different curriculum 'ideologies'?

Curriculum is sometimes accepted as a given thing – something conceived and written elsewhere, which the teacher simply delivers as efficiently as she can. But there are alternative perspectives on 'curriculum' coming from particular philosophies of education. To understand curriculum making, it is helpful to think of curriculum as a process and as enactment – the curriculum only becoming real as it is enacted. To understand the significance of this, consider how differently the standardised national curriculum set out for English schools is taught from one school to another (see Roberts 1996). The teacher matters hugely to what is actually taught (the enacted curriculum). The field of curriculum studies commonly distinguishes between curriculum as content and product, and curriculum as process and development (see Kelly 2008 and Schiro 2013). Curriculum making aligns more with a process model.

But the notion that the curriculum can be dictated from afar, and is largely independent of the teacher runs deep. The origins of such a notion (the content-product model) can be traced back to nineteenth century utilitarianism and social reform and to the enlightenment, in which science introduced analysis and 'effectiveness' to society. The content-product curriculum model became well-established in the early twentieth century through a Fordist model of production with Franklin Bobbit (1916) likening education to a steel factory and the notion of inputs, outputs and efficiency. Tyler (1949) influenced curriculum planning in England during the years of the post-war settlement, before economic recession destabilised educational thinking and called curriculum into question in the late 1970s. Tyler's model began with a set of questions, reflected in Graves' (1979) argument for curriculum planning. The assumption was that if the educational purpose is clear, then the curriculum can be designed to provide the knowledge, experiences and assessment to achieve that purpose. Tyler's (1949) model, built upon by Peters (1965) and Hirst (1974) established a notion of the 'rational curriculum', justifying subjects on the basis of providing the (objective) knowledge necessary for educational purposes.

The content-product model of curriculum has been much examined through the lens of value/belief systems or 'curriculum-ideologies' (see Davies 1969, Scrimshaw 1983, Roberts 1996, Ross 2000, Rawling 2001 and Schiro 2008, 2013) and linked to particular ways of thinking about education. These are: first, a behaviourist view of knowledge – particular knowledge will lead to particular behaviour; secondly, the ability to control the individual – the knowledge (the curriculum) is imposed from outside; thirdly, an emphasis on accountability – the delivery of content should lead directly to a measureable product; fourthly, an atomistic approach to planning (see Pring 2013, Kelly 2008 and Schiro 2008) – because content is pre-determined and not negotiated or contingent on the learner, it can be broken down into a detailed set of objectives to be 'delivered'.

The process-development model of curriculum, by contrast, takes a more 'learner-centred' perspective of education and a more social-realist view of knowledge. A learner-centred 'curriculum ideology' has a long history. Dewey (1916) is a key figure in the modern era, but the notion of education allowing the flourishing of the child's innate goodness can be traced to Rousseau (1762a, 1762b) and Pestalozzi in the early 1800s (Heafford 1967). The related notion of learning by experience or 'doing' can be traced further still, to Comenius' theory of education according to nature in the seventeenth century (1657). Piaget (1964) contributed to a resurgence in child-centred education in the 1960s and 70s and Howard Gardner's multiple intelligences (Gardner 1983) gave quasi-scientific support to learner-centred educators and spurred a fashion for schools emphasising 'learning styles' (White 2006).

Schiro (2008) argues that a learner-centred 'curriculum ideology' in the classroom is revealed by several characteristics. These include: a tendency to see the child as autonomous and to be guided, rather than instructed or coerced; learner choices; an experiential approach, emphasising activity; concern for the growth of the whole person; a tendency to integration of curriculum (rather than discrete subject teaching); focus on the present; avoidance of grading and measuring performance normatively. The learner-centred curriculum ideology sees curriculum more as process (than product) and tends toward knowledge as constructed such that growth and learning comes first, knowledge second. The learner's experience is sought and knowledge, to an extent is a by-product. Experience is sought over knowledge (Barth 1972: 108). Curriculum making reflects a learner-centred curriculum ideology by recognising that the teacher's curriculum thinking must account for the learner's experiences.

A learner-centred educational perspective should not be confused with 'learning' in contemporary schooling rhetoric. 'Learnification' (Biesta, 2013) can be argued to be the antithesis of a learner-centred philosophy. 'Learning' has been linked to the performativity agenda and 'deliverology' (Pring 2013). The term 'performativity' has origins in how language creates an identity (see Austin 1962, Butler 2010 and Kohn 1999). In curriculum literature 'performativity' is used to describe how teachers and students 'perform' to take on the identity of 'effective' teacher and learner by attaining measureable results (see Pring 2013 and Brooks 2016, 2017).

Popular theories of how attention to learning can transform teaching effectiveness, such as Claxton's 'building learning power' (1999) have been criticised as a performativity tool which, if used uncritically, can undermine curriculum making (Mitchell and Lambert 2015). The emphasis on learning in contemporary schooling is concerned with attainment and measurement of performance, which is a characteristic of the content-product curriculum model, which breaks curriculum into measurable objectives. 'Learning' as measured performance can be seen as 'social-efficiency' disguised by the gentler language of 'child-centredness' (Schiro 2008).

Curriculum 'as process' has been advocated as a response to the threat posed by the performativity of late capitalism. Kelly (2008) argues that the understanding and use of 'curriculum' has become anti-educational. Curriculum, he argues is understood only in narrow terms, as given content to be delivered effectively. In such an understanding, the teacher's role as curriculum 'maker' or 'thinker' is weakened. For Fielding and Moss (2011), Apple (2004) and Morgan (2011), such use of 'curriculum' amounts to government using schooling to control people for instrumental ends, to become willing producers and consumers. Kelly argues that thinking about curriculum as a process can restore curriculum balance and freedom for teachers to engage intellectually with education to develop the curriculum and a stronger, intrinsically worthwhile education for young people. Curriculum making resonates with Kelly's argument (2008).

Lambert and Morgan's (2010) notion of curriculum making is located more in learner-centred education and a process model of curriculum, than in the content-product model and a 'social-efficiency' curriculum ideology. However, 'curriculum making' is more nuanced than simply being a learner-centred and 'curriculum as process' argument. The notion of curriculum making arose from a concern for the 'emptying' of subject knowledge from schools (Lambert 2005, 2009a, Lambert and Morgan 2010), which helps to explain Lambert's care to locate geographical curriculum making within an argument for robust subject knowledge. Young and Muller's (2010) notion of three curriculum futures, in which a social-realist view offers 'powerful knowledge', which changes, but is not 'over-socialised' (2010: 14) has been incorporated in Lambert's notion of curriculum making (Lambert 2011, Lambert and Young 2014, Lambert and Biddulph 2015).

A social-realist epistemology underpins curriculum making. Social realism views knowledge as constructed and social, but also accepts there is an objective (realist) world and therefore boundaries between disciplines have to be made, to make sense of theoretical knowledge. A social-realist position guards against two positions, which both fail to give access to 'powerful knowledge'. These are excessive 'instrumentalism', which removes knowledge boundaries on the one hand, and excessive 'conservatism' on the other, which defers to the status quo and does not allow knowledge to evolve (Moore and Young 2001). A social-realist view of knowledge in education gives access to 'society's conversations' (Bernstein 1999) through powerful knowledge (Young and Muller 2010, Wheelahan 2010).

Curriculum making (Lambert and Morgan 2010) emphasises the teacher's agency and the connectedness of pupil, subject and teacher in a curriculum making process. The model lacks explicit reference to how the curriculum making process is situated in value/belief systems. As Apple (2004) stressed, hegemonic control can be hidden, unless the 'common-sense' and 'taken-for-granted' elements of schooling are critically deconstructed. However, using a four-fold value/belief system categorisation (Schiro 2008, 2013), the curriculum making model can be located in a combination of the 'scholar-academic' (which values subjects as allowing humanity to pursue a 'better' knowledge) and the 'child-centred' value/belief systems, with some elements of the 'social reconstructionist'.

An element of the 'social reconstructionist' 'value/belief' system is indicated by the importance which curriculum making attaches to independence from central control. For example, curriculum making requires the teacher's critical thinking and encourages practitioner research. Furthermore, there is an emphasis on the educational purpose of the subject, which can include for social change. Lambert and Morgan (2010) refer to geography and geographical knowledge as a 'curriculum resource', the purpose of which is education. Education, in their argument, is interpreted in different ways (including individual growth or social reconstruction) but not as the neoliberal goal of using schooling for economic efficiency and maintaining the status quo in society and economy. This leads me to the conclusion that 'social-efficiency' does not drive curriculum making.

So, 'curriculum' and the teacher's relationship to it is complex, contested and value-laden. But it is not controversial to say that teachers have a crucial role to play in the quality of the curriculum as it is enacted. (What 'quality' looks like will always be contested – although there are ways to examine 'quality' to which I return later in the book when I look at the potential of 'powerful knowledge' and 'capability' as tools to explore curriculum quality). Nor is it particularly controversial to say that, therefore, teachers should take on a leadership role and responsibility for the curriculum they enact. This leads us to the notion of 'curriculum making' as the fundamental role of the teacher.

What is 'curriculum making'?

'Curriculum making' is a theoretical model presented as a diagram by Lambert and Morgan (2010: 50) (see Figure 2 in the introduction). The great strength of the model is to show a balance of three sources of 'energy' in a process of 'making' the curriculum: the student's experiences; the subject; the teacher/teaching choices (Lambert, 2009a: 124). However – and absolutely key to the argument in this book – the model is distinctive from the teachers' curriculum work in practice (curriculum enactment). Curriculum making is very helpful as an idealised model to strive toward – but, it cannot be assumed that curriculum making necessarily takes place in such perfect balance in practice. The model hides many other influences and controls over the teacher's curriculum enactment. It is with this understanding that I explore the influences over teachers as they struggle to be the curriculum makers of the idealised model. But to grasp the notion of curriculum making as an ideal to aim towards, it is first necessary to understand how the model is conceived in relation to the teacher's professional role and a particular way of thinking about curriculum at different scales.

Scales of 'curriculum' and the curriculum making model

Curriculum making is located in an understanding of curriculum as process, rather than as predetermined or fixed content to be 'delivered' the 'balancing act' of attention to the three curriculum-making 'sources of energy' is an ongoing process by which a local curriculum evolves and it requires the teacher to think about 'curriculum' at different time scales and different levels of action. Oram (1973) uses the analogy of theatre to contrast perspectives on 'curriculum'. Curriculum can be as: envisioned (script writing); produced (rehearsed); and enacted (performed and experienced by actors and audience together). Curriculum can be as 'intention, plan or prescription' or as 'what does in fact happen' (Stenhouse 1975: 2). Ball and Bowe (1992) emphasise the crucial difference between curriculum as 'text' (planned and imagined) and as 'context' (played out in different schools). 'Curriculum', they argue, can only be understood when text and context are examined together. The implication is that teachers must play a part in making the curriculum (in context), as well as the part played by government policy, subject association guidance or textbook (as 'text').

The intended curriculum can be distinguished from the 'real' curriculum (see Oates 2011, Mitchell 2013a and Stenhouse 1975). Oates (2011) emphasises curriculum as the pupils' total experience, not just the teaching, and includes unintended learning outcomes. Roberts (1996) validated the importance of considering the teachers (as the geography department) and the local context when she showed that the National Curriculum, as enacted and embodied in schools, is not a uniform 'national' experience, but is strongly mediated by differences between teachers, departments and schools. Different values and department 'cultures' or 'ideologies' play a significant part in the enacted curriculum (Roberts 1996: 189). This reminds us once more that the teacher matters – we cannot assume the 'delivery' of a standard, documented curriculum, whether or not that curriculum is prescribed in great detail and accompanied by supporting textbooks or materials.

Curriculum making is located in view of 'curriculum' as enactment at a local level. The teacher's role is emphasised in the enactment, more than curriculum as learner experience, which may be unintended and out of the teacher's control. While curriculum making recognises some co-construction of knowledge between teacher and learner by being underpinned by a social-realist epistemology (Bernstein 1999, Lambert and Young 2014), curriculum making does not emphasise the learner as controlling curriculum. Rather, curriculum making forms part of a wider argument for the teacher to take professional responsibility or a 'curriculum leadership' role (Mitchell and Lambert 2015: 377).

The roots of 'curriculum making' – in geography education

Curriculum making builds on earlier notions of teacher-led curriculum development (Stenhouse 1975, McElroy 1980, Rawling 1996, 2001, Kent 2000, Sachs 2003, Mitchell 2006) and curriculum planning (Graves 1979, Marsden 1976) in geography education. In these notions, teachers are viewed as critically engaged in decisions over *what to teach* (often working in groups or as a community). Curriculum making concurs in viewing teachers as critically engaged in this curriculum question. Lambert and Morgan (2010) define curriculum making as the teacher's work 'in between' curriculum planning and curriculum development. The conception of a theory of curriculum making is therefore dependent upon these two earlier ideas. However, curriculum making differs in three main ways, first by emphasising every individual teacher's curriculum responsibility, secondly by the 'local' (classroom) scale of the process, and thirdly by the notion of balancing concern for the subject, the teaching and the student.

The emphasis on the teacher and the 'local' scale are clear in the literature. 'Teachers are the curriculum makers' (Lambert and Morgan 2010: 50). 'Curriculum making firmly places the ownership of the local curriculum in the hands of each geography teacher.' Brooks (2006: 77). The notion of the teacher as a dynamic actor builds on a long-standing tradition of geography teachers as actors shaping the curriculum in an 'activist profession' Sachs (2003), notably in the Schools' Council curriculum development projects before the statutory National Curriculum for England and Wales (Kent 1996, 2000 and Rawling 1996). In the 2000s, the Geographical Association favoured a 'local solutions' approach to curriculum development projects (Mitchell 2006: 150), but this still kept a notion of curriculum development as a long-term process, with teachers working together to produce materials that might be disseminated through the semi-formalised route of the subject association (Cordingley, Bell and Thomason 2004, Crombie White 1997).

Curriculum making is more fluid and immediate than the longer-term processes of curriculum planning and curriculum development. Curriculum making represents a dynamic, ongoing teacher's enactment of curriculum as process. It is not the same as lesson planning or curriculum planning but is the act of translating curriculum planning into lesson sequences (Lambert and Morgan 2010). The sequences should be 'driven by some broad aims and goals' (2010: 50). Curriculum making is thereby a shorter-term reflection of Graves' (1979) curriculum planning model. Catling describes curriculum making as 'medium-term planning' (2013: 17). Puttick makes a distinction between the very short-term acts of the teacher's re-contextualisation of subject knowledge in the classroom, and curriculum making at the level of whole schemes of work (2015b: 33).

Curriculum making emphasises teacher-student interaction more than 'curriculum planning' and 'curriculum development'. 'Young people's geographies' (Biddulph 2011a, 2011b, 2013) have highlighted the significance of the student and using 'student voice' (Biddulph 2012) in curriculum making. Biddulph (2013) asks 'Where is the curriculum created?' (2013: 129) and argues that curriculum making helps to show that curriculum is 'created' not by any single power or authority, but by the interaction of subject, student and teacher.

Curriculum making encourages teachers to see curriculum as praxis – an ongoing enactment of balancing the three equally important educational 'pillars' or 'sources of energy' (subject, child and teacher). These sources of energy are constantly changing. Curriculum making is therefore always contingent, requiring the teacher to be dynamic. Lambert has described teachers as 'the ultimate boundary workers' (2011: 257). This represents a shift from Graves' (1979) longer term, more stable or 'solid' curriculum planning to a more unstable, immediate or 'fluid' concept of curriculum making. Such a shift resonates with contemporary social theory, in particular, Bauman's (2001, 2005) notion of how life has become 'fluid' or 'liquid', faster, more intense and requiring more immediate responsiveness from people. Graves' model of curriculum planning assumes a stability to the geography teacher's position, allowing for advance planning. Lambert and Morgan's (2010) notion of curriculum making is a more immediate and dynamic representation of the teacher's work.

Curriculum making, then, has evolved (in geography education) from a long tradition of the teacher as deeply committed to a relationship with the subject curriculum. Curriculum planning and development laid the foundations for the contemporary (or post-modern may be more appropriate) idea of curriculum making for a more fluid, uncertain and speeded-up world. In this book, I am arguing that the nature of current society – the times in which we all live – affects curriculum enactment, and that we must understand this if we are to support teachers to make a curriculum of high quality and contemporary significance for young people. Later in the book, I analyse four case studies of curriculum enactment in light of social theory and social change to develop this argument. However, at this point it is important to clarify what I mean by 'society'.

What is 'society'?

I refer to 'society' as the structures and patterns of human relationships, which operate more widely than the geography department or school. The social structures and patterns, which define wider 'society', operate at the global scale (including late capitalist and neoliberal society) but are mediated at the national and local scale, as politics and culture are a part of the structuring of social relationships. The teacher, the department and the school operate 'within' the wider social structures, patterns, norms and expectations of the particular time. The notion of 'structure' is central to the meaning of society used in my research and therefore warrants closer examination here.

In discussing contemporary social theory and answering the question: 'What is society?' Elliott (2009) emphasises the structures and structuring of social interactions and social institutions. Key social theory drawn upon in my research includes Giddens (1990, 2000) and Bourdieu (1984) who propose theories of how the actions of the individual are structured by, and linked to, their deep and sub-conscious understanding of societal norms – a sense of 'the rules of the game'. Theories of structuration build on the seminal work of Saussure (1916), which showed how people are not free agents, but constantly read 'signs' around them, interpreting these signs and 'signifiers' to make meaning and to act accordingly. Saussure (ibid) emphasised the role of language as 'signs', which structure the thoughts, actions and lives of people.

Foucault (1972) makes visible the unseen 'layers' of structure on which our assumptions about 'normality' are based. Significantly for my research, Foucault (1977) shows how social structures exert power and control over the individual. To live in any society, we all (to some extent) 'self-discipline' to avoid falling foul of what we understand to be normal or correct ways to behave.

The research on which this book is based also draws on postmodern social theory, particularly Bauman (2001, 2005) and Baudrillard (1994) and the intersection of political economy and postmodernity, in the notion of 'late capitalist society' (Jameson 1992). While it does not contradict a definition of society as structures and patterns, which affect human thought and behaviour of the times, postmodernity draws attention to tensions and contradictions in these structures and patterns.

Also significant for my research is a common understanding that 'society' involves some degree of collaboration. So, while theories of structuration, control and even domination can give a rather bleak picture of what 'society' is and how it functions, most definitions of 'society' emphasise an enabling function – a shared understanding by people of the society at that time, so that they can live and work together.

The findings of my research suggest that 'society' at the wider scale is closely reflected at the local scale, both by controlling structures such as Foucauldian 'surveillance' and the 'self-disciplining' of teachers and the collaboration of geography teachers as they enact the curriculum. This 'playing out' of wider structures as observable patterns in school and curriculum enactment becomes evident in the case studies and the overall analysis I offer later in this book. Ultimately, teachers do have some agency and can make curriculum choices that enhance curriculum quality. But, there is a something of a battle to be fought against powerful wider influences, which can draw teachers away from the beautifully simple balance of the curriculum making model. The goal of balanced curriculum making is hard won by teachers.

Taking a historical view of the society-curriculum relationship

To really understand the relationship between society, curriculum and teachers, a historical 'long view' is enormously helpful. Taking such a view is not only interesting to chart the swings in the ideas and practices of schooling and curriculum 'enactment', it shows that society and curriculum are always connected – in a two way or dialectical relationship such that each reproduces the other. A historical analysis of schooling can also be used to produce a set of themes, as I do here, which becomes an analytical tool to examine the current situation. The next chapter offers such an examination of the society-curriculum relationship from the late nineteenth century to the present.

2

LESSONS FROM THE PAST – SOCIETY, CURRICULUM AND TEACHERS

It is easy for teachers to imagine that they are making 'rational' decisions about what and how to teach a subject (like geography). But, to a large extent, we are all controlled by the times in which we find ourselves. This chapter takes a historical 'long view' to show that society, curriculum and teachers are always connected. The theory of a society-curriculum dialectic (Bourdieu and Passeron 1977) suggests that the teacher has limited agency in curriculum choices, but she is nonetheless empowered by a realisation of how 'the times' influence her work. Examples of the 'ideological battleground' of education in which the teacher has played a curriculum-making role in the past include a socialist educational movement of the late nineteenth century in response to poor working conditions and imperialist expansion, and a radical curriculum movement in the 1980s calling for teachers to develop a curriculum for social change. This chapter concludes with the growing dominance of a neoliberal ideology from the late 1980s into the early twenty-first century (late capitalism) in which teachers are increasingly restricted and controlled, so that their agency as curriculum makers is diminished.

Locating curriculum making – a historical analysis of curriculum and society

The emphasis on the teacher in curriculum making can be understood as the continuation of a tradition of teacher-led geography curriculum development. However, I argue that curriculum making is also a response to the threat of the de-professionalisation of subject teachers in the contemporary educational climate of performativity. The argument is underpinned by the position I take (justified by a historical analysis) that the teacher's role in the curriculum at any given time is largely controlled by the society in which they are located. I present five recurring themes, present in each historical phase. These are power/control, conflict, scale, change and value/belief systems. These themes help to understand how society influences teachers and how curriculum making can be understood as a product of conflict between educational values and beliefs and as a call for teachers to shape the curriculum locally, as they enact it in their own classrooms.

Ross (2000) Walford (2001) and Schiro (2008) identify four periods of curriculum change and I use these to base my historical analysis in this chapter. They are:

1.   Pre-1920 (ideas of education, schooling and geography curriculum).
2.   1920–1976 (social democratic consensus, into the 'golden age' of teaching and geography for modernisation).
3.   Mid-1976–1988 (crises of capitalism, the 'new sociology of education' and debate over the roles for geography education).
4.   Late 1988–2008 (neoliberal hegemony and the 'emptying' of subjects).

More recently the accounts of Morgan (2011) Lambert and Young (2014) and Mitchell and Lambert (2015) identify a fifth period:

1.   2008–2016 (a new crisis of capital and a 'knowledge turn' in the curriculum).

Each period is now discussed in turn to construct five recurring themes in the society-curriculum relationship.

Pre-1920 (ideas of education, schooling and geography curriculum)

The educational debates of the late nineteenth and early twentieth centuries (which saw school geography become established) make four key points. These are: a conflict between the needs and values of the ruling classes of imperial Britain and the utopian ideas driven from the deepening social problems of industrialisation; a school-driven foundation of geography as legitimate academic discipline; enlightenment and the domination of science as high status knowledge; and the ongoing influence of pre-enlightenment thinking, including the Greek philosophers and ancient belief systems.

Huckle (1985) argues that geography in the late Victorian age served the utilitarian needs of the upper classes in the exploitation of natural resources and to legitimate imperial expansion. With deepening social problems of industrial society in the late nineteenth century came socialist thought in the utopian ideals of Owen, Marx and Engels. Kropotkin (1885) brought an early notion of radical geography, proposing how geography should be anti-militarist, anti-imperialist, anti-capitalist, and fostering harmony and mutual aid.

The establishment of geography as an academic subject was driven upwards, from the needs of school geography teachers in the late nineteenth and early twentieth centuries, rather than downwards, from the university into school (Goodson 1998, Walford 2001). This is significant for the geography curriculum. The 'rational' school curriculum later argued for by Hirst (1974) and Peters (1965) views the university disciplines as leading the school curriculum in what Schiro (2008) calls a 'scholar academic curriculum ideology'. Goodson (1998) challenges the assumption that the university discipline of geography holds power over the school subject, arguing that the school-society relationship is dialectical, or 'two-way', such that school influences university geography and vice versa. Goodson's 'two-way' relationship has been challenged by the argument that a 'great divide' has developed between the university discipline and the school subject (Goudie and Spooner 1993, Stannard 2003).

Critiques of how curriculum can be distorted by the competitive marketisation of schooling are frequent in the twenty-first century, yet such was also the case in the mid-nineteenth century when elementary schools in England were given 'payment by results'. Victorian teaching of 'the facts' was encouraged by the state's 'payment by results' funding of elementary schools (Walford 2001). The geography curriculum was criticised by Her Majesty's Inspector of Schools:

> Geography teaching is sometimes too much restricted to the pointing out of places on the map and to the enumeration of such details as the names of rivers, towns, capes and political divisions.
>
> *(Her Majesty's Inspector of Schools 1885, quoted in Walford 2001: 38)*

With the recession of the 1890s, a reform movement in education and progressivism developed what Huckle (1988) calls a more 'humane pedagogy' which Schiro (2008) charts with the rise of the child-centred movement and experiential education, drawing on Dewey (1916). Huckle argues that these reforms still lie within his own theory of education serving the needs of the ruling class, there being just enough to adjust people to new forms of economy and society without threatening the underlying order.

Through this and each successive era, five themes are constructed from a historical perspective on the geography curriculum (Table 1).

1920 to mid-1970s – consensus, into the 'golden age' and geography for modernisation

This was a period of relative stability in education. There was consensus and a social settlement toward school and curriculum. This was a post-war 'golden age' of teacher autonomy that embraced modernisation. However, 'modernisation' was accompanied by a school geography often reactionary and backward looking (Huckle 1985, Morgan 2011). Toward the end of the period, the 'new sociology of education' was influential in the academic field of curriculum studies, arguing that subjects are social constructions, rather than 'rational' disciplines. This period thus shows both striking elements of change, and curriculum development, but also resistance to change.

Huckle (1985) argues that by 1920 working class resistance to the dominant capitalist class had been defeated. The lack of a viable technical or vocational alternative to academic subjects meant that a social democratic consensus was

TABLE 1 Themes from curriculum studies applied to the geography curriculum, pre-1920

Theme	Ways in which theme is constructed pre-1920
Power and control	Economic forces hold power over curriculum. The establishment of mass schooling and school geography was controlled by an elite class, driven by economic motives. The elevation of science to the highest status in school subjects in this period has been argued to be driven by the power of political economy rather than 'rational' human knowledge (Unwin 1992).
Conflict	Class conflict existed between utopian socialist education and schooling to preserve the status quo, and serving the interests of the elite. There was also conflict between viewing children as intrinsically 'good' to be nurtured, and seeing children as essentially a social threat to be controlled or 'mended'.
Scales of influence	The nation state became influential with mass schooling established. The influence of the global economy (imperial need for trade) was apparent in the early geography curriculum which focused on regions and their valuable resources, but the scale of the individual teacher was also influential as their needs shaped the discipline in the university (Goodson, 1998).
Value/belief systems	Different educational value/belief systems can be constructed in the conflicts over schooling and curriculum, particularly those of child-centred education, social reconstruction (in the utopian education movement), and social efficiency (education to serve social stability and economic growth). Social-efficiency dominated the period Huckle (1985), argues.
Change	The 1870 Reform Act changed education dramatically, with mass schooling established for the first time. The late nineteenth and early twentieth centuries saw geography change from an embryonic state of a collection of facts about the world, to a more coherent discipline based on the concepts of region and integration.

reached and persisted until the 1970s. School geography was able to capitalise on the relative autonomy of subject teachers, Huckle (1985) argues, but he also points to textbook and exam research showing that this suited the interests of the dominant class in society, and that school geography, therefore, continued to act as ideology despite the lack of obvious state intervention.

After the war, much social reform took place, and a welfare state was rapidly established. The 1944 Education Reform Act established secondary education for all, however, as Jones (2003) notes, this was not as radical as it might have been. A tripartite system of grammar schools, secondary moderns and technical colleges, reinforced social roles and the class system, with academic geography serving the elite. Immediately after the war, Britons wanted the security of a settled, imagined past and the post-war education settlement appears to reflect this, looking backwards rather than forward (Jones 2003). School subjects played their part in this 'reproduction' of national culture, as Morgan (2003) examines through the geography curriculum, which constructed a nostalgic, imagined Britain through the selective representation of geography for pupils.

By the 1950s, post-war scarcity had abated and consumerism was on the rise (Ross 2000). The 1950s to the early 1970s was a period of wide-ranging and large scale modernisation in Britain. This became known as a 'golden age' for geography teachers (Lawton 1980). This is less a comment on the quality of education received, and more on the way teachers were treated. This was an age of teacher autonomy, and the dominance of subjects in the curriculum, marked toward the end of the period by large scale, well-funded and teacher-controlled curriculum development projects, such as the Schools' Council geography projects. Schiro (2008) – though basing his research in American history – concurs that this was a period in which the 'scholar academic' curriculum ideology flourished and so, established subjects, like geography, thrived.

However, as Jones (2003) points out, drawing on the vivid accounts of failed education, such as Blishen (1955), the experience for working class children in secondary moderns was less 'golden', as their rejection of the academic subject curriculum and of school itself, intensified. Huckle (1985) argues that the curriculum development projects in geography were an elitist exercise and the management of social and economic change, rather than the triumph of teacher autonomy, which the 'golden age' implies. He also points out that the 'New Geography' was associated with a 'new professionalism', and that geography teachers' self-interest was driving aspects of the curriculum, just as Goodson (1998) found during the establishment of the discipline in the nineteenth century.

Rawling's (2001) account of curriculum change in geography picks up the story of school geography in the late 1960s. The geography curriculum, she notes, had changed little since before the war, and the 'modernisation' of school geography really appeared with the positivist shift to quantification and reductive modelling of the 'New Geography' led by Chorley and Haggett (1967) and disseminated into (mainly independent) schools via an elite group of geography teachers.

The period from 1965 (the introduction of comprehensive education) to 1976 (Callaghan's Ruskin speech, which led to the National Curriculum) is an important sub-section of this overall period. Rawling (2001) suggests this period was one of change following curriculum consensus. But Huckle argues that the New Geography was neither revolution nor the crisis suggested by Graves (1975) but profoundly adaptive and conservative, 'an elitist exercise from the start' (Huckle 1985: 300), this was 'enlightened traditionalism' (also described as such by Walford, 1981) rather than radical change. Huckle saw the New Geography as part of the reforms:

> to further modernise and expand provision as one means of sustaining post-war economic growth and political consensus.
>
> *(Huckle 1985: 300)*

At the very end of this period, in the early 1970s, there was a challenge to the unquestioned assumption that geography (and other school subjects) was a 'rational' body of knowledge. As the 'New Geography' gave the school subject a positivist turn, the 'new sociology of education' was doing the opposite. Seemingly 'rational' or 'neutral' subject knowledge in a liberal humanist view of education (such as the geography envisaged by Peters 1965, and Marsden 1976) could be rejected when shown that knowledge, far from being neutral, was socially constructed to serve the interests of 'the powerful' – dominant elite groups, exerting control over society (Young 1971). Morgan (2003) considering the curriculum both during this period and more recently, argues that school geography was profoundly subjective. Geography textbooks reveal the interests of the powerful behind representations of Britain and Britain's place in the world. This resonates with the argument that education serves to reproduce culture (Bourdieu and Passeron 1977, Huckle 1985) and also that textbooks can legitimate knowledge, making curriculum knowledge 'official' (Apple 2000.

> Though curriculum texts and textbook interpretations are written so as to give the impression that they offer a transparent 'window' on reality, they are, in fact, cultural productions and are capable of being read in different ways.
> *(Morgan 2003: 460).*

The later part of this period (1950s and 70s) was one of relatively flourishing geography curriculum development and so is a suitable place to briefly examine which agents can enable and influence geography curriculum development. These agents sit within the value/belief systems of the times (the social–economic context) and they are not separate to the overarching societal influence. The impetus for curriculum change comes from 'ideological', technical and economic changes (Taylor and Richards 1985). Therefore, changing society drives curriculum change. However, agents of change can be considered both as transmitters of wider value/belief systems and as having agency in their own right. In the context of curriculum development in the 1960s and 70s, an examination of the agents that facilitate curriculum change draws attention to the varied scales at which influences over the curriculum operate (Figure 3).

Taylor and Richards' (1985) 'agencies of curriculum change' serves to illustrate two points. First, they show how power to influence curriculum is dependent on the prevailing social, economic and political conditions of the time. Secondly, they show how agencies operate at a range of scales. National scale initiatives are arbitrated by the local scale, the classroom and ultimately the individual pupil. However, the 'agency' of organisations and individuals is contested. A structuralist approach, as Huckle (1985) takes, argues that agency is overestimated and is often 'false consciousness', ultimately controlled by deep and hidden social and economic structures.

The themes constructed in this period are summarised in Table 2.

1976 to 1988 – crises of capitalism and the State takes control

In this period two concerns can be seen to dominate. The first is that, as a response to economic upheaval, the state sought to increase the accountability of schooling to national economic need. This appears most obviously in the (statutory) National

Scale	Agent of curriculum change
Global	Impetus for change from ideological, technical and economic changes.
National	**Schools council** curriculum study group (established by Ministry of Education) and **Nuffield Foundation** – teacher-led curriculum development projects facilitated. **Universities** – new knowledge for courses, resources, staff and facilities for subject teams. **Central government** – stronger than sometimes recognised before 1970s (an indirect impact on curriculum, e.g. through funding) and since 1976 involved in the 'great debate' and providing guidance materials to schools. **Exam boards** – in responding to school developments and in introducing new subjects for examination (human biology, general studies, and computer studies). **Subject Associations** – aiding teacher-led curriculum development. **Media** (e.g. BBC programmes for schools) Commercial publishers – both in reflecting and pioneering new thinking and publishing individual teachers'work.
Local	**Local education authorities** – teachers' centres and advisory services (teachers' centres/teams of local authority inspectors and advisers).
School	**Headteacher or Deputy Head** with curriculum responsibility – recognise and support geography curriculum. **Heads of Department/teacher teams** – enact and develop geography curriculum. **Parents** – influence but on teachers' terms.
Teacher (classroom)	**Teacher** – 'mediates everything', with considerable autonomy (though less than the myths suggest).
Pupil	**Pupils** along with teacher are 'final arbiters' of curriculum.

FIGURE 3 Agents of curriculum change – scales of operation
Source: adapted from Taylor and Richards (1985: 41–53)

Curriculum. The second is that value/belief systems rose to the surface in heightened debate over curriculum purpose and content.

By the mid-1970s, mounting economic pressure was driving educational debate. Jones (2003) suggests that there had been a tacit assumption that through the 1950s and 60s education contributed to economic growth, and state spending on education was high. As British industry began to fall behind its competitors, questions about the effectiveness of education to support economic growth and competitiveness began to be asked. To this point, decisions over what to include in the

TABLE 2 Themes from curriculum studies applied to the geography curriculum, 1920–1976

Theme	Ways in which theme is constructed 1920–1976
Power/control	The 'new sociology of education' illuminated hidden structures of power within school subject knowledge, changing the notion that subjects (including geography) were neutral bodies of knowledge. During the 'golden age' teachers enjoyed (relative) power and control over the curriculum.
Conflict	A relative lack of conflict is notable in this era of a social settlement and relative consensus in education. However, the tripartite system created class division and class conflict, appearing in the rejection of the curriculum offered by much of the working class (Jones 2003). There was also conflict toward the end of the era, between progressive (child-centred) education and both the scholar-academic and social-efficiency educational value/belief systems.
Scales of influence	The 'golden age' allowed the teacher to exercise relative power over curriculum. This extended to the regional and national scale of groups of teachers, supported by the nation state through projects such as the Schools' Council curriculum projects. However, the global scale was still exerting influence in the geography curriculum serving the interests of a modernising national economy, driven by competition in global markets (Huckle 1985, Morgan 2011).
Value/belief systems	A scholar-academic value/belief system strengthened during this period in which grammar schools were established and teachers gained relative autonomy to focus on their subject. However, the tripartite system was elitist, and social efficiency could also be seen in educational beliefs of an academic curriculum for the elite and a vocational curriculum for the majority, who would become willing workers and consumers. There was also a resurgence of progressive, child-centred value/belief systems in the 1960s.
Change	Modernisation and curriculum development, including the 'New Geography' appeared to drive forward curriculum change. But the accusation was made by the new sociology of education (and later Huckle 1985) that such developments were profoundly elitist, and part of a deeper resistance to change. There is also a lack of change framing the period of settlement and relative stability – in a sense this is the calm before the economic, social and political storm of the late 1970s and 80s.

curriculum and how to teach subjects were made 'in house' by subject communities of teachers, universities and teacher educators (Rawling 2001). Callaghan's Ruskin speech of 1976 calling for education to become more accountable to the economy, marked a turning point in state intervention and control over curriculum decisions, culminating in the National Curriculum.

The accountability of education driven by the seismic social and economic shifts of the 1970s was to become implemented by the publishing of school performance 'league tables' and high stakes inspections. Teachers were to find themselves subject to constant surveillance in their work, such that they must account for exam results, compliance to the National Curriculum and other measures by which their school could be judged by inspection at any time. This was a form of the 'panopticon' leading to schools and teachers self-disciplining under ever-present surveillance (Foucault, 1977). This marked the end of a (relatively) 'golden-age' of teacher autonomy and (after something of a battle in the early 1980s) a narrowing of scope for different 'curriculum ideologies' in school geography.

The term 'ideologies' is consistently used by research into how education and curriculum can be divided and classified into distinct value/belief systems. Ross (2000) describes 1976 to 1986 as a period of 'turmoil' in the curriculum. Rawling (2001) sees the decade leading up to the Education Reform Act of 1988 and the National Curriculum as one when contrasting 'ideologies' came to the surface of educational debate. Huckle (1985) similarly identifies an intensifying of educational debate during times of social change. Education of the time mirrors the political and social conflict of Thatcher's 'neoliberal state' (Plant, 2012) ending the consensus politics of the post-war years. Rawling (2001) emphasises the influence of the political 'New Right'. She suggests two distinct 'ideological traditions' were operating within the New Right, those of neoliberalism (emphasising market-forces and choice) and neoconservatism (emphasising the restoration of culture). These 'ideologies' can be argued to have different purposes for school subjects; neoliberalism placing little value on subject knowledge beyond skills and utility, but neo-conservatism (cultural restoration) placing high value on knowledge for the transmission of 'high' culture.

It is important to avoid confusing neoliberal politics (associated with vocational and utilitarian educational ideology, which tends to downplay the importance of subject knowledge) with liberal-humanism (an educational ideology that tends to elevate the importance of subject knowledge as an end in itself). But the tension (and to some extent contradiction) in the New Right ideologies within Thatcher's administration, of simultaneously seeking cultural restoration and modernising efficiency, were reflected in tensions in the National Curriculum.

Rawling (2001) argues that the geography curriculum is more than pure ideology. She sees a deeper philosophical basis to justify geography as a subject, drawing on Hirst's (1974) notion of 'forms of knowledge'. Nonetheless, Rawling argues that the period immediately before the National Curriculum 'orders' of 1991 is one in which debate over the purpose of school geography reveals systems of belief and principles or 'ideologies'. While different educational ideologies can be traced to the late nineteenth century and earlier, this period of 'turmoil' is a suitable context to consider how value/belief systems interrelate.

Rawling distinguishes between six 'ideological traditions', whereas as Schiro (2008) and Walford (1981) make a four-fold distinction. Ross (2000), again drawing on this period, takes a political slant in his use of 'ideology' and curriculum and makes an eight-fold classification. These analyses suggest that belief and value systems drive different purposes for subjects. Though this period brought curriculum and educational value and beliefs to the fore, classifications of educational 'ideologies' (the word ideologies is consistently used) pre-date this period. Davies (1969) gives a four-fold classification of conservative (cultural restorationist), revisionist (modernisation or social efficiency), romantic (child-centred) and democratic (for social change). Notably, a scholarly/liberal-humanist category is absent from Davies' argument. Scrimshaw (1983) uses five categories of: progressivism (child centred/the individual), instrumentalism (social-efficiency), reconstructionism, classical humanism (cultural heritage transmission), and liberal humanism (subject disciplines for a participatory democracy). Eisner (1979) gives six 'educational ideologies' and offers a distinctive perspective which, unlike any other classification, takes account of religion, and argues for an education to allow for 'cognitive pluralism', which accepts different forms of intelligence and knowledge. His six categories are: religious orthodoxy (following the Jesuit tradition, which is common in American schools), rational humanism, progressivism (child-centred), critical theory (reconstruction), reconceptualism (modernisation/social efficiency), and cognitive pluralism (acceptance of different forms of intelligence and knowledge).

There is some consistency between the analyses, for example all accounts identify value/belief systems of child-centred, social reconstruction and modernisation-efficiency. The majority also recognise 'scholar-academic' and 'cultural restorationist' value/belief systems. However, the simplicity of models such as those proposed Schiro (2008, 2013) and Walford (1981) can belie tension and complexity within one category. There appear to be sub-systems within systems, and classifications such as these are to some extent arbitrary human constructions.

It is helpful, at this point, to clarify the purpose of Schiro's (2008) work, which is distinctive by its focus and depth of analysis on curriculum value/belief systems. Schiro aims to provide a classification that reveals hidden value and belief systems (or 'ideologies' in his words) and so provides a 'diagnostic' tool for the curriculum and the teacher. Schiro (2008) invites the reader to self-diagnose their 'ideology' through coded multiple choice questions. Both Rawling (2001) and Walford (1981) similarly suggest that a teacher's personal educational ideology can be 'diagnosed' or revealed by their language:

> The casual remark over staff-room coffee lifts the curtain for a moment ... 'Of course, the fundamental thing is to give them a grasp of the basic ideas of the discipline' ... 'I don't really care what they got from it but the trip was a tremendous experience' ... 'We are really here to get them an O level aren't we, that's all' ... 'If they just understand how the system gets at them, I'll be happy'.
> *(Walford 1981: 222)*

Schiro's work is helpful in the use of a historical account to trace four 'ideologies' from their early roots to current influences, in the context of American schooling (these roots and influences being philosophical, social, economic and political). Although based on American schools, Schiro's classification has a place in making sense of the contemporary curriculum in England by drawing clear boundaries between 'ideologies'. However, the fourfold categorisation can belie the complexity of curriculum and the belief/value systems that inform it.

Rawling (2001) suggests that the decade leading up to the 1988 Education Reform Act was a period when the child-centred (progressive) educational movement, which had become influential in the 1960s and 70s clashed with the growth of the ideas of the New Right (both cultural restorationism and utilitarianism). Ross (2000) concurs in his view that the curriculum shifted in the late 1970s to become objectives-driven, having been content-driven since the early twentieth century, and additionally process-driven in the progressivism of the 1960s and early 70s.

Huckle (1985) explains this period within his theory of geography education as social reproduction. Huckle (1985) sees the late 1970s as economic crisis and the end of social democratic consensus playing out through an educational response, which was needed to restore profitability. Educational budgets were cut, though disguised as a drive to increase accountability, raise standards and give more choice. Huckle (ibid) writes during the ideological conflict and curriculum uncertainty of the mid-1980s. This was also a time of a new awareness of issues facing humanity (such as environmental loss and unequal development) about which geographers could offer an analysis. Huckle (ibid) emphasises the possibilities for radical or socialist school geography in such times and suggests that increased state control over education was causing some geography teachers to become 'radicalised'. Huckle, reflecting Freire (1970), outlines his vision of a critically aware geography teaching:

> Through a process of dialogue, teachers and pupils would seek a critical awareness of their own identity and situation, would analyse causes and consequences and would then examine ways reflectively to transform that reality.
>
> *(Huckle 1985: 303)*

A group of geography educators in the 1980s were considering futures and critical perspectives on 'environment' and 'development' at this time (Huckle 1985, Fien and Gerber 1988, Pepper 1989, Hicks 1995, Huckle and Stirling 1996). This group can be classified as 'reconstructionist' in curriculum ideology (Walford 1981, Rawling 2001, Schiro 2008). Their view that the curriculum should serve to change society is captured by Fien and Gerber's (1988) 'Teaching Geography for a Better World'. The 'reconstructionist' educational ideology has a distinctive view of subject knowledge as the focus of conflict over curriculum content. The reconstructionists accept that curriculum knowledge is political and contested (Schiro 2008). Thus the 'supercomplex' world (Lambert 1999) and 'wicked problems' like climate change with all their controversy and uncertainty (Morgan 2006), are embraced by such geographers, rather than avoided as conjecture. But this notion that all subject knowledge is political construction is itself contested. Standish (2009) and Marsden (1997) reject a reconstructionist view of knowledge on the grounds that subject knowledge becomes used for 'good causes'. An overly flexible (entirely socially constructed) view of knowledge in a curriculum setting out to develop values and emotional well-being also risks education becoming 'therapy' (Furedi 2009, Ecclestone and Hayes 2009). These contested views reflect ideological conflict and philosophical difference in the meaning of 'education'. Only when underlying educational principles and beliefs are revealed, do such curriculum conflicts make sense.

Huckle was pessimistic in that he saw the positivistic 'New Geography' as still dominant during this period, but he was optimistic in the humanistic and structuralist alternatives in academic geography at this time. Fien and Gerber's (1988) edited volume captures the spirit of radical, reconstructionist school geography among a significant minority of geography educators and teachers. But as Morgan (2011) shows, critical perspectives were to lose ground as the hegemony of neoliberalism became established, and schools became increasingly bureaucratic and managerial.

The themes constructed in this period are summarised in Table 3.

Late 1980s to 2008 – neoliberal hegemony and the 'emptying out' of subjects

Three matters relating to curriculum debate in the context of ideologies can be drawn from the late 1980s to 2008, a period characterised by the National Curriculum and state intervention in schools and teaching. The first is the argument that neoliberal hegemony became established, the second (and related to the first) is that the teacher's role as curriculum maker was weakened. The teacher as public intellectual was replaced

TABLE 3 Themes from curriculum studies applied to the geography curriculum, 1976 to 1988

Theme	Ways in which theme is constructed 1976–1988
Power/control	The state exerted its power and control over education through the statutory National Curriculum (though as Roberts 1996, showed this does not mean teachers lost all agency over the enacted curriculum).
Conflict	Teachers and government came into conflict over control of the curriculum; the 1988 Education Reform Act was the culmination of a steady rise in state control over education during this era. Conflict between curriculum value/belief systems come to the fore in times of social and political change.
Scales of influence	The nation state became increasingly and visibly influential, though the global economic context was also evident in influencing educational reform for competition in a global economy, and teacher resistance showed that the local (school and classroom) scale still mattered.
Value/belief systems	Value/ belief systems became more explicit in curriculum debates. Economic forces driving curriculum change also became explicit, and increasingly dominant with the curriculum and teachers challenged to be accountable for national economic growth.
Change	This period was one of turmoil and uncertainty, leading to a shift from relative teacher control over the curriculum to explicit central government control, albeit with geography given a secure position in the National Curriculum. It was a period in which recontructionist school geography reached its zenith in the modern era, offering hope of a geography 'for a better world', before neoliberalism gained ground.

by teacher as skilled technician. The third is the tension between curriculum as 'text' and 'context' (Ball and Bowe 1992) – the curriculum as enacted can be very different to that intended. Curriculum differences between departments can be argued to be more noticeable than similarities of a supposedly 'national' curriculum (Roberts 1996).

Several accounts of curriculum change expose and critique a social efficiency ideology which fails to serve the interests of all in society (Hartley 1997, McCullogh, Helsby and Knight 2000, Goodson 1998, Ball 2000, Kelly 2008, Fielding and Moss 2011, Giroux 2005a and Morgan 2011). A common theme in these critiques is of the totalitarian and controlling force of the state, increasing since the late 1970s. In response to a weakening state and declining economy the state sought to induct young people into 'mechanical obedience' (Goodson 1998). This efficiency and effectiveness movement in schooling, has been criticised by Rawling (2001) and McCullogh, Helsby and Knight (2000) for de-professionalising subject teachers and downgrading a teacher's role to that of classroom technician. With the control and obedience required, comes accountability, as Kelly (2008) examines.

Kelly (2008) argues that the schooling model of social efficiency misses the point of education altogether by forgetting that education should be for the flourishing of life. He uses a Confucian proverb to illustrate this:

> Confucius once said, if you have two pence to spend, spend a penny on bread and a penny on a flower, the bread to make life possible, the flower to make it worthwhile.
>
> *(Kelly 2008: 80)*

Kelly thus draws attention to the importance of the philosophical question of what education means and what schools are for, explored by Carr (2003). These central, philosophical questions underpin Schiro's (2008) explanation of how ideologies account for the tensions and contradictions in school curricula.

Morgan (2012) comments on the currently dominant geography curriculum model of given package or product to be delivered, rather than a process. In this view of curriculum, Morgan both reflects Kelly's (2008) argument for curriculum as process, and gives further credence to Schiro's (2008) categorisation of 'social efficiency' curriculum ideology.

> The curriculum is written and handed down from on high by 'experts'. School subjects are presented as a package or product – received consensual knowledge – and not as a process that mediated an active reading and writing of the world.
>
> *(Morgan 2012: 63)*

Morgan's (2012) critique of school geography reflects Schiro's argument that social-efficiency ideology is revealed in an atomistic approach to knowledge. Physical and human geography are encouraged to be seen as separate, with knowledge split into small pieces with little room to see how these fit together (for example, of a physical system and social relations). Knowledge is thus seen as regurgitation. Morgan examines how school geographical knowledge, in being seen as uncontested (the way the world is) serves to reinforce capitalist ideology. An example of this is the shift to the global scale from the national. Morgan, drawing on Herod (2011), argues that the scale of representation is a social construction. The view that the world has become globalised and the privileging of the global scale over the national serves a view of living within a system of overarching dominance that is beyond control and therefore must be accepted. In this accepting view, any measures to improve the world (for example for 'sustainable development') must operate within the system. This, Morgan argues, is the recent approach of school geography and a different view of knowledge is needed for geographical understanding. Using 'ideological' in the sense of 'false consciousness' he argues:

> dominant forms of school geography have promoted ideological under-standings of society and environment, and that, to enable students to understand how geographies are made and remade, there is a need to develop forms of geographical understanding that are rooted in political economy and social construction.
>
> *(Morgan 2012: 152)*

Huckle (1985) also argues that schools provide an ideology that supports capital, and in doing so diverts attention from human agency and social explanations of the world. Huckle (1985) Pepper (1989) and Morgan (2012) all argue that understanding how people and nature relate (a concern at the heart of geography) is bound up with ideology. Huckle (1985) and Morgan (2012) argue that a dominant ideology exists in school to serve capitalist interests. This is seen through the uncontested nature of knowledge, acceptance of ecological modernisation, and an approach to controversy that does not encourage analysis through political economy or historical perspectives. Morgan (2012) and Huckle (1985) provide accounts of the geography curriculum which, examined through Schiro's (2008) classification, critique a dominant 'social-efficiency' value/belief system, positioning their arguments as 'social reconstructionist'. However, such accounts, which bring ideology (in the sense of 'false consciousness') to light, bring an additional layer of complexity to Schiro's classification, in their examination of the role of capitalism in school geography. While Schiro's (2008) classification is helpful, it must be considered in light of other accounts of 'ideology' and curriculum.

The theme of the neoliberal state taking power and control over the curriculum in late capitalist times is common among critics of education for social efficiency. Apple (2000, 2004) argues that 'official knowledge' flows from the unquestioned power of the neoliberal state and applies Gramsci's (1971) notion of hegemony to schooling. Rawling (2001) and Walford (2001) argue that state control has changed school geography through such a process in which teacher agency over curriculum is reduced. Education policy at the level of the nation state is influenced by the advance of globalisation. Butt (2011, 2017) uses globalisation to provide an explanation for the increased use of performance management and deregulated competition in schools. In the globalised world, he argues, 'educationists are tasked to deliver greater international competitiveness and economic growth' (2017: 13) influencing educational reform, teacher education, schools and curricula.

Academic disciplines are not immune from political economy at university level, which further problematises any notion of the existence of pure or 'rational' subject knowledge. State-sponsored marketisation of universities has had damaging effects, according to Unwin.

> The process of socialisation is complete. The pursuit of a creative, critical knowledge is dead.
>
> *(Unwin 1992: 17)*

It has been argued that New Labour education policy (1997 to 2007) deepened neoliberal hegemony (Fielding and Moss 2011, Kelly 2008). New Labour policy can be seen to have been a mix of belief and value systems, or hybrid of ideas. This is reflected in educational belief and value systems. New Labour policy can neither be seen as politically far right, nor social-democratic left. It borrowed from ideas of neoliberalism and social democracy, but did not fully embrace either (Jones 2003). While operating in the rational scientific framework of neoliberalism and 'efficiency', it drew on the 'Third Way' (Giddens 2000) for the conceptual and philosophical framework behind the New Labour project. Giddens' 'Third Way' represents neither the dominance of society as structuring the individual, nor of the individual creating society. Giddens argues that society structures individual life, but society is reproduced by individual actions. Thus Giddens seeks to break the society-individual dualism (Elliot 2009).

This belief system ambivalence is apparent in the ideas of educational advisor to New Labour, Barber (2009), Breslin (2005) and Beare (2001) who argue that traditional school subjects are no longer fit for purpose. Beare, with overtones of postmodernity (particularly Bauman's 2000, 'liquid modernity') argues that changing times have made schools and curriculum structures redundant. He argues that industrial society needed ordered, divided parts, to serve the production line economy. Society, and schooling, similarly, was ordered and divided, with bells and timetables, uniformly sized and aged classes and a curriculum to match, of cleanly divided, discrete subjects, taught by subject teachers. Beare (2001) suggests the post-industrial world of fluidity, organic change and wholes, warrants an education to match. So, in this vision, subjects overlap and learning becomes interdisciplinary, concerned as much with process of learning as with knowledge. The emphasis is on 'drawing out' the person's potential, rather than 'stuffing in' knowledge.

The notion of drawing out the individual's potential suggests child-centred beliefs, as well as social-efficiency, and the utility of encouraging young people to develop skills and the ability to be flexible. However, as Hartley (1997), Apple

(2004), Kelly (2008) and Fielding (2011) argue, what may superficially appear as child-centred interest, may be economic interest, and thus a social-efficiency 'ideology', which makes the child accountable themselves for a developing a skill set to succeed in work. Curriculum purposes at the national scale during the New Labour years, therefore, fit with a social-efficiency 'ideology' (value/belief system) and a modernisation narrative. However, elements of other 'ideological traditions' (Rawling 2001) including the utilitarian, the progressive and the vocationalist are also present in this period, suggesting schooling under New Labour's 'Third Way' was a hybrid of ideas.

The teacher's role – from public intellectual to technician

This efficiency and effectiveness movement in schooling has been criticised by Rawling (2001) and McCullogh, Helsby and Knight (2000) for de-professionalising subject teachers and downgrading the teacher's role to that of classroom technician. With the control and obedience required, comes accountability, as Kelly (2008) examines.

Kelly (2008) offers a way of looking at curriculum as either process (emphasis on principles) or product (emphasis on aims and objectives). Kelly argues in favour of teacher agency in curriculum design, using Stenhouse's (1975) view of the teacher as researcher and Eisner's (2002) argument for teacher action research. Kelly (2008) gives a historical account of curriculum to illustrate how teacher autonomy has since been increasingly undermined since the 'Golden age' of 1944 to the 1970s (Lawton 1980) by the 'power-coercive' strategies of the state, such as inspections and public league tables. Kelly (2008) thus contributes to the notion that the curriculum is increasingly controlled by the state.

Moore (2004) drawing on Ball (2000, 2003) approaches dominant 'ideology' from the field of teaching, with the rise of the discourse of the professional teacher as the 'competent craftsperson', which reveals an ideology of social efficiency and neoliberalism in seeing the teacher as technically skilled, but anti-intellectual in a culture of managerialism. The 'competent craftsperson' discourse is part of a wider social efficiency curriculum ideology in a narrative of 'modernisation'. A modernisation narrative justifies the teaching profession driving toward order and completeness in the curriculum, so that an uncontested, finished curriculum product can be delivered. 'Modernisation' may be interpreted as 'state control' and a shift away from teacher autonomy in 'the death of progressive education' (Lowe 2007). With curriculum making subsumed by technical concerns of effective teaching there has been 'a narrowing of teachers' work' (Morgan 2012: 157). The possibilities for the teacher's engagement as curriculum maker are not helped by curriculum change becoming an increasingly centralised process (Rawling 2015, 2016).

Several arguments have been made for the teacher to be curriculum 'developer' including a critical view of the competent craftsperson discourse, seeing this as downgrading of teacher to effective deliverer of an imposed curriculum, for example Connelly and Clandinin (1988), Crombie-White (1997), Brighouse

(1994), Skilbeck (1990), McKernan (1996), Eisner (2002) and Sachs (2003). Lambert and Morgan's curriculum making (2010) is located in the same, critical perspective, which argues for the teacher as public intellectual rather than as 'competent craftsperson'.

Curriculum as 'text' and 'context' – the importance of local differences

Some literature in the field of geography and curriculum 'ideologies' during this period, such as Rawling (2001), pays close attention to the values, traditions and ideologies revealed in the process of producing the National Curriculum, a written document to be delivered by teachers, by law. Ball and Bowe (1992) and Roberts (1996) focus on the National Curriculum as it is enacted and embodied in schools. The important conclusion from both is that the National Curriculum is, in reality, not a uniform 'national' experience, but is strongly mediated by differences between teachers, departments and schools. These differences are often in values and cultures, or 'ideologies' in Roberts' words (1996).

Ball and Bowe (1992) contest the meaning of 'National Curriculum'. They argue that the 'texts' of the policy and written orders are not implemented evenly, but are subject to different interpretations of the 'context'. These four contexts are a school or department's capacities, contingencies, commitment to existing approaches, and innovation histories, each of which will vary, thus affecting how 'National Curriculum' is interpreted. Drawing on Barthes (1974), Ball and Bowe (1992) argue that 'texts' can be interpreted in a 'writerly' way (active and dynamic) or a 'readerly' way (passive and accepting). Ball and Bowe's research, in stressing the importance of local context and the role of 'writerly' teachers to develop their local curriculum, resonates with the Geographical Association's 'local solutions' approach to combining curriculum and professional development work (Mitchell 2006) and the notion of the teacher as 'curriculum maker' (Lambert and Morgan 2010. Ball and Bowe's (1992) argument is that 'curriculum' can only be understood when text and context are examined together. This implies that individual teachers 'make' the curriculum, as well as government policy, subject association guidance or textbook, for example.

Roberts (1996), building on the notion that the curriculum is not evenly 'delivered', but enacted in contexts, adds the perspective of department 'ideologies'. Using both values and 'ideologies', Roberts (1996) draws on research into the earlier centralised curriculum initiatives of the Schools' Council projects, and rejects the argument that differences between a centralised 'text' and the experience in the classroom are due to problems of communication from centre to periphery. Rather, there are different values or 'ideologies' at work. Her empirical work identified three department 'types':

- Type A – curriculum as content knowledge
- Type B – curriculum as framework of ideas, skills and values
- Type C – curriculum as developmental process for students

These categories resemble the various classifications of curriculum ideology and relate to Young and Muller's (2010) different purposes of knowledge. But the significance of Roberts' work is to argue that different department 'ideologies' produce a different version of *a* national curriculum, despite the intention of *the* National Curriculum (a text) to remove difference and to control teaching. Her final remark suggests department contexts hold greater power over the enacted curriculum, than the 'text' of the National Curriculum:

> in 1993 departments A, B and C resemble their former selves more than they do each other.
>
> *(Roberts 1996: 204)*

1988 to 2008 saw state control over curriculum extended and with it a deepening of neoliberal ideology in schooling. However, the teacher and the geography department could still influence curriculum enactment.

The themes constructed in this period are summarised in Table 4.

TABLE 4 Themes from curriculum studies applied to the geography curriculum, 1988–2008

Theme	Ways in which themes are constructed 1988–2008
Power/control	Power and control of the state (often at 'arm's length') over curriculum decision making deepened through further versions of the statutory National Curriculum, inspections and published league tables. Academic subjects became less powerful curriculum influences than bureaucratic concerns to show that 'objectives' were achieved and 'results' produced.
Conflict	Conflict is less noticeable in this era than a lack of conflict. A new settlement for teachers was reached with growing acceptance of a technicist model of teaching and a social efficiency curriculum value/belief system. Resistance to radical change deepened in schools, such that propositions to rethink the curriculum were seen as lacking common sense. However, a counter position and source of resistance to the 'efficiency' curriculum continued through geography educational research arguing for the importance and power of subject learning (such as Roberts 1996, 2003, Rawling 2001 and Morgan 2002, 2003).
Scales of influence	The nation state deepened its influence, albeit indirectly. Locally devolved decision making was influenced by government-controlled curriculum and inspection frameworks.
Value/belief systems	A social efficiency value/belief system dominated and neoliberal hegemony was established (Apple 2004).
Change	State control over the curriculum changed the relationship between teachers and the curriculum, making their professional role more technical/managerial and less intellectually engaged with the subject content of curriculum. There was curriculum change, driven for 'efficiency' and economic motives rather than radical (reconstructionist) or scholarly-academic motives.

2008 to 2016 – a new crisis of capitalism and a knowledge turn

Since 2008, the economic, social and political landscape has changed again, with effects on education and curriculum. A single broad theme can be drawn from this period, of intensified debate over education in all respects; its purposes, the level of accountability of schools to economy and society, the role of teachers and the curriculum. In this intensified debate, just as in the late 1970s and 80s, different value/belief systems are revealed. Debate over the curriculum, encouraged by a White Paper (DfE 2010) and a curriculum consultation, ahead of a new National Curriculum, has tended to focus on the role of knowledge. A 'knowledge turn' can be discerned (Lambert 2011) in which the power of knowledge is contested. In the recent debate over the role of knowledge in curriculum, 'ideologies' and their associated educational narratives can be identified, such as radical education for social change (Morgan 2009, 2011) and a blend of schooling for conservative cultural restoration and neoliberalism to provide workers and consumers for economic growth (DfE 2010, 2016).

Contested purposes of knowledge in the curriculum

In this period, contributions to the recent debate about the purpose of subject knowledge (or 'knowledge turn') include the notion of 'core knowledge' and 'powerful knowledge'. Hirsch's (1987) argument for cultural literacy includes a notion of 'core knowledge', used by the government (DfE 2010) and re-interpreted by the Geographical Association in their curriculum proposals (GA 2011). The significance of 'core knowledge' to teachers is evident in its presence in public documents which inform the statutory National Curriculum (DfE 2010).

However, the meaning of 'core knowledge' is contested. Hirsch (1987) uses the term in the context of cultural literacy. 'Core knowledge' is 'what every American needs to know' (ibid) to be able to engage with cultural life. Hirsch (1987) concludes his argument with a long list of words and phrases, the important facts, or core knowledge, which should be learned by American children. The UK Coalition government uses the term 'core knowledge' in their white paper (DfE 2010)

> The National Curriculum should set out clearly the core knowledge and understanding that all children should be expected to acquire … It must embody their cultural and scientific inheritance, the best that our past and present generations have to pass on to the next. But it must not … become a vehicle for imposing passing political fads on our children and must not squeeze out all other learning.
>
> *(DfE 2010: 38)*

This passage reveals an ideology of 'cultural restoration' in celebrating the past and, in the anxiety over 'political fads', it reveals a suspicion of 'social reconstructionist' ideology. The use of 'core knowledge' is apparently a neutral term, suggesting a belief in scholarly academic principles of education. However, the notion of 'core knowledge' is contested and, in the White Paper (DfE 2010) it is undefined. In this period, subject knowledge, including the notion of core knowledge, has been examined and theorised (Firth 2011a, 2011b, 2013, Lambert and Young 2014) as will now be considered.

The White Paper uses the term 'essential knowledge' as well as 'core knowledge'. Lambert (2011) has suggested the importance of interrogating these terms. Core knowledge can be seen as an exhaustive list of facts which excludes the possibility of any deeper, conceptual understanding of the subject. Such deeper understanding is necessary to access the powerful knowledge of the subject. Lambert (2011) explores the notion of extensive and intensive knowledge. The former can be likened to core knowledge in the Hirschian sense, the latter to subject knowledge, which is more specialised, going beyond the 'essential' to allow deeper understanding, through subject knowledge.

The analogy of language illustrates how the Hirschian sense of core knowledge is insufficient to explain the importance of subject knowledge (Lambert and Morgan 2010, Lambert 2011). Lambert (2011) likens the extensive, core knowledge or 'facts' of geography to subject 'vocabulary', but without conceptual knowledge or 'grammar' the subject, like language, makes little sense. Without conceptual understanding, Hirschian 'core knowledge' is fragmented and likely to be incoherent to the pupil. An important part of Lambert's argument (ibid) is the role of the teacher in helping pupils to construct subject knowledge in a coherent way. Both Hirsch (1987) and the White Paper (DfE 2010) fail to recognise this role (despite the White Paper's title 'the importance of teaching'). Lambert's ideas (ibid) are reflected in the Geographical Association (GA) curriculum proposals (GA 2011), which are a pro-active measure by the GA to influence the government's National Curriculum Review. The proposals use the notion of 'core knowledge' and suggest that this is important, but only when accompanied by 'content knowledge', which can be likened to subject 'grammar' in concepts such as 'place' and 'scale' (Lambert and Morgan 2010) and 'procedural knowledge', or the knowledge of the processes of 'doing geography', such as geographical enquiry and fieldwork (GA 2011).

Lambert (2011) and the GA proposals can therefore be seen as viewing the role of 'core knowledge' in the curriculum differently to Hirsch (1987) and the White Paper (DfE 2010). However, Lambert (ibid) appears to be embracing a notion of core knowledge and welcoming a 'knowledge turn', which reasserts the position of subjects, such as geography, in the curriculum. Lambert (ibid) offers a theoretical rationale for core knowledge, which goes beyond Hirsch's notion (1987) of knowledge as a list of facts for cultural literacy, to a notion of 'procedural knowledge' for 'human capability' and 'powerful knowledge', which is only available through subjects and thus distinguished from the 'everyday knowledge' of life experience.

'Powerful knowledge' underpins the curriculum making model by providing a rationale for the teacher's attention to the subject. A brief examination of powerful knowledge is helpful, here, because it holds the potential for geography teachers to use their subject knowledge to assert their control over the enacted curriculum. Powerful knowledge is thus a means of subject teachers' resistance to weaker forms of knowledge which downgrade their professional role to that of 'technician' (Lambert and Young 2014, Mitchell and Lambert 2015).

Key to the significance of powerful knowledge is its social-realist theory of knowledge. This sees subject knowledge as dynamic and changing, but still bounded by the discipline. This is best illustrated through Young and Muller's (2010) three futures for subject knowledge (Figure 4).

Young and Muller (2010) argue for F3 as a 'social realist' theory of knowledge. They show that F1 is an under-socialised theory of knowledge (which in effect denies that knowledge is produced in a social context), while F2 is over-socialised (which denies that knowledge has any objective 'reality' that is not socially constructed). F1 is reluctant to recognise that subject knowledge changes over time and is knowledge taken as given: unless students can be persuaded to 'defer gratification' such knowledge is seen as irrelevant and boring and is rejected. F2 on the other hand fails to provide access to the 'powerful knowledge' needed to access life opportunities, and perversely conceals from the students the real world knowledge that contributes to their being educated.

For subjects, including geography, the significance of a social realist theory of knowledge is that subject boundaries are seen as permeable and able to stretch – they are strong and maintained, but they can move and be crossed in the construction of school geography. This resonates with Lambert and Morgan's (2011) notion of curriculum making in geography and teachers as 'boundary workers'. Lambert (2010) recognises the important contribution of both 'powerful knowledge' and 'core knowledge' by arguing that a synthesis of both supports a notion of 'geographic capability' (Lambert, Solem and Tani 2015).

'Powerful knowledge' in Young and Muller's (2010) conception, is potentially emancipatory by its inclusivity. Their social realist view of knowledge is different to the view of knowledge put forward by the White Paper (DfE 2010) or Hirsch (1987). Both Hirsch and the White Paper see core knowledge as unchanging facts, backward looking and emphasising the best of the past; a view that accords with F1 knowledge, knowledge of the powerful, exclusive and seemingly irrelevant to

Future scenario	View of knowledge	Implication for school subject
F1	Under-socialised *Knowledge for the powerful*.	Elitist – subject boundaries are fixed and maintained. Knowledge is fixed, backward looking.
F2	Over-socialised *Knowledge lacks power*.	Subject boundaries are removed. Generic learning outcomes, such as skills, become the aim – a turn away from knowledge.
F3	Social realist *Powerful knowledge*.	Subject knowledge boundaries are maintained but also crossed for the creation and acquisition of new knowledge. Subject knowledge is dynamic and forward looking.

FIGURE 4 Three futures for subject knowledge
Source: adapted from Young and Muller 2010

working class children who are not inducted to middle-class educational values (Young and Muller 2010).

Young and Muller's F2 knowledge helps to understand the context of English schooling policy immediately prior to the 'knowledge turn' marked by the White Paper in 2009. New Labour's focus on soft skills for a flexible workforce downplayed subject knowledge. A culture of learning soft skills, pedagogy and teacher performance, persists in schools (Roberts 2010, Mitchell and Lambert 2015). Roberts (2003) and Lambert (2011) are critical of the impact that policy aiming for learning and teaching effectiveness over subject knowledge emphasis (an F2 approach) is having on school geography. The perceived weakening of subject knowledge has been critiqued from different perspectives. Such perspectives include those of teacher de-professionalisation (Hartley 1997, McCullogh, Helsby and Knight 2000, Rawling 2001), a therapeutic turn to education (Ecclestone and Hayes 2009, Furedi 2009) and an ethical turn to geography education (Marsden 1997, Standish 2009).

The marketisation of schooling in this period is reflected by the growth of multi-academy trusts (MATs), which run more than one academy and in some cases 10 to 15 academies or more. In November 2016, there were 1,121 active MATs in England, including both primary and secondary age groups. By comparison, in March 2011, there were just 391 MATs (House of Commons 2017). The 'academisation' of schooling warrants consideration with respect to curriculum enactment.

MATs are often formed by taking over or replacing failing schools. This puts pressure on the MATs to demonstrate rapid success, or 'improvement', leading to a focus on the narrow measure of examination result metrics. This is likely to encourage a focus on 'teaching to the test' and 'effectiveness', rather than a risk-taking curriculum leadership. MATs may therefore, tend to reflect the 'technician' model of teacher professionalism, rather than that of 'curriculum leader'. MATs have been linked to a standardisation of procedures. In the most extreme cases it is claimed that MATs lead to 'teachers being told to "just stick to the script" like staff in a call centre' (Guardian 2017). Wilkins (2017) argues that MATs draw the 'gaze' of government to the practices of the schools (academies) concerned. The rise of MATs therefore reflects an increasing 'self-disciplining' of teachers' and headteachers' work under the accountability felt under such a 'gaze'.

MATs self-evidently remove an element of school autonomy. This makes the curriculum leadership of the 'future school' envisioned by Lambert and Young (2014) unlikely because key decision making is centralised and taken away from the 'local' (school level) both for the headteacher of the academy and the head of the geography department. Some larger MATs operate a centralised MAT curriculum, planned outside the school, to be 'delivered' and assessed consistently across the academies – the 'script' to be 'stuck to' (Guardian 2017). This leaves little room for the teacher to be a curriculum maker. Academies are also exempt from government requirement to cover the National Curriculum, which further influences curriculum enactment in their geography departments. The proportion of young people educated in MATs is predicted to rise still further (House of Commons 2017) and so MATs will remain a significant influence on the enactment of the geography curriculum in England, posing a threat to the praxis of curriculum making in school geography.

Under Lambert's leadership, the Geographical Association's 'Manifesto for Geography – A Different View' (2009a) calls for teachers to engage in curriculum making. In arguing for curriculum making, Lambert and Morgan (2010) call the relationship between the state, the teacher and geography (the school subject) into question. Since 2010, the argument for geography teachers to be 'curriculum makers' has continued to be made by Lambert and other geography educators (Lambert 2011, 2015a, 2015b, Lambert and Hopkin 2014, Biddulph, Lambert and Balderstone 2015, Mitchell and Lambert 2015, Mitchell, 2016).

The notion of curriculum making was thus produced by Lambert and Morgan in a societal context of government aiming for schooling to prepare children for the 'knowledge economy'. In this aim, government held a deficient view of subject knowledge (Lambert 2011). The argument for curriculum making has been refined, focusing on the central question of how geographical knowledge is educationally valuable. This work led to the notion of geographic capability or 'geocapabilities' (Lambert, Solem and Tani 2015) drawing on the notion of human empowerment, borrowed from the field of development economics (Sen 1995, Nussbaum 2013). 'Geocapability' offers a rationale for how the geography teacher's curriculum making may be underpinned by 'principled thinking' (Morgan 2014). Geocapabilities is an attempt to be 'convincing' in the case that geography education matters (Lambert, Solem and Tani 2015: 1).

Geocapability is a refinement of the educational rationale for the geography teacher as curriculum maker. It is significant that this refinement has been made in the 2010s because these are times in which pressure on teachers and students to perform has become intense. In his work to make a case for why the geography teacher should be the curriculum maker, Lambert has been increasingly concerned with the rationale for why the teacher should be in an ongoing relationship with geography (the discipline from which they make their school subject), or put simply, why geographical knowledge matters in education. In his collaborations, Lambert has explored the teacher's role in the geography curriculum (Lambert and Morgan 2010), the nature and importance of geography as a 'powerful knowledge' (Lambert and Young 2014) and the value of geographical knowledge for human 'capability' (Lambert, Solem and Tani 2015).

Powerful knowledge and geographic capability are relevant to my research because they can be interpreted as extensions of curriculum making as an argument for teachers' resistance to the pressurised times of performativity and 'learnification'. Curriculum making was proposed as a case for why geographical knowledge matters in a child's education. 'Powerful knowledge' (Lambert and Young 2014) and geographic capability (Lambert, Solem and Tani 2015) extend the explanation of why geographical knowledge matters, supporting the curriculum making argument for teachers to use geographical knowledge as they make curriculum choices. Lambert and Young (2014) argue that teachers should be 'knowledge workers' and 'principled thinkers' with the subject discipline geography framing teachers' curriculum work. This emphasis on subject knowledge is part of a wider 'knowledge turn' in education since 2008.

Curriculum making is located in a particular view of educational purpose and so can be interpreted with the lens of curriculum value/belief systems. Curriculum making rejects an instrumentalist argument for education primarily for skills to serve national economic needs. Lambert and Young (2014) and Lambert, Solem and Tani (2015) make a case for curriculum making serving education as subject knowledge for human growth and individual flourishing. However, curriculum value/belief systems and educational philosophies are complex and they can change as society changes.

While there is much recent discussion about the importance of knowledge in the future curriculum, less has been made of the significance of assessment. How the curriculum is evaluated and how pupils' curricula learning and experiences are assessed influences the teachers' enactment of the curriculum. Consideration of how curriculum is to be assessed and evaluated is critical to how curriculum 'knowledge' and 'understanding' is approached, in either narrower or broader ways as Eisner (1982, 1998a, 1998b, 2002) has discussed. Slater (1982, 1993) Lambert and Morgan (2010) and Roberts (2011) argue that the goal of geography education is 'making meaning' and 'understanding' rather than 'efficiency' or narrow behavioural objectives, such as recalling disconnected facts.

Taylor and Richards (1985) note the power of examination boards to change curricula in the 1970s and 80s. The marketisation of schooling and assessment by which examination boards compete to provide schools with the 'commodity' of GCSE and A level grades (which schools in turn use to market their services to parents) was brought sharply into the public eye late in 2011 with a scandal of examiners giving hints to paying teachers at conferences. There is a debate over how far the assessment system serves educational goals, and calls for a restructuring of school assessment were extended into policy documents (DfE 2011).

In this period the 'two-way' relationship between university and school geography (Goodson 1998) has been challenged by the argument that a 'great divide' has developed between the university discipline and the school subject (Goudie and Spooner 1993, Stannard 2003). The university discipline has increasingly fragmented into disparate specialisms and geographical research and thought has recently developed at a pace that outstripped school geography curriculum development. Butt (2008) points out that this has particularly been so where the more traditional examination boards are concerned to the extent that 'it is hard to make connections to recent developments in academic geography through these specifications' (ibid) and this is harmful:

> the uncoupling of school and university geography continues to be mutually damaging – their drift apart has meant that universities have virtually no influence on the nature of school geography, and vice versa.
>
> *Butt (2008: 163)*

Unlike the more self-regulating university discipline, school geography suffers from exposure to the whims and swings of government policy. Although the Conservative government in power at the time of my research values geography as a school subject (albeit as a limited version of geography) there is an existential threat to school geography in the long term as pressures for the school curriculum to be 'relevant', 'engaging' and 'issues-based' can override the academic argument for subject boundaries (Standish 2003, 2004). Stannard (2003) argues that a 'reconnection' of academia with schools is necessary for the health of the discipline itself. Arguing that improved collaboration between universities and schools is important to secure the future for school geography, Butt (2008) calls for further government support for geography curriculum development collaboration, such as the 'Action Plan for Geography' which ran from 2006 to 2011.

Goodson's 'two-way relationship' is therefore nuanced and cannot be taken for granted. Nonetheless, the relationship remains vital for the existence of school geography – past, present and future.

A crisis of capitalism – an opportunity to make a radical geography curriculum

The recession that followed the banking crises of 2007 to 2008, has been interpreted as a crisis of capitalism, illustrating the inbuilt tendency of the global economic system to be destructive (Harvey 2010. The social repercussions of this (such as unemployment and loss of some services) provide an opportunity for a 'social reconstructionist' curriculum to make headway. In 2009, Morgan argued that the time was ripe for geography teachers to challenge the dominant assumption being promoted by the government, that schools and the curriculum existed to bolster existing social arrangements. The narrative was that subject knowledge did not really matter as much as effective learning 'for the knowledge economy' (Morgan 2009: 115). Morgan has consistently argued that a model of school geography which sees subject knowledge as fixed and static is deficient, by failing to recognise that what is taught and learned in school has direct bearing on social relations (between the individual and the state), and so must always be challenged by the curriculum maker (the teacher) (Morgan 2002, 2009, 2011, 2012, 2014a, 2014b)

Morgan (ibid) draws attention to the significance of 'the hidden curriculum' for curriculum enactment. The 'new sociology of education' (Young 1971) showed that neither the curriculum nor schools are 'neutral' vehicles for education, but both pass on messages about values and societal norms to young people. Schools, the curriculum, teaching and learning are structured in certain ways, for example, children are commonly divided into setting by attainment, which is often referred to as 'ability', and elite, fee paying schools send 'hidden' messages to children about the ordering of people in society. Most schools (and examination systems) are structured so that children coming from middle-class homes are better equipped to succeed, as they are more likely to have already been introduced to the value of reading, writing, and expectations that they will engage in 'higher' forms of culture valued by schools. Young people are therefore endowed with varying levels of 'cultural capital' from the home (Bourdieu 1984). Giroux (2005a) argues that the 'hidden curriculum' builds on this cultural capital to inculcate an acceptance of the unequal structuring of society through schooling.

There is a 'hidden' curriculum of values and norms in the school geography curriculum. Morgan (2012) argues that capitalism as the 'natural' way of things is an implicit message perpetuated by school geography. He calls for geography teachers to teach the underlying political–economic causes of the relations between people, nature and place, rather than simply acceptance, which renders these underlying causes invisible. The school curriculum is both reflection and transmitter of societal values, but this is rarely brought to light for or by teachers (Bourdieu and Passeron 1977, Huckle 1985). The 'hidden curriculum', and how far it is revealed, is significant for curriculum enactment. Morgan (2012) and Huckle (1985) argue that when geography teachers become aware of the hidden curriculum of norms, values and political–economy, they are better placed to challenge them in the curriculum they enact.

The themes constructed in this period are summarised in Table 5.

TABLE 5 Themes from curriculum studies applied to the geography curriculum, 2008–2016

Theme	Ways in which themes are constructed 2008–2016
Power/control	Power and control can be identified, not only in the exertion of control by the state over schools, teachers and curriculum, but also in the notion of powerful curricular knowledge. The term 'powerful knowledge' (Young and Muller 2010) is used in a government sponsored curriculum document (DfE 2011), evidence both that a 'knowledge turn' has taken place, and of a broadening debate over the power that the curriculum holds. This raises the possibility of teachers taking greater control as curriculum makers.
Conflict	A renewed debate about curriculum knowledge brought schooling based on efficiency and soft skills into conflict with arguments for academic subject knowledge, and social reconstructionist arguments for how subjects are used.
Scales of influence	The economic crash of 2008 was global in both cause and impact. The crash and following recession have led to cuts to school and university budgets, the election of a centre-right government and a renewed debate over the role of education. The global scale thus drove curriculum change during this period. However, the nation state remains influential in the production of curriculum 'texts' in the 2014 Geography National Curriculum (GNC). However, some teachers, geography departments and wider collaborations of teachers, such as the Geographical Association, engaged in a consultation for the 2014 GNC and teachers may still have agency over the enacted curriculum.
Value/belief systems	The 'knowledge turn' reveals different value/belief systems in the approach to knowledge. The Coalition government (DfE 2010) reveal cultural restorationist and scholar-academic value/belief systems, but the debate about subject knowledge and disillusionment with consumption and debt-fuelled economic growth has also brought social reconstructionist value/belief systems to light (Morgan 2012).
Change	The 2008 economic crash marked the beginning of social and economic change which Morgan (2011, 2012) suggests is of a similar magnitude to the oil price shocks of 1973, which led to 'the great debate' and ultimately, direct state control over curriculum. The role and purpose of the curriculum is under scrutiny and remains the source of debate.

Themes constructed from the historical analysis

From the historical description of curriculum, five themes have been constructed. These are: power/control, scale, conflict, change, and value/belief systems. Aspects of each theme are significant for my research. These aspects are summarised below.

Power/control

In each of the historical eras the question arises of who or what holds power and control over the curriculum. Understanding the relationship between subject knowledge and power helps to answer this question. Taylor and Richards (1985) remind us that curriculum debate and contestation is a matter of consequence for political power. They argue that the political struggle between different curriculum ideologies:

> is a struggle for the power to define education and to transmit particular beliefs and values to the young.
>
> *(Taylor and Richards 1985: 36)*

The curriculum is a transmitter of belief and value systems. Hidden structures in economy and society control and influence the curriculum (Huckle 1985, Morgan 2012, Apple 2004). However, power over curriculum is complicated by curriculum existing as text (in documents, materials and ideas) and in context (as interpreted and enacted by teachers and pupils in the classroom). There is, therefore, a complex multi-layered relationship of influences over the curriculum. The global economic system, the nation state, the school and the classroom teacher each have influence over curriculum, which leads to the second theme.

Scale

References from the global to the personal in the literature allow the construction of scale as a theme in curriculum studies. The teacher enacts curriculum in the classroom. But the notions of hegemony and ideology connect the global scale of society and economy to the personal scale of curriculum embodied by the teacher and pupil. This connection is made through the spread and adoption of ideas, beliefs and values. These scales may be nested, as in Taylor's (1981) sense, so that a belief/value system is reproduced at each scale, or they may exist independently of one another, so that, as Roberts (1996) argued, an 'ideology' at the national scale is mediated by distinct 'curriculum ideologies' at the local scale. The scale of the nation state influencing curriculum through governance and regulation is a theme running throughout the history of mass schooling in England. Other influences over curriculum lie at a meso-scale, such as regional differences, and collaborating groups of teachers, who were particularly effective in the 1960s and 1980s (Taylor and Richards 1985) and have potential to empower teachers as agents of curriculum change (Skilbeck 1990, McKernan 1996, Sachs 2003 and Mitchell 2006).

The notion of the network (Herod 2011) is also useful in considering power over curriculum, through the communication, sharing and uptake of materials and ideas over the internet, including the role of the subject association and informal geography teacher networks. This is an area in which there has been little research in geography education, but which is a significant part of these research findings.

Conflict

Conflict is a central theme in the literature in both more direct and more hidden ways. Conflict is accompanied by difference. In the literature, conflict is indicated between: the working class and the elite, teaching and bureaucracy, positivism and social construction, the local and the national (and global), economy and humanity, education for change and education for the status quo, idealism and pragmatism. The chief realm of conflict in this literature review is that of beliefs and value systems. Lambert and Morgan's (2010) curriculum making argument opposes the belief that subjects are less important than 'learning' and rejects the role of teacher as effective 'deliverer' of a curriculum fixed and controlled at a larger scale. A lens through which conflict can be viewed is the geographic (space, place and scale). There is conflict between the curriculum enacted by the teacher in the classroom and the curriculum 'text' of policy (and other influences) operating at the national, global and network levels.

The literature also reveals the opposite of conflict – consensus – which is also helpful in understanding the power and control behind the geography curriculum, for example in the notion of hegemonic control, which can lead to consensus around accepted 'common sense' beliefs.

Change

Change is an overarching theme of this historical analysis. There is change in curriculum, schools, teachers, subject, society/economy and policy, ideas, and value/belief systems. Attention to the theme of change helps to understand power and control over the curriculum by illuminating causes and effects of changes in the curriculum. The notion of change is fundamental to the role of teacher as curriculum maker, but the opposite notion, that of stasis and inertia, is also a useful way to look at control over the curriculum, and helps to show that the notion of change is a relative concept. An example of this is that change to the National Curriculum can be met by resistance from teachers and geography departments.

Value/belief systems

Distinctive categories of value/belief systems can be discerned from a broad analysis of curriculum differences (the term curriculum and educational 'ideologies' is widely used and defined as value/belief systems). There is considerable agreement over categories of curriculum value/belief systems, and they become a useful tool for identifying how curriculum decisions are made – and thus how value/belief systems have powerful influence over curriculum. Since the 'new sociology of education' (Young 1971), there has been an increasing volume of critical literature arguing that curricula knowledge (and schooling more broadly) is not neutral but structured and controlled by the dominant values and beliefs of society and economy. However, it is inadequate to accept that a single value/belief system can come to control 'the geography curriculum' as it is enacted in countless different classrooms. Apple (2004), Huckle (1985) and Morgan (2010, 2011) bring hidden value/belief systems to light, but we are reminded by Roberts (1996) and Lambert and Morgan (2010) that individual departments and teachers still have some agency over curriculum making.

Conclusion to historical analysis

I argue that history shows that the curriculum, at any given time, is largely controlled by the society in which the teacher is located. Furthermore, a historical 'long view' shows that teachers, curriculum and society are linked together by relationships of power, control, conflict, scale and value/belief systems. These (relationship) themes help to understand how society influences teachers in their curriculum work. Crucial for my research, is that the historical analysis enables the location of both curriculum making (a recent theory of how teachers *ought* to relate to producing a curriculum) and curriculum enactment today (the actual practice of teaching a curriculum) as part of the long story of how teachers encounter conflicting curriculum ideas, values and beliefs as society changes.

Curriculum making is a response to a changed society from a particular value/belief perspective and a particular epistemology of geography education. In the next chapter, I focus on current times to examine curriculum making through the lens of late capitalism. By doing so I argue that late capitalism is changing the teacher/student/subject relationship with profound implications for how teachers enact the curriculum.

3

CURRICULUM MAKING – A RESPONSE TO LATE CAPITALIST TIMES

In this chapter, I examine the distinctiveness of late capitalist society arguing that the changed way in which late capitalist society conceives of the individual is particularly significant. Teachers must manage a tension created by a changed conception of the individual (the student) they teach. The effect of the tension can be a pulling of the teacher's attention away from the subject. Curriculum making can be understood as a call for teachers to assert their power over curriculum at the local scale, as resistance to late capitalist pressures.

The times – late capitalism (and its relationship to neoliberalism)

My research uses 'late capitalism' as its main theoretical lens in approaching the issue of how society and economy relate to curriculum enactment. However, the use of 'neoliberal' has become 'near ubiquitous' in contemporary social science (Ganti 2014), while 'late capitalism', though less common in curriculum studies, is used to analyse the same concern of educational failings in recent times by Hartley 1997. Similarly, Morgan (2011) describes 'contemporary capitalism' with attention to its global and disorganised stage, to analyse those same failings for geography education. Thus, both 'late capitalism' and 'neoliberalism' are used pejoratively in the field of curriculum studies, offering an explanation for how market-oriented government policy becomes harmful to a broad and balanced curriculum.

However, late capitalism and neoliberalism are not interchangeable terms and there is a distinction between them in three ways. First, late capitalism is more closely linked to postmodern culture (Jameson 1992) and post-Fordist economy (Hartley 1997). Secondly, 'late capitalism' originates in Marxian analysis to describe capitalism since the mid-twentieth century (Mandel 1998, Lash and Urry 1987, Harvey 1990). Thirdly, late capitalism describes a phase of time, with an end point, rather than a potentially timeless ideology and (its Marxian roots notwithstanding) 'appears to be a relatively neutral term' (Ganti 2014: 93).

Neoliberalism, unlike 'late capitalism', is often described as an 'ideology' (Apple 2004, Mirowski 2009) and a 'philosophical movement' (Ganti 2014: 91). The pro-neoliberalism argument is that individual freedom can only flourish in a society that protects private property and a competitive market (Mirowski 2009, Steger and Roy 2010).

Viewing the (social and economic) times as both 'late capitalism' and 'neoliberal' is complex and nuanced but helpful to understand curriculum making because both views allow a social-economic analysis of the influences over teachers' curriculum making and so help to shine a light on how far geography teachers can be curriculum makers in current times. In my research, a socio-economic lens can help to uncover power, control and influence in education. A fundamental difference in my research to accounts such as Hartley (1997), Apple (2004), Kelly (2008), Morgan (2011) and Fielding and Moss (2011) is that the phenomenon to which I apply a social-economic lens is not curriculum, but *curriculum making*, which is distinctive by emphasising the teacher's role in curriculum.

Late capitalism

A late capitalist view recognises the influence of financial capital through globalisation and the multinational corporation across all aspects of society (Lash and Urry 1987, Mandel 1998). The notion of late capitalism derives from Marxian economic analyses of society after the Second World War, but differs from classical Marxism by rejecting the belief that proletarian uprising would overthrow capitalism. Rather, late capitalism sees a gradual weakening toward a possible, eventual collapse as the corporatist phase of capitalism leads to growing dissatisfaction and the replacement of entrepreneurial values with more democratic or 'labourist' values (Schumpeter 1994).

Postmodernism is a cultural relation to the economic and social theory of late capitalism and is a way of understanding education in current times. Hartley (1997), Biesta (1995) and Morgan (2002, 2014a) argue that a weakening of belief in subject knowledge indicates a postmodern rejection of the modernity project, as Morgan explains:

> The extent to which schools and teachers seem to have given up on knowledge is a reflection of how society has given up on ideas of Enlightenment and modernity.
>
> *(Morgan 2014a: xii)*

In his educational analysis of late capitalism, Hartley (1997) connects the post-Fordist economy of late capitalism to postmodern culture in his argument for educators to take a critical stance against the bureaucratic managerialism and individualism of late capitalist society. Postmodern perspectives bring into question 'what counts' as knowledge, which supports the argument that technology is changing the relationship of teacher, learner and curriculum as formal authority structures are broken down. Such perspectives include Lyotard's (1984) fragmentation of knowledge, Baudrillard's (1994) tendency toward simulation and Bauman's (2001, 2005) notion of the 'melting' of the once solid structures of society into more 'liquid' forms.

Late capitalism and postmodernity provide twin lenses with which to analyse teachers' curriculum enactment. They explain how changes in society and economy have altered the way students, teaching and knowledge are conceived, such that knowledge becomes more fluid and less structured. The instrumental purposes of knowledge become more important than the knowledge itself. Here, the tension between Lambert and Morgan's (2010) argument for teachers to be curriculum makers and the pressures of the times upon teachers comes to the fore. Curriculum making requires teachers to be 'knowledge workers' (Lambert 2011) engaged with their discipline and the school subject, a part of which requires maintaining the boundaries of 'powerful knowledge', but the performance pressures of the times coupled with the fragmentation and fluidity of knowledge encourages teachers to 'give up on knowledge' (Morgan 2014).

Neoliberalism

Neoliberalism provides a distinctive societal-economic lens with which to analyse the influences over teachers' curriculum enactment. Critical accounts of neoliberal society explain how intensified competition and privatisation in recent times have influenced schools, teachers and curriculum (Apple 2004 and Fielding and Moss 2011). An acceptance of neoliberalism as a critical economic theory (frequently used in the field of curriculum studies) is compatible with the acceptance of the social-economic theory of late capitalism. This compatibility is illustrated by Hartley's (1997) use of both to explain the influence of society on schooling.

After 'classical neoliberalism' (Smith 1993) became widely discredited by society following the World Wars and depressions of the twentieth century, neoliberalism offered a future for free market competition (Steger and Roy 2010) gaining support in the West during the Cold War as an alternative to collectivism, centralised planning and socialism (Ganti 2014). This support accelerated with recession and the breakup of state sponsored industry in Britain in the 1970s (Prasad 2006). By the mid-1980s the 'neoliberal state' led by Margaret Thatcher had established a principle of government intervention and control – not to temper the freedom of the competitive market as post-war welfarist governments had done – but to encourage it (Steger and Roy 2010, Plant 2012). Since then, in Britain, the neoliberal state has been reinvented in the New Labour Project of 'The Third Way' (Giddens 2000) providing a 'softer' version of neoliberalism for more social justice and public-private partnership (Barber 1997). New Labour and the subsequent Coalition government were nonetheless essentially neoliberal in their commitment to private enterprise and competition.

The rise of the neoliberal state ended the post-war social settlement and, over the decades which followed, took control of the curriculum away from teachers (Rawling 2001, Morgan 2002). New Labour education policy (1997 to 2007) deepened neoliberal hegemony, according to Fielding and Moss (2011) and Kelly (2008), but New Labour policy was a mix of belief and value systems, and a hybrid of ideas, borrowing from neoliberalism and social democracy, without fully embracing either (Jones 2003). The Coalition and subsequent Conservative governments have continued a neoliberal agenda in schools, through academisation, which embeds the market and competition in education. Schools and teachers remain accountable for student performance, which becomes ever more crucial as schools (often in academy chains) compete for survival and growth. Such a climate raises the question of how the teacher's curriculum enactment is affected by pressure to achieve results that will help their school to compete.

Curriculum making (Lambert and Morgan 2010) is an argument for teachers to take control of the (enacted) curriculum and to assert their power as professional 'knowledge workers'. Key to this argument is that the teachers' curriculum role has been diminished in recent times. The curriculum making model is therefore both a product of and a response to social and economic change. Furthermore, curriculum making is an idealised model in tension with increased pressures on teachers to enact a curriculum driven by performativity.

Curriculum making remains a significant and potentially powerful concept for the teacher, but society is changing both how teachers enact the curriculum and how young people (as individuals and students) are conceived. The teacher's professional identity becomes particularly important in times of pressure and change. It becomes increasingly important that the teacher identifies as a curriculum maker if they are to 'recontextualise' the knowledge of their discipline into a high-quality school curriculum.

The teacher – recontextualising geography to make the curriculum

Curriculum making is located within a particular view of the teacher's relationship to subject knowledge. In this view, the teacher works upon and changes or 'recontextualises' subject knowledge for the purpose of teaching a young person (Bernstein 2000). Such an act of subject knowledge recontextualisation is a key process of curriculum enactment. Understanding how teachers recontextualise subject knowledge can help to explore the influences over the teacher as they enact the curriculum and the way that the teacher responds to those influences. For example, helpful questions are raised by considering the teacher's knowledge recontextualisation such as, from where and whom is subject knowledge coming? How far is the teacher in control of both subject knowledge choices and how knowledge is changed into an enacted curriculum?

Rather than being a transmitter of 'inert' knowledge in an 'under-socialised' curriculum, the notion of the teacher as curriculum maker views knowledge in a more dynamic way. Curriculum making emphasises the teacher as knowledge 'boundary worker' (Lambert 2011: 257) and holding a 'balance' between their knowledge of pedagogy, subject and learner (Lambert and Morgan 2010: 50). Curriculum making involves 'translating a curriculum plan' (2010: 50). Brooks (2008) argues that 'the interpretation and implementation of the geography curriculum is done by geography teachers' (2008: 355). The notion of curriculum making is thus connected to the teacher as actor upon subject knowledge, transforming that knowledge into an enacted curriculum, as Puttick identifies:

> There is a substantial tradition of discussing the transformation of (mainly disciplinary) knowledge into school curricula, a process described by Dewey as psychologising; by Bruner as conversion; and by Schwab as translation.
>
> *(Puttick 2015a: 29)*

Bernstein's (2000) notion of the recontextualisation of knowledge by teachers is significant in understanding curriculum making. Bernstein argues that the recontextualisation of knowledge produces subject boundaries, which are legitimised through social power relations and communicated through social control structures. Young (2009) and Young and Muller (2010) use Bernstein's ideas in developing the notion of 'powerful knowledge' and the case for boundaries to be maintained but also crossed for a subject-based school curriculum of powerful knowledge (Young and Muller 2010: 16). These ideas inform the notion of curriculum making and its representation as a balanced Venn diagram model (Lambert 2009a, 2011, Lambert and Morgan 2010, Young and Lambert 2014, Lambert and Biddulph (2015).

Puttick's research (2015b) examines curriculum making at the very short term, as 'micro processes'. He argues that the complexity of curriculum making 'might be present in each act of recontextualisation' (2015b: 33). In order to understand how geography teachers transform their subject knowledge as they enact the curriculum, Puttick (2015b) applies Bernstein's (2000) pedagogic device of the official recontextualising field (ORF) and the pedagogic recontextualising field (PRF) to an ethnographic study of geography departments. Puttick's significant contribution to understanding curriculum making is to refine the 'knowledge work' of geography teachers to five degrees of recontextualisation (2015b: 369). However, he also sheds light on the nature of contemporary curriculum making. Puttick (2015a, 2015b) identifies the internet, accountability for examination results, and teacher-department identity narratives as prominent in geography teachers' curriculum work.

Puttick's (2015a, 2015b) notion of five degrees of recontextualisation recognises that teachers sometimes change subject knowledge substantially from a source (such as a textbook, website or television programme) and sometimes they change it very little. This raises the question of what influences the teacher in these acts of changing knowledge and how far they have agency over the curriculum knowledge they produce. Drawing from Young and Muller (2009) and Bernstein's (2000) arguments, Young and Lambert (2014) argue that the teacher is pivotal in a relationship between themselves, a changing discipline of geography, the school subject and its educational purposes. This raises questions of: 'What is influencing the teacher as they enact this pivotal role?' and, 'Does the teacher have agency in the process, or are they reacting to outside (societal) influences, with little control over the curriculum produced?'

The teacher's identity and curriculum making

Curriculum making is bound up with teacher identities and teacher identities change as schooling and society changes. The relationship between teacher identity and curriculum making is therefore significant for my research and is helpful in analysing teachers' descriptions of curriculum making and their personal curriculum making 'story'.

Mitchell and Lambert call for teacher training to initiate new geography teachers into a particular 'self-image' (2015: 377).

> Curriculum making must become integrated into the teacher's professional self-image – into how they identify themselves as 'geography teachers'. This may require a substantial shift as the common self-image of the 'professional' teacher has moved toward the 'competent craftsperson' in recent years.
>
> *(Mitchell and Lambert 2015: 377)*

The relationship between the geography teacher's identity and curriculum has been explored through research into the teacher's use and conceptions of subject knowledge. Brooks (2012) shows that the geography teacher's self-identity as a 'professional' is subject to the influence of changing times and educational trends. She examines the shift from curriculum to pedagogy in educational discourse in the 2000s, how this affects teachers' professional identities and the importance of the formative stages of a teacher's 'geographer' and 'teacher' identity to provide a point of reference and stability through changing times. However, this identity is not static. Teachers are 'reforming and remaking their professional practice in the light of their changing contexts' (2012: 305). Drawing on Barnett's (2011) notion of professionalism as 'being' and 'becoming', Brooks (2012) argues that geography teachers draw on and change their professional identity to make sense of changing circumstances to 'navigate' the changing times. Professional communities are particularly significant to this process of 'being' and 'becoming'.

Brooks had earlier identified a tension in teachers' curriculum making, in the difficulty of reconciling their personal view of 'good geography' with 'good lessons' (2008: 367), which required teachers to be strategic.

> Teachers, as curriculum developers, have also had to use their subject knowledge in a strategic way in order to enable them to act within their values framework.
>
> *(Brooks 2006: 367)*

Brooks develops the analogy of teacher as navigating changing times in her notion of the teacher's 'professional compass' (Brooks 2016). Subject expertise is tied to the geography teacher's professional identity and therefore shapes their practice (Brooks 20016.

Puttick (2016) concurs with Brooks in two ways. The first is the importance of subject-based professional identity in 'sustaining' teachers' work. The second is the recognition of the significance of professional (subject teacher) communities. Brooks (2012, 2016) and Lambert (2010b) emphasise 'communities of practice' in geography teachers' work. Puttick focuses on the individual teacher in the department context. He finds that the teacher's individual beliefs about geography, shaped from early childhood, affect how the teacher 'locates' themselves in the department – however, the department has a strong influence on the teacher's identity, through a shared geographical narrative.

> There was strong evidence in Town Comprehensive of a shared narrative through which individual teachers' histories and specialisms were re-told and re-framed to construct the cohesive whole of their department.
>
> *(Puttick 2016: 15)*

The communities and cultures in which teachers practice affect the development of their subject identities, which in turn affects their practice. Alexander (2009) shows that 'culture' can be at both a wider societal scale and at the school level.

> Teaching is located in the larger cultural context. But students and teachers also create their own micro-culture.
>
> *(Alexander 2009:15)*

At the national and international scale, Morgan and Lambert (2005) and Brooks (2006, 2012, 2013a, 2016) refer to a geography education 'community' in connection to teachers' curriculum work. The subject association plays a substantial role in disseminating ideas including curriculum making and associated concepts, such as 'geocapabilities' (Lambert, Solem and Tani 2015) and 'powerful knowledge' (Lambert 2008, Lambert and Morgan 2010, Young and Lambert 2014). At the local scale, Puttick (2015) and Roberts (1996) draw attention to the significance of a shared geography department identity or culture in shaping curriculum.

A 'performativity culture' (Winter and Firth 2007: 352) is deeply embedded in contemporary schooling, but there are 'micro-cultures' (Alexander 2009:15) within teacher communities, which may help to 'sustain teachers' by strengthening shared identities within a community (Puttick 2016). The notion of teachers developing a 'professional compass' (Brooks 2016) is also informative when considered alongside the argument for geographical knowledge to underpin teacher's curriculum work to 'resist the flow' of the times (Firth 2011a, 2013, Lambert 2011 and Mitchell and Lambert 2015).

Attention to teachers' identities and how they change helps the examination of how changes in society are influencing curriculum enactment. A 'performativity culture' in wider society has permeated schooling and threatens to dominate teachers' curriculum thinking but geography teachers' identities are resilient. This raises the questions of to what extent are teachers' identities shaped by 'the times'? And how are teachers drawing on their identities as they enact the curriculum in pressurised times? Teacher identity is thus a helpful perspective with which to examine the society–curriculum enactment relationship. Changing identities and response as 'resistance' to the pressures form a key part of the findings.

Students' identities are also changing with the times. This is a similarly significant perspective for examining teachers' curriculum work and so it is to student identity which we now turn.

The student – a 'new individualism'

Two branches of social theory show a changed society in late capitalism. These are economic change, with a shift from Fordist to post-Fordist production, and cultural change with a shift from modernity to postmodernity. These changes can be linked to society's conception of the individual and the child in school (Hartley, 1997). The pervasion of the internet in almost everyone's lives, and most intensely in young lives outside school, is changing the way in which the individual relates to others, and it is changing the teacher–student–curriculum (subject knowledge) relationship, with potential implications for pedagogy and curriculum (Kress 2006, Somekh 2006, Lave and Wenger 1991, Moore 2015, Morgan 2014b).

Morgan (2011:118) argues that a 'neoliberal turn' has taken place with a shift from 'Fordism to post-Fordism' (Aglietta 1979 in Morgan 2011: 118), and from 'Organized to Disorganized capitalism' (Lash and Urry 1987 in Morgan 2011: 118), which is passed on to how schools imagine the student.

> A third phase aimed at the construction of a new consensus – this involved focusing on the image of the new model student/worker committed to the goals of team work, flexibility and the desire to learn.
>
> *(Robins and Webster 1989, in Morgan 2011: 119)*

Hartley (1997) presents neoliberal society's influence as a deep-rooted tension playing out in schooling. His argument runs that there is a tension driven by two contradictory forces in the late capitalist world. One is the drive to produce, more, better, faster – an economic imperative. The other is to consume, as a self-centred individual – a cultural imperative. These forces are difficult to reconcile in many aspects of society, including schooling where they affect how the individual is being conceived. On the one hand the post-Fordist economic world is driving a technical and competitive individualism, in which there is pressure to make a highly skilled and effective workforce. On the other, postmodern culture encourages a 'self-centred and narcissistic individualism' in which the person is a consumer (Hartley, 1997: 3). This, Hartley argues, encourages teachers to adopt a 'pedagogy of pleasure' (1997: 77) while at the same time finding themselves subject to 'total quality management' (1997: 132) passed on to their students through Foucauldian assessment practices of close surveillance and standardised measurement (1997: 113–114).

'Consumerism' has been identified as a growing, global trend in both higher education and schools (Naidoo, Shankar and Veer 2011, Postman, 1996). The student is increasingly recognised as a consumer, with individual needs and demands to be satisfied (particularly connected to the economic utility of the education offered). Postman (1996) argues that these – consumership, economic utility and separatism (the individual), and also technology – are the new 'gods' of education:

> The gods of economic utility, consumership, technology and separatism are to be found in our schools now, exerting their force and commanding allegiance. They are gods that come from outside the walls of the classroom.
>
> *(Postman 1996: 60)*

The origin of the new 'gods' in Postman's argument is particularly significant for my research, which is concerned with how curriculum and wider society relate. He argues that they come from 'outside' school, in wider society. Wider society is thus the driver of change in school and Postman's language portrays schools as subject to an overwhelming power from 'outside'.

Turner (2010) argues that a 'demotic turn' or 'turn to ordinary people' has taken place. His argument is located in cultural studies and the internet and social media enabling such a 'demotic turn'. Morgan (2014b) suggests a 'demotic turn' can be seen reflected in a changed teacher-student relationship in schools, aided by the internet and social media.

> This is … a shift away from the notion of the expert who has authority and status by dint of their social role, towards the recognition that ordinary people are potential experts. In schools it is reflected in the rise of 'student voice' initiatives, the trend towards the 'gamification' of learning, and the cult of 'personalised learning'. This ceding of 'power to the people' is aided by the widely held notion that social media is allowing for the flourishing of creativity, sharing and innovation. Simply put, we have reached the point where the question, 'why do I need a teacher when I've got Google?' requires a serious answer.
>
> *(Morgan, 2014b: 1)*

The internet is causing a shift in the power and authority that the teacher holds over the learner's curriculum. Moore (2015) argues that using the internet to 'learn' is fundamentally different to the way knowledge and learning is structured in school. Kress (2006) argues that comparing the homepage of a website to a 'traditional' page shows such a fundamental change. The homepage offers a variety of entry points and paths to the information the reader wishes to acquire. Unlike a traditional (book) page, it does not assume an order to be followed. In other words, it does not assume to 'know the audience' (2006: 164). This represents a shift in the power/authority of the author. Kress (2006) argues that children's 'habitus' (2006: 167) is shaped by using the internet – yet in school they encounter 'an entirely different model of the relationship (between themselves and knowledge)' (2006: 167). Kress (2006) draws attention to an inversion in power and authority taking place from the institution of the school, to the life-world of the learner. The teachers is in a difficult position here. Kress identifies that teachers have a 'need for their consent' (2006: 167) when offering a curriculum to the learner.

> Children in school are users of these media, they have become subjects whose 'habitus' in terms of their power/authority relationship to knowledge and interest is shaped by that use ... children now come to school only to meet there an entirely different model of the relationship. This poses the problem ... the power of institutional authority versus the interest of the learners, and the need for their consent, in a world where, ideologically at least, the directionality of power, authority and knowledge to learner and life-world has been inverted.
>
> *Kress (2006: 167)*

The internet-led shift in how 'learning' takes place at home and outside school learning can be linked to teacher and learner identities. Somekh (2006) argues that the universal availability of facts and knowledge necessitates a shift from a 'teaching curriculum' (McCormick and Murphy 2000: 229) to a 'learning curriculum' (Lave and Wenger 1991: 97), which recognises that teachers become more concerned with the learners' experiences, than with pre-set knowledge. Teachers become improvisers rather than knowledge transmitters. Moore (2016) suggests that the effect of this is that:

> Knowledge is as often invoked in support of practice and experience, as the other way round and the relationships between teachers and learners, and indeed between teachers, learners and curriculum, undergo a radical change in which learner and teacher identities themselves become blurred within a set of joint learning ventures.
>
> *(Moore 2015: 94)*

As Somekh (2006) describes, 'teacher and learner roles are interchangeable' in the collaborative learning environment of an internet-driven information age. The 'blurring' of the line between teacher, learner and curriculum has implications for reading the curriculum making model. Lambert and Morgan (2010) see the teacher as curriculum maker, using and balancing the three 'resources' of teacher, student and subject. But such an act may require a clarity in the separation of the three resources, which becomes difficult when the resources are blurred or even 'interchangeable'.

Conclusion to Part I – What is happening now?

In a historical analysis in Chapter 2, I concluded that neither curriculum nor teachers can be separated from the society in which their curriculum is enacted. In this chapter, I have argued that the curriculum making model is a response to late capitalist times. However, there is a tension between curriculum making (an idealised model of teacher agency) and a persistent controlling influence of society and economy upon curriculum. Curriculum making requires considerable teacher autonomy, but that autonomy may be compromised, even controlled, by outside pressure.

Previous research has explored the curriculum-society relationship, but not the relationship between *curriculum making* and society. Curriculum making is an important idea for geography education with widespread currency, but there has been little empirical research to examine its usefulness and applicability. It is this gap that I sought to fill in my research, and the findings of which inform this book. As a community of teachers and educators we need to understand the potential for geography teachers to be curriculum makers as they enact the curriculum in changing times. After a theoretical examination (including the historical analysis I have presented) there is little doubt of a dialectical relationship between society and curriculum. But, we are left asking – what is happening now? The questions remain, which invite empirical study:

- What is the relationship between society and geography curriculum enactment?
- How are teachers responding to societal influences over their curriculum enactment?

These were my key research questions as I set out to make such an empirical study by looking closely at four geography departments.

The next part of the book first explains how I carried out my research. Then four case studies of geography departments are presented, each showing a distinctive 'character' with respect to how they approach their curriculum choices, and the influences and controls over their curriculum 'enactment'. Using this evidence, I go on in the final chapters of the book to argue that late capitalist times are driving 'hyper-socialised' curriculum enactment.

PART II

Curriculum enactment: case studies of geography departments

Introduction – Researching curriculum enactment in late capitalism

This introduction to Part 2 of the book describes the empirical basis for my argument that teachers' work has become 'hyper-socialised'. In my research, four geography departments in London schools provided the case study data.

'Curriculum' has tended to be downplayed in schools, despite the powerful forces of late capitalist society acting to shape it. Therefore, the role of teachers as potential curriculum makers warrants close attention and empirical evidence in such times, as I have argued in part one. Before embarking on empirical work, a literature review developed my theoretical position on the influence of the changing times on schools, teachers and curriculum (see Chapters 1 to 3). I was also careful to adopt an open, inductive approach as far as possible, so as not to be overly led or constrained by a theoretical perspective. With this in mind, I observed and listened to the teachers' narratives of curriculum enactment. Alongside this I developed a set of analytical statements by coding and grouping data (lesson observations, curriculum planning meetings, in-depth interviews and department curriculum documents). As I analysed the data I found connections between the themes drawn from my historical analysis of literature and contemporary social theory. From these connections, I constructed a description of how current society influences teachers' curriculum work. I articulate this description as 'hyper-socialised' curriculum enactment (see Figure 5).

Why a case study approach?

Readers may have noted, at this point, that the empirical support for my argument in this book is founded on an interpretivist view of knowledge. Some may be inclined toward 'proof', probability or large samples or randomised controlled trials when

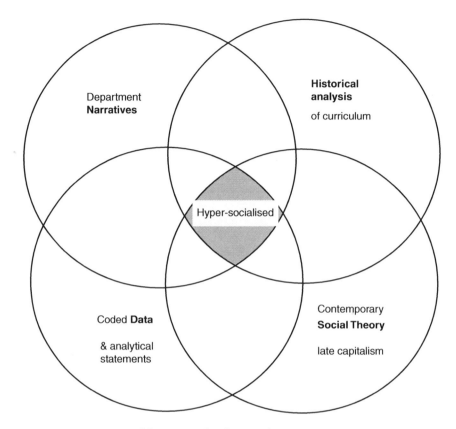

FIGURE 5 Construction of 'hyper-socialised' curriculum enactment

examining evidence in educational research. I do not claim I can 'prove' anything about curriculum enactment, and I make no apology for this. I do however claim to offer a robust interpretation to help understand the very complex phenomenon of 'curriculum' as enacted by teachers in all the 'messiness' of the real world setting.

A case study approach is highly appropriate for such research. Case studies can allow an often taken-for-granted phenomenon (like curriculum) to be seen anew, with fresh insight, and I believe this has been so in the case studies and conclusions drawn from them, which I present in the next section.

I should point out I am aware of the knowledge assumptions made and the limitations to an interpretivist case study approach such as this. I am assuming that readers will not want a full discussion of these here, nor a detailed methodology, but these are explored and available in the thesis on which this book is based (Mitchell 2017). It may, however, be helpful to give a brief overview here, of how the research was designed and how the four case studies were selected, before going on to present each case of a geography department's curriculum enactment, given their own chapter.

Research design, data collection and analysis

Figure 6 summarises the final research design showing five key aspects to the empirical work or 'methods' used:

1.   Four, in-depth case studies of geography departments.
2.   A range of data sources (lesson observations, department planning meetings, interviews and documents).
3.   A theory-informed, inductive coding system.
4.   The production of robust analytical statements about curriculum making, through a rigorous process of reducing and interpreting coded data.
5.   The production of 'portrait' descriptions of each department case study (and as a sub-set of each, teachers' own stories).

The case study departments

The geography departments were known to me beforehand through my work as a teacher-educator. They were selected because they offered differing 'human' (teacher) contexts and different school 'cultures'. But also these were schools broadly in the same part of one city, teaching the national curriculum under, ostensibly, the same 'rules' of accountability. The sample thus gives potential for fruitful findings into the nuance of influences on teachers' curriculum making.

Key Stage 3 (KS3), the 11–14 age group, or the first three years of a young person's secondary schooling in English schools, was chosen because there is no 'high stakes' public examination for this age group. The teacher enacts the curriculum with more autonomy than for examination courses with more tightly prescribed content. The relative autonomy to choose what and how to teach in KS3 gives potential to illuminate wider influences over curriculum enactment than in the more restricted curriculum of GCSE and A level (examination) courses.

The four cases are:

●   Comprehensive, state schools
●   Large, established departments with a mix of experience levels (4–6 dedicated geography specialists, the Head of geography in place for several years)
●   Inner/suburban London
●   Mixed catchments (serving a range from privileged middle class to socially/ economically disadvantaged).

School A – 'Arnwell' – Mixed boys/girls. The school has an integrated 'skills' curriculum for Humanities in year 7 (rather than discrete subjects). Much teaching in KS3 is by non-specialists. Literacy and behaviour are whole school priorities in the younger year groups. Academic achievement (using the common league table measure) is close to national average.

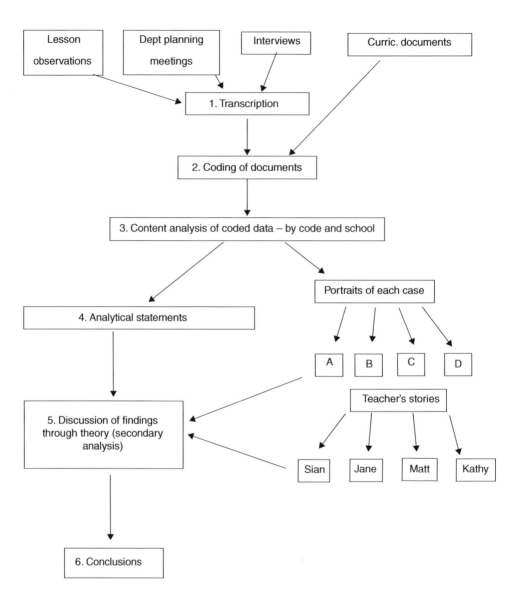

FIGURE 6 Summary of research design

School B – 'Brightling' – Girls. Academic achievement (using the common league table measure) is slightly above national average. There is challenging behaviour and pupil motivation can be low.

School C – 'Claymore' – Girls. Academic achievement (using the common league table measure) is well above national average. The school is in an inner-city area with pockets of deprivation but it is highly 'desirable' with middle-class families. Pupils' families are from wide extremes of income.

School D – 'Derwent' – Mixed boys/girls. The most suburban location and the highest proportion of middle-class pupils. Academic achievement is well above national average. The school is very popular and oversubscribed (like School C this school tends to be very desirable to middle-class parents). The Head of Geography was completing a Master's degree in Geography Education at the time of data collection and is active in the geography education community – for example, participating in an externally funded geography curriculum project (a universities-schools alliance).

The following four chapters present each department's curriculum enactment story.

4

ARNWELL HIGH SCHOOL – A CURRICULUM FOR ENGAGEMENT AND SKILLS

Introduction – how the case study chapters are structured

The following four chapters present the empirical findings from my research by describing each geography department's curriculum enactment as a case study 'portrait'. Together, these chapters illustrate the differences in geography curriculum enactment between schools. After these chapters, I examine the common aspects of curriculum enactment across the four departments. These commonalities are interpreted with the lens of late capitalism and the five themes from the historical analysis to describe how society and economy are influencing teachers' curriculum enactment.

Each portrait is described as it relates to student, teachers and geography (adapted from the three pillars of the curriculum making model) and the constructed themes of accountability and technology. The themes constructed from the historical analysis of literature (Chapters 2 and 3) are discussed in the conclusion of each of the following descriptive 'portrait' chapters and in the analysis of the commonalities of curriculum enactment across the four departments. Each of the case studies is introduced with a brief summary of its distinctive aspects. Then the school and department context is described, as this context is itself an influence on curriculum enactment, before the full case study is portrayed.

The differences between the departments show teacher agency in curriculum enactment. Some geography teachers, especially the Heads of Department, portray a concern for curriculum making, in particular by giving attention to the school subject and the discipline of geography as well as the experiences of the child and their (teacher) choices. The portraits show that school context is a control over the geography teacher's work, either supporting or restricting the geography teacher's integrity to make their own curriculum choices. In the final analysis looking across all the departments, I articulate a common process of curriculum enactment in late capitalism.

Arnwell High

'Arnwell High' is an inner-city school with many students in challenging socio-economic circumstances. A key aspect of curriculum enactment here is a link between student behaviour, the perceived 'relevance' of curriculum content, and the development of 'learning skills'. School management and whole school curriculum organisation restricts the Head of Geography's power to lead geography in the school curriculum at Arnwell.

Head of Department, 'Sian's story' is one of struggling to develop a dynamic geography curriculum in a school context that does not place high value on subject content in Key Stage 3 (KS3). Her story is also one of wanting students to enjoy their KS3 geography lessons. But behind this there is a larger vision to develop particular values and attitudes in the students. Sian wants her students to grow into confident and capable adults who 'care about the world'.

School and geography department context

The school context helps to explain the teacher's emphasis on behaviour and engagement through 'relevance' and the whole school emphasis on cross-curricular skills and depth of content (over breadth), which restricts teacher agency to make subject-led curriculum choices. The local area (inner city and exceptionally high inequality) connects to the Head of Geography's description of her personal aim for geography education to take these young people out of their small, inner-city 'bubble'.

Arnwell High is an inner-London 11–18 mixed comprehensive of average size (1,284 students). The school serves a mixed catchment, in an area of very high economic inequality. Many of the wealthier families in the area send their children to independent schools, and Arnwell has a relatively under-privileged student body. Students on free school meals, with special educational needs (SEN)/disabilities and children learning English as an additional language (EAL) are 'well above average' according to their Office for Standards in Education, Children's Services and Skills (Ofsted) report. The school's most recent (2011) Ofsted report rates Arnwell as 'good' overall. This is an improvement from earlier inspections but working toward the 'outstanding' Ofsted grade helps to explain the close monitoring and control of teaching (such as direction over the amount of teacher talk in lessons) portrayed in the data analysis. Behaviour was a significant problem at Arnwell and has improved in recent years (evidenced by the testimony of teachers who have been at the school for many years, my own experience visiting the school over a ten year period, and in Ofsted inspections). The school underwent a major rebuild in 2006 to 2007. There is a carefully enforced uniform and a business-like atmosphere in the school with open plan teacher office areas and suites of computers in all classrooms.

The staffing structure has a humanities division with a Head of Humanities responsible for geography, history, religious studies and citizenship. However, there is a group of geography specialist teachers and a teacher responsible for geography (Sian) to whom I refer as 'Head of Department' (HoD). At Arnwell, KS3 is organised as 'integrated humanities and skills' (IHS) in year 7, before geography appears as a discrete lesson in the timetable in year 8.

The geography teachers are summarised in Table 6.

These are the geography specialist teachers. Geography lessons in KS3 are also taught by non-specialists. All but one of the geography team are very experienced teachers and are well established at the school. Six geography specialist teachers are an impressive team in a school of this size. However, all the team – with the exception of Sian, HoD and Mike, the newly qualified teacher (NQT) – have additional responsibilities, two being in senior management. Furthermore, they all teach other subjects in addition to geography and so are pulled away from a geography focus. Sian says that several years have passed since the geography team last met together.

Analysis of curriculum enactment – students

Behaviour (using relevance and enjoyment)

Behaviour, relevance and enjoyment are recurring themes in interviews with Sian and Clare, in lesson observations and in curriculum documents. Behaviour has improved over the last seven years at Arnwell, according to teachers interviewed. But concern for behaviour appears to be never far from the surface of teachers' thinking and actions around curriculum.

> Past behaviour has been SO terrible in this school. It's a funny school to teach in, you almost have to entertain them. It has to be about that experience for them otherwise it's not going to work for you.
>
> *(Sian)*

> Our philosophy is to make sure that their learning is relevant and connects to their own experience.
>
> *(Clare)*

TABLE 6 The geography teachers at Arnwell

	School responsibilities (beyond Geography)	*Age and time at the school*
Sian (HoD)	None	30s 6 years
Sally	Assistant Head	40s 15 years
Clare	Deputy Head	40s 10 years
Sean	Head of year	50s 20 years
Dave	Head of year	30s 12 years
Mike	None (NQT)	20s <1 year

During a geography department planning meeting, new national curriculum topics of soils and glaciation were discussed. Sian expresses disappointment about having to teach these physical geography topics. She jokes that talking about soils leads to poor behaviour because the topic is dull.

> Podsol, bags of soil … (groans) soils are worse than rocks! … See, just starting talking about soils and there's low level disruption!
>
> *(Sian)*

Students are involved in curriculum decisions. They are asked to choose which places they study in parts of KS3.

> We do a lot of interviewing of the students. We've done an awful lot on student voice this year, speaking to them about what they enjoy and what things work well … to plan for next year.
>
> *(Sian)*

There is an extended project on the local area, which Sian relates to fostering students' interest and engagement. One observed lesson featured the 2014 Brazil Football World Cup. Brazilian football stadiums were used as a way to learn population distribution and settlement pattern in Brazil. Another lesson, which focused on skills of data analysis, investigated crime in the local borough. Crime and football are both topics featured in the former government-funded Qualifications and Curriculum Authority (QCA) programmes of study, and are described as having been in the department's curriculum for many years, and they are topics that are a part of the everyday life experience of children attending Arnwell High. Data analysis of two observed lessons portrays crime and football as vehicles for learning skills (such as numeracy and graphicacy) through an engaging 'relevant' topic, rather than being used to understand or think through geographical concepts (such as space, place and environment).

Clare (Deputy Head and geography teacher) describes the need to 'engage' students with 'relevant' content. Content for 'the kids in the school' is often linked to an issues approach. Analysis of other interviews, lesson observations and curriculum documents further support the portrayal of an 'engagement through relevance' theme.

> We don't get much 'what's the point?'. Our philosophy is make sure that their learning is relevant and connects to their own experience – where there are going.
>
> *(Clare)*

> We've moved more towards an issues-based curriculum over the last five years and issues are the sort of things the kids in the school grab onto and engage with. We thought that was the best way to teach the geography.
>
> *(Sian)*

The theme of engaging students by selecting 'relevant' content is illustrated in the portrayal of an 'issues' approach. Sian's portrayal of curriculum making, and KS3 curriculum documents, describes teaching issues of pollution, local and global inequalities, unfair trade and 'blood diamonds'. Sian emphasises sustainability as the main geographical concept being learned through these issues and she downplays some geographical concepts (such as physical process), as one observed lesson illustrates. The lesson was part of the 'wild weather' unit and was titled 'What can we do to develop sustainability?' The learning objectives were given as: 'to investigate what actions can now be taken to limit the impacts of global warming'; and 'to evaluate who can affect the most change, individuals or governments'. Although ostensibly part of a physical geography (weather) unit, observation showed that the lesson was about addressing a global issue (climate change) by considering responsibilities and political positions (the role of individuals, state and international governance). Other lessons observed, taught by a different geography teacher, used topics of crime in the local area, and the Brazilian Football World Cup 2014 to make geography 'relevant' to these students. Observation revealed the lessons were about mathematical skills with little geographical content other than framing the mathematics in a location and an engaging 'relevant' topic.

'Active' approaches to learning are mentioned frequently. HoD (Sian) talks of 'nice' lessons and when asked what this meant she refers to 'active' learning with students talking and the teacher as more of a facilitator than a giver of knowledge. 'Active' learning was observed in lessons, where paired and group work involved solving problems and in one activity, leaving their seats, still working in groups, to gather information from seven sheets stuck on walls around the room. The emphasis placed on 'active' and 'relevant' learning helps to explain the teachers' resistance to topics (like soils and glaciation) that are far from these students' life experience and so can be perceived as more difficult to teach through such 'active' student learning.

The data analysis shows a connection between the portrayal of curriculum for engagement (for good behaviour) and school policy to integrate the humanities subjects in year 6. The integrated curriculum means that children are taught by the same humanities teacher four times a week, because, regardless of their specialist subject, humanities staff teach geography, history and religious studies to 11–14 year olds. This implies closer teacher-student relationships, which foster good behaviour.

Developing skills (over subject knowledge)

In KS3, particularly in year 7, there is an emphasis on students developing the generic 'learning skills' needed to succeed in their later studies. Sian describes these skills as 'quite basic' and when probed, she says this means listening well, following instructions, working together and behaving appropriately, as well as reading, writing and numeracy. The emphasis on basic learning skills in KS3 is whole school policy enshrined in an 'Integrated Humanities and Skills' (IHS) curriculum in Year 7. Both this 'subject' title and a statement on the school website present 'learning skills' as treated in school policy with (at least) equal importance to subject content.

> All students follow an Integrated Humanities and Skills course. This covers all Humanities subjects, as well as a focus on learning to learn skills, literacy and group work.
>
> *(Arnwell website, curriculum pages, 2014)*

Figure 7 highlights the emphasis on learning skills (blue), other humanities subject content (red), and the small amount of distinctively geographical content or skills (green). Subject (geographical) content is not emphasised. Two thirds of the curriculum overview document is given to literacy and general learning skills.

The analysis of three lesson observations illustrates how the influence of a generic skills agenda is enacted in the curriculum. The first observed lesson illustrates soft skills or 'learning to learn'. Students were asked to 'evaluate' and 'investigate'. They worked in small groups pooling their ideas together, drawing from their existing knowledge and experience, combined with stimulus material, to solve an issue (unsustainable use of the environment). Students were encouraged to 'reflect' on their own learning, for example they were asked how they found the difficulty of a task and how they tackled the learning problem. In such ways teachers build 'learning to learn' into the curriculum.

The second lesson illustrates the dominance of basic numeracy skills and a diminished geography in the aims of the (geography) lesson. The lesson title is 'developing skills in researching crime' and learning objectives are given as 'to be able to use mathematical skills to work out the percentage of specific crime figures' and 'to be able to analyse data and make conclusions about crime in certain areas of London'. The outcomes of the lesson were practice in calculating change as a percentage and knowing the difference between absolute and proportional figures. There was some geography (students are taught that Kingston is safer than the local borough and London's crime is decreasing overall). However, questions implicitly raised by comparing two boroughs' crime statistics, such as 'why is crime different between boroughs?' are not discussed. The places mentioned have no bearing on the numeracy skills being practised. The place context and geographical aspects of crime (such as urban processes) are used superficially, to give a 'relevant' local context to a mathematical skills lesson. In one episode of the lesson, a student wanted to think about 'place' and asked a general question about London, but their question was dismissed by the teacher as not relevant to the lesson.

The third lesson illustrates the dominance of basic numeracy skills over geography, not in the aims of the lesson, but in the distraction of skills such that the enacted (implicit) aim shifts away from that which is stated. This lesson objectives were geographical – 'to investigate the locations of world cup stadiums' and 'to investigate Brazil's level of development'. However, most of the lesson was given to calculating and drawing proportional symbols to represent city population. The proportional

Title	Humanities Content	Literacy Focus	PLTS (personal, learning and thinking skills)
First Impressions of (Arnwell)	–	Writing to Explain. Written article for youth magazine outlining their own and others first impressions. Modelled on Zadie Smith article.	Reflective Learners RL1 RL2
Geography Focus – (borough x) Talk Tour	Geography skills and fieldwork. Maps, grid ref, scale, aerial, satellite, thematic and topographical map.	Speaking: presentation, formal, pace, structure. Enter literacy level for speaking.	Independent Enquirers IE 1 Develop questions to solve (using maps). IE3 Explore different perspectives of place (in Camden).
Poverty and Wealth	Thematic: Definitions of poverty,Causes of poverty, Christian/Islamic views of poverty, Victorian study of poverty/wealth, Development categories, The impact of trade on development, Wealth distribution in the USA.	Speaking To explain. News report explaining various aspects of poverty and wealth. Vocabulary – more academic.	Team Workers TW 1 Collaborate with others to work towards common goals. TW 2 Reach agreements, managing discussions to achieve results. TW 3 Adapt behaviour to suit different roles and situations.
RS Focus – Religious Festivals	Knowledge and understanding of six different religious festivals.	Writing to Compare. Change the assessment question from significance to a comparative piece about the six different festivals studied. Enter literacy level for writing.	ReflectiveLearners: Based on feedback and drafts of comparative writing. RL 1 Assess themselves and others, identifying opportunities and achievements. RL 2 Set goals with success criteria for their development and work. RL 3 Review progress, acting on the outcomes.

FIGURE 7 Arnwell: KS3 (Yr 7) integrated humanities skills (IHS) curriculum plan for Sept 2014

Changing London	Thematic Settlement, How the settlement has changed, London as the seat of power, Move from monarchy to parliament, Historical events in London, Religion in medieval London, Changes in religion in London, Sustainability, London in the future.	Writing to Analyse.	Problem Solving **PS 1** –I will generate ideas and explore possibilities. **PS 2** –I will ask questions that lead to the best solutions.
History Focus – The Battle of Hastings	(To be planned)	Reading for Meaning Enter literacy level for reading.	Independent Enquirers IE 5 Consider the influence of circumstances, beliefs and feelings on decisions and events. IE 6 Support conclusions, using reasoned arguments and evidence.
Citizenship Focus - Fair Trade	Voluntary groups and citizens working together. Active citizenship. What is Fair Trade? How does Fair Trade benefit farmers? How can we be part of the solution? Active citizenship.	Speaking to persuade.	Team Workers TW 4 Show fairness and consideration to others. TW 5 Takeresponsibility, showing confidence in themselves and their contribution. TW 6 Provide constructive support and feedback to others.
Community?	Thematic		

FIGURE 7 (Cont.)

symbols were not actually proportional. The instruction was given to draw symbols as 'Sao Paolo – 11million = 11mm diameter, Manaus – 2 million = 2mm diameter'. This made the symbol area disproportionately large for the more populous cities and so proportional symbols were taught inaccurately. The lesson did not substantially deal with the planned geographical objectives. The enacted curriculum prioritised basic numeracy and graphicacy skills over planned geography.

The 'skills' theme portrayed in the analysis of lesson and HoD interview data are connected to the whole school approach. Clare (Deputy Head and geography teacher) refers to the school's learning skills policy as an influence on curriculum. She explains that independent learning, group work and 'active learning' enabled by good behaviour and levels of engagement is expected. Clare explains how the Headteacher gives guidelines about the maximum permissible time in lessons given to 'teacher talk', to ensure lessons are 'active'. Sian describes how such policies are monitored by senior management taking unannounced 'learning walks' to classrooms.

Sian's attitude to the learning skills emphasis is somewhat ambivalent. She agrees with active ('nice') lessons being taught, and she enjoys teaching through group work and engaging students in issues (such as sustainability), which readily allow discussion, speculation and links to students' experience. However, she is frustrated by how 'learning skills' have replaced geographic skills, and she sees the geography curriculum as weakened by the integrated skills curriculum. The IHS curriculum reduces time for geographical content in year 7. The GCSE curriculum begins in the summer term of year 9 and KS3 geography is thus 'squeezed', as Sian expresses: 'We lost a lot of geography skills when (the integrated Year 7 curriculum) came in … year 7 is lost.'

Lesson observations corroborate the interview data in which teachers emphasise skills. In David's lessons geographical enquiry was marginalised by the priority of numeracy and graphicacy skills. In Sian's lesson (on environmental sustainability) there was more balance between geographical enquiry and learning skills. The learning skills were the 'soft skills' of independent work, group cooperation, speculation and problem-solving. These were balanced by more geographical skills of gathering geographical data from text, maps, photographs and diagrams, and decision-making using geographical concepts (such as governance at different scales – personal, national and global, and social, environmental and economic impacts). However, analysis of all data at Arnwell presents the emphasis of skills over subjects in KS3 curriculum making.

Analysis of curriculum enactment – geography

Depth over breadth

The prominence of behaviour, 'relevance' and learning skills in the portrayal of curriculum making at Arnwell is reflected in the department's portrayal that depth is preferred to breadth of geography at KS3 to allow students to settle into and engage with a topic (through activities) rather than 'jumping' from one topic to another.

> We're trying to avoid 'lily pad' learning, where they jump from one thing to another, where there is one lesson a week, etc. We are aiming for more depth.
>
> *(Clare)*

Deputy Head and geography teacher, Clare's 'lily-pad learning' conjures an image of incessant and sudden leaps, like frogs, from one thing to another. She uses the analogy for thinking about how students can become unsettled by studying too many different topics in too quick succession. The depth over breadth approach is most apparent in year 7 where a theme is developed over an extended period. Some themes are clearly geographical, such as the local area study, while others cross disciplines and there is a less clear subject lead, for example, 'fair trade' and 'poverty and wealth'. Sian presents herself as trying to lead more geographical curriculum thinking in the team and she describes the new 2014 Geography National Curriculum (GNC) as an opportunity for this by giving authority to her expectation that the team engage in geography curriculum planning.

Assessment and accountability - the GNC and skills for examinations

There is some tension between the time and depth of the thematic (and skills focused) approach favoured in the department and the new geography national curriculum for 2014 (GNC), which has an emphasis on broad 'core knowledge' of the discrete subject. The HoD's attitude towards the GNC is ambivalent. She describes that her wish to be compliant although she is concerned that new topics, in particular glaciation and soils, may be difficult to teach in engaging ways. To an extent, she welcomes the 'guidance' of the GNC, on balance preferring it to the last GNC iteration of 2007. She describes the 2014 GNC as 'more prescriptive' but that she prefers this as she can clearly 'tick-off' content.

> I quite like ticking things off almost like a GCSE spec … where you're going to cover. I like that guidance.
>
> *(Sian)*

Sian links the department's attention to geographical skills in their KS3 curriculum as preparation for GCSE exams. She portrays the influence of the examination board over curriculum making, even at a different key stage as 'obvious'. She implies the power of GCSE is automatic, if GCSE changes, 'obviously' KS3 needs to change to prepare students for GCSE success.

> GCSE has changed now, so OCR has to have a skills paper, so obviously our KS3 now needs to be a lot more rigorous with geographical skills so they are well supported further up the school. So after the last few years there is almost a skills lesson within every module within Key Stage 3.
>
> *(Sian)*

Assessment and accountability influence curriculum making at the level of school policy for measuring and reporting students' progress. Sian relates school policies ('the school improvement plan') on assessment and feedback to the use of lesson time, which in turn means that curriculum content is lost, or 'chopped'.

Assessment has been a big focus in terms of the school improvement plan, that's influenced an awful lot in terms of the, sort of, content we can get through. They must be assessed formally at least twice every half term and that assessment must also have some feedback on, and evidence that the students have gone back to that work and improved on that work. And that all of a sudden takes up an awful lot of curriculum time so you don't get through your having to chop some bits of the curriculum in order to do that properly'.

(Sian)

University geography

University geography is most noticeable by its absence in the portrayal of curriculum making at Arnwell. 'Relevance', engagement and learning skills are dominant and active (explicitly referred to by Sian and Claire in interviews). References to changes in the discipline of geography in universities, are rare. The only explicit references to the university discipline are Sian describing her degree (which was geography and English) as an influence in bringing sustainability and issues into the curriculum. Sian struggles to remember details but she describes her degree as shaping the way she sees geography as 'changing all the time' and influencing how she sees her role as a geographer/ geography teacher to keep geography 'relevant'.

One of the modules I did at uni was called 'new horizons in human geography'. That was... lots of issues and I think that has influenced... I mean health was new back when I did my degree (laughs) what else was new? ... I can't even remember, but it was health ... I think it was something else that really influenced me ... but it's that idea that geography is changing all the time, that we shouldn't keep the same things and that we should always keep an ear to the ground and change it to keep it relevant all the time.

(Sian)

Sian describes her university degree as guiding her principle that geography changes and needs to be kept updated or 'relevant'. However, this contradicts her description of the sources of new geography in the department coming mainly from other school teachers (such as websites which share lesson materials), local issues and the students' own lives, rather than the university discipline directly, as a source.

Analysis of curriculum enactment – teachers

Other teachers' work

The department portrays using 'other' geography teachers' work. These others can be in the department, but also from outside, meaning teachers or other educators who share lesson materials on websites. Lesson observation corroborates interviews to show a practice of downloading 'lessons' (objectives, materials and activities) prepared by another teacher, sometimes at the point of entry to the classroom and somewhat uncritically. All the geography teachers except Sian indicate that they have school priorities other than teaching geography, which may account for the high level of reliance on other teachers' lessons 'on the system'. Sian describes how there is variability between the geography teachers in how far they use the shared system 'properly' (to support careful planning):

> Some people will pick it up and teach it straight from the PowerPoint ... other people will pick it up and prepare properly and amend it and change it.
>
> *(Sian)*

The ease with which 'other teachers' work can be used (and re-used) is portrayed as a threat to curriculum making. Sian describes how 'writing the curriculum' is an important teacher's skill, which can be lost through excessive sharing from 'the system'.

> (We are trying) to make sure that everybody does have a turn at it (writing the curriculum) ... otherwise we become just quite stale ... people don't know how to ... just become de-skilled in being able to start from scratch and just write something.
>
> *(Sian)*

Sian expresses how she draws from other teachers' work (through websites) but taking a critical approach. She also portrays trying to adapt geography materials on the department intranet, (which she refers to as 'the curriculum').

> I thought a lot of the curriculum that was there was stuff that had been taken from the Internet from other people's work, so there were four modules there that I didn't feel were particularly written for our kids or particularly suitable for our kids.
>
> *(Sian)*

Sian's story: leading the geography curriculum in isolation

Sian describes her frustration at leading a geography department where all but one (the NQT) in her team tend to prioritise other (non-geography) responsibilities. Most of the team therefore, prefer to minimise geography curriculum change.

> A lot of people have been here a long time and are reluctant to change things.
> I'd like (the integrated skills curriculum) to be more focused on geography so we get more content in there ... I'd like more opportunities to be able to take the kids out.
>
> *(Sian)*

Sian is responsible for geography in the school. The school structure recognises humanities as a department and geography does not have formal status as a department. She has not been able to hold a meeting of all the geography teachers 'for years'. Nevertheless, Sian appears committed to geography teaching and building a geography 'department' through the team of six experienced specialist geographers at the school. Sian has taught at the school for six years and, although she portrays herself as supporting much of the 'Arnwell approach' to using curriculum for engagement, behaviour and skills, she describes trying to build a more subject focused curriculum and a more subject-focused team.

Sian recognises that her 'team' teaching geography lessons must rely on each other to plan and prepare lesson plans, schemes of work and materials (largely by PowerPoint) on the school's intranet. These are partly 'ready-made' lessons that are sometimes 'pulled off' the system and delivered without amending them. Sian would like more creative use of materials and more commitment from the geography teachers to curriculum-making.

> They (teachers) don't necessarily change it they just teach it from that Power-Point and I don't feel that you can just teach something from someone else's PowerPoint. Unless you put it together you don't know their thinking. People will miss out those bits that you've made notes on, you want to expand on.
>
> *(Sian)*

Sian expresses a feeling of isolation as a geographer at two levels – in Arnwell and in the wider community. In the school she feels frustration at the commitments and responsibilities of other teachers of geography, although she understands and accepts these pressures as part of the wider priorities of the school. She would like the team to be more critically engaged in geography curriculum development. In one part of an interview, Sian describes how she deliberately 'stirred up' a response from one of her team, to engage them in critical curriculum development:

> actually getting them to look at what's there and realise the state of thing … whereas if it's me just looking…Dave wrote quite an irate, almost, email (saying) 'This is terrible!' But I thought 'brilliant!' That's exactly the sort of thing I want, is to be passionate about it and care about it. That worked as a strategy.
>
> *(Sian)*

On several occasions, Sian referred to the youth of teachers as positive for geography curriculum-making. 'I'd like some young geographers coming in with new ideas' (Sian). She links young teachers to the 'nice' (ibid) or active lessons common in the school, but she expresses some frustration that the geography 'department' consists of several older teachers who have senior roles in the school or responsibilities pulling them away from geography curriculum work.

Sian's approach to the GNC hints at a sense of isolation in the wider community of geography teachers. She says she would like more opportunity to interact with this community. Sian describes her commitment to developing the department's geography curriculum. But because bringing the team together is so difficult, she describes the GNC almost as a surrogate for meeting with other geographers. She hints at a lack confidence in her own selection of content and she finds a prescriptive GNC reassuring.

> I like the fact that I can say 'that's what we need to be covering', because you don't speak to many other heads of department do you? It's quite nice to know what you have to cover almost. Whereas with this old one (NC 2008 programme of study) it could have been anything, which makes you very unsure about what it is you're producing.
>
> *(Sian)*

Sian describes engagement with the geography education community in a virtual way, to a degree, through the Geographical Association (GA) and online areas of shared geography materials, including the Staffordshire Learning Network (SLN), the RGS schools' website, 'geography all the way' and 'geography pods'. However, she is not entirely positive about shared materials on the web. She prefers to develop curriculum ideas and materials within the department and she encourages her team to take part in this endeavour.

Sian describes her university background as fostering her interest in issues (of relevance to her students) and she expresses how she wants her students to develop informed attitudes and values. Her description of the purpose of the geography curriculum links to the locality (their 'small bubble') and is one of empowerment 'to do things' and values 'to care'.

> (I want them to) know what's going on but they don't live in this small bubble that's (borough X) that there is nothing else out there, that nothing else matters. I want them to expand their horizons want them to go off and see places and do things and care about the world.
>
> *(Sian)*

Sian's view of curriculum purpose is also expressed more simply;

> I just want it to be enjoyable. I want kids to come to geography and enjoy the lessons and be engaged in the lessons and want to find out more.
>
> *(Sian)*

Sian's story is one of a head of geography struggling to develop a dynamic geography curriculum in a school context which does not place high value on subject content in KS3. Her story is also one of wanting students to enjoy their KS3 geography lessons. But behind this there is a larger vision to develop particular values and attitudes in the students. Sian wants her students to grow into confident and capable adults who 'care about the world'.

Conclusion to Arnwell – 'student engagement' and 'skills'

Arnwell's geography curriculum making is distinctive by the themes of 'student engagement' and 'skills'. While these themes are present in all four case study departments, data analysis shows that they are prominent in Arnwell. The 'engagement' narrative is that if students are to learn they must behave in lessons and to behave in lessons they must enjoy the process of learning and they must perceive content as 'relevant' or meaningful to their lives.

There is an integrated skills-focused curriculum in year 7, which downplays broad subject knowledge and emphasises skills and engagement with learning. Subject knowledge is not as strongly emphasised as the other case study departments. The KS3 curriculum is portrayed as being for engaging students in learning and developing generic skills as much as (or more than) subject understanding. The school's senior management principles of a curriculum for engagement and learning skills (influenced by a legacy of poor behaviour and low academic motivation still in the memories of most staff) are a controlling curriculum influence, and Sian struggles to develop a curriculum based on geographic (disciplinary) principles. The teachers of geography are pulled away from working closely as a geography team by other priorities (pastoral, senior management, other subject teaching). Nonetheless, Sian appears happy to embrace the narrative of 'enjoyment' (through 'relevant' content and 'active' lessons). Sian appears less enthusiastic about the 'learning skills' narrative, which remains a KS3 curriculum making influence.

The themes constructed from the literature review are reflected in curriculum enactment at Arnwell. There is a conflict between Sian's concern for the subject of geography and senior management pressure to focus on learning skills. This plays out within the geography team as Sian struggles to draw her geography teachers to curriculum making as they are pulled toward other schooling concerns. The dominant curriculum value/belief systems evident are social-efficiency (in concern for developing useful skills) and child-centred (in the concern for the child's flourishing, particularly by pursuing their own interests). Sian is trying to bring change to the curriculum, using internet communities (websites that share geography teaching materials) but she describes curriculum inertia caused by a team under time pressure who re-use materials on the department intranet and are resistant to change.

The teacher has some control over curriculum making (the enactment of geography curriculum varies substantially between individual teachers); however, a common engagement and skills narrative informs curriculum making. The engagement and skills narrative comes through senior management of the school, but in turn power is held over the school by public accountability for results and the expectations of the young people at the school to be engaged in lessons.

5

BRIGHTLING GIRLS' SCHOOL – NAVIGATING 'LEARNIFICATION'

Introduction

The analysis of curriculum making at 'Brightling' Girls' School shows some aspects in common with Arnwell, in particular concerns for student enjoyment, compliance to the GNC, generic learning skills and the practice of sharing curriculum materials on an intranet. However, there are differences. At Brightling, engagement with the discipline of geography is more evident, GCSE and A level geography is a prominent driver of the KS3 curriculum, and the teaching team is portrayed as more focused on geography.

School and geography department context

Brightling Girls' school is an 11–18 comprehensive school of average size, just over one mile away from Arnwell High and within the same inner-London borough. There is (like Arnwell) very high socio-economic inequality in the catchment, with some of the most privileged Londoners living close to some of the most disadvantaged. The proportion of students on free school meals and with EAL are 'well above average' according to the 2013 Ofsted report. The proportion of SENs is described as 'above average'. GCSE results at Brightling are above the national average, but they have varied somewhat in the last three years, which is the prime reason cited in the Ofsted report (2013) for being awarded 'good' (rather than 'outstanding').

Jane has been teaching at the school since she first qualified eight years ago. She has been Head of Geography for four years. There has been high turnover of staff in the department and Jane's team are young and relatively inexperienced teachers. But, the teachers in the geography department meet regularly and their prime responsibility is teaching geography. The geography teachers have recently moved into the same office, which Jane says helps them to communicate as a department (see Table 7).

TABLE 7 The geography teachers at Brightling Girls' School

	School responsibilities (beyond Geography)	Age and time at the school
Jane (HoD)	None	c 30 8 years
Rhona (resp. for KS3)	None	20s 3 years
Katie	None (NQT)	20s <1 year
Alan	None (Teach First)	20s <1 year

Analysis of curriculum enactment– students

Enjoying 'relevant' geography

Jane (Head of Geography) reveals a number of factors influencing the department's approach to curriculum making in interviews. Students' enjoyment 'drives' her curriculum thinking, she says, and she links student enjoyment to four points: subject content (a matter of what is taught, not just how it is taught); teacher enjoyment (which teachers enjoy, students will enjoy); a modern geography (up-to-date and accurate); and relevance (students must relate content to their own lives). Data analysis produced four subthemes at Arnwell, illustrated in the excerpt below.

> I'd say it (student enjoyment) is the driving force, more so than anything else. When I took over as Head of Department … we had a … very old-fashioned geography. We were teaching them about Japan as an economic superstar. And the idea that all the latest technology was coming out of Japan things like that and it just wasn't true anymore, and the girls were getting disengaged and I hated teaching it other teachers hated teaching it … the girls just didn't see the relevance of geography to their lives.
>
> *(Jane)*

On several occasions, Jane describes how 'student voice' comes into KS3 curriculum decisions. Student voice (giving their feedback, opinions or preferences to the teacher) is a subtheme of student enjoyment.

> (Student voice activities are) … a focus group essentially, with a cross-section of girls from that year group at the beginning and end of a scheme of work, the planning stage of the scheme of work, to really think about what the girls want to learn about. But also how they found the scheme of work, what they think could be worked on for next year.
>
> *(Jane)*

The 'fantastic places' unit illustrates how the teachers 'listen' to students and take account of what they want.

We found 20 places and gave images to the girls to choose their top 3 to learn about.

These were their top 10:

- A garden in Kyoto
- Glass Beach California
- Salt Flats Bahrain
- Central Park
- Stacks China
- Giant's Causeway Ireland
- Glowworm Caves New Zealand
- Love tunnel Ukraine
- Victoria Falls Zimbabwe
- Glacier Iceland.

> We tried to get a wide range of environments and localities. We found by (Google) searching on 'fantastic places', and '10 most beautiful places'. We guessed got the top one right the Glowworm Caves because it's pink like a fairytale!'
>
> *(Jane)*

Data analysis produces an 'engagement' narrative. Jane says how she asks three questions in curriculum making:

> What do these girls need? What are they going to find interesting? What do they want to learn about?
>
> *(Jane)*

The second two questions appear to drive many choices, particularly at the level of the lesson – the particular location or case study for example. The principle of engaging students is sometimes linked to the use of internet searches, as in 'fantastic places'. In an observed lesson, the specific geographical process learned (columnar jointing whereby volcanic rock cools and contracts and wave erosion exposes hexagonal columns) was influenced by Jane searching for an 'interesting' place to illustrate a physical geographical process. The unique and dramatic landscape of the Giant's Causeway, Antrim, Northern Ireland, was chosen. The distinctive physical process and the place was dictated partially by Google searching. The internet also influences Jane's curriculum making through news websites, which she describes as being used 'an awful lot'.

The order of Jane's curriculum questions suggests that her starting point for curriculum-planning is what the students 'need'. This goes beyond the students' immediate interest, curiosity and enjoyment. The 'need' she refers to can be related to the notion she describes as the 'finished geographer', which, Jane explains, cannot be achieved without some hard work and struggle (on the learner's part) to acquire geographical knowledge. Jane describes how superficially engaging topics are successful up to a point, such as learning about the drama of hurricanes and tornadoes, but without understanding air pressure, the limit to geographical understanding is quickly reached. Nonetheless, data analysis produces a prominent 'enjoyment' and 'relevance' theme within a broader narrative to keep the curriculum 'up-to-date'.

The 'relevance' theme of department B's curriculum making is reflected in the use of news and current affairs. Jane says that the department 'use news websites an awful lot' and, when asked where the department tend to go for lesson activities and ideas, the news is her first response (mentioned before textbooks and geography teaching websites). The department portrays a high value placed on bringing the everyday and the 'relevant' to the curriculum. The drive to keep curriculum content 'relevant' and current may not change the geographical concepts that are to be learned (the department's curriculum aims are planned, sometimes years in advance) but it does affect the specific content of the enacted curriculum, for example, on which places are studied to illustrate a geographical process, or even which process will be learned.

Analysis of curriculum enactment– geography

Skills and looking to GCSE and A level

Jane refers to KS3 as preparation for GCSE and A level. To support her department's KS3 curriculum planning meeting, Jane provides her team with copies of the Department for Education (DfE) GCSE requirements for geography (published just one month before the meeting) as well as the 2014 GNC programme of study, and she repeatedly refers to thinking about preparation for GCSE and A level when talking about the KS3 curriculum.

> I think it's (GCSE and A level results) a huge driver absolutely huge but not from the data perspective. I don't look at it from a results perspective I look at it from a … we want these finished geographers at the end of it.
>
> *(Jane)*

Jane describes her aim as to develop 'geographers'. GCSE and A level are mentioned a great deal and they appear to be influential in the department's curriculum-making. However, she describes them as a strategy and a guide for her geography curriculum-making, rather than examination results being an end in themselves. The 'driver' of GCSE and A level also featured prominently in the geography department's KS3 planning meeting. Jane tells her team how they should 'start' with A level and a notion of a 'finished geographer', then work backwards to plan KS3 saying 'We need to focus on what A level needs, so what GCSE needs and so what KS3 does.' (Jane). The planning meeting revealed Jane's emphasis on developing geographical skills in KS3, which could then be applied in KS4 and A level.

> The team wrote out a 'dream student' at year 9. We then completed skills sheets, what skills that students would have, and broke it down … 7, 8, 9, an aspect of skill in each year.
>
> *(Jane)*

Assessing progress (by using GCSE and A level as a guide)

Jane describes a strategic use of GCSE and A level to develop 'finished geographers'. She identifies the weakness of students' inability to recognise their own progress toward becoming 'geographers'. Jane also suggests that the geography teachers are ill-equipped to assess this progress. Much of the department's curriculum making narrative, voiced by Jane, relates to developing clear steps of progress, which can be articulated for teachers and students, measured and assessed. This 'systematic' approach to steps of progress was particularly apparent in the KS3 planning meeting in which the team attempted to identify and order a progression of geographical skills. Jane claims that her attention to GCSE and A level was primarily to develop 'finished geographers'. But she indicates a resignation to the power of exam performance accountability for needing to teach some skills (such as writing and exam technique).

> It's all very well and good if they can understand it but if they can't get it down onto paper then … it doesn't really matter how they're doing … it doesn't matter in the educational system that we work in if they can't get it down on the paper they're not going to get the marks … My feelings on that matter are fairly unimportant.
>
> *(Jane)*

Jane describes strategies, techniques and her ambitions for assessing students' learning and progress. She talks of having 'detailed frames and checklists for self-assessment and marking' and of 'training' students in self-assessment so they can be 'very self-aware and critical'. She expresses frustration at the time and effort to design their own assessment systems for KS3 geography and she would like to be relieved of this burden. 'As much as we hate to admit this, I just want someone to give me something.'

Emphasising sustainability

The first of Jane's three questions, which guide her KS3 curriculum making, is 'What do these girls need to know about?' Skills, preparation for examination success and enjoyment are recurring themes in Jane's words and other evidence from the department. But there is also a rationale based on how geographical knowledge will affect the girls' lives. Jane talks about geographical concepts.

The island of Yap (Micronesia) for culture, rice fields (China) for inter-dependence, slums (la Rochina, Rio) for sustainability.

(Jane)

Jane describes how geographical concepts inform the selection of places and processes to be studied. There is a balance between the child's immediate interest (their enjoyment), the skills they are developing for exam success, and the conceptual grasp of geography they are developing. In particular, the concept of sustainability is portrayed as influencing curriculum making, in interviews, lesson observations and curriculum documents.

I think it (sustainability) is huge, absolutely huge. I would say every single scheme of work has some element of it in. And I suppose that's because it's the context that we as teachers have developed in. It's such a global issue that it's kind of infiltrated our consciousness, I'd say and therefore it's kind of indoctrinated into us so we indoctrinated into the scheme of work (laughs).

(Jane)

One of the lessons observed was a 'trading game' lesson (taught by Jane) sourced from Christian Aid, whose mission is to end poverty. The lesson raises the 'issues' of poverty and unfairness, and questioning in the lesson draws out a notion of unequal power and unfairness through the global trading system. The department's KS3 curriculum overview (see Figure 8) uses language that presents geography as 'issues', often exploring human problems and solutions. Wording is sometimes emotive including, 'wasteful societies', which refers to 'consumerist lifestyles', 'life on the edge' referring to the impacts, costs and benefits of exploiting landscapes, the sustainability of flood management, 'hot and bothered', dealing with the uncertainty of climate change and 'current population issues that face the UK'. There appears to be a link between Jane's emphasis on enjoyment and relevance and issues-based geographies of sustainability. The topic titles give a 'spin' to make geography 'sound' exciting for children.

Jane portrays a strong personal purpose and vision for her department's curriculum. She wants her students to be empowered and to become 'global citizens'. Empowerment is seen as the ultimate result from her students being freed from a parochial world view (by understanding how they connect to the world). But the nuances revealed in Jane's words are significant to understand how Jane approaches curriculum making. The 'bubble' from which Jane wants her students to be 'taken out' evokes a notion of escape and liberation through knowledge. Jane emphasises the 'inner-city' and specifically 'London' students and she is strongly aware of the need for the curriculum to educate young people in a locally specific context. Jane's vision of curriculum purpose tempers idealism (to be 'better global citizens') with pragmatism (employability).

I think our ethos has always been about to ensure that inner-city students … inner-city London students understand their place in the wider global context and taking them out of their little London bubble and showing them how they connect to the

	Year 7	Year 8	Year 9
Autumn 1 **Skills Focus:** **Atlas Skills**	**Fantastic Places:** A unit of work that allows students to develop their understanding of the core concepts studied in Geography through investigating a series of different places around the globe.	**Risky World:** During this unit students will explore a range of different extreme weather phenomenon, including hurricanes and blizzards and will investigate the complex causes of these as well as the impacts on people and the environment.	**For Richer and Poorer:** During this unit students will examine the reasons why there are such large differences in levels of development at a global scale and how different regions of the world are developing at different rates. Students will be asked to form opinions on different approaches to tackling uneven development.
Autumn 2 **Skills Focus:** **OSMapping** **Skills**	**Look at it this Way:** A unit that examines how and why landscapes vary and the part that people play in landscape changes. Students will consider why landscapes are important, our perceptions of different landscapes represented in the media.	**Processes and Pressures:** A unit that examines the causes of river flooding as well looking at the likelihood of flooding both in the local area and other locations around the world. Human interactions with the environment that can lead toflooding is also addressed and students will be encouraged to consider the sustainability of our approach to flood management.	**Conflict Geographies:** A unit that examines the nature of conflict at a range of scales. The impacts of these conflicts will be evaluated and possible solutions will be discussed.
Spring 1 **Skills Focus:** **Graph work** **and** **Quantitative** **data analysis**	**Moving Stories:** Students will investigate the changes that are happening to the UK's population. They will examine the processes that lead to population change and will be encouraged to express their own views on current population issues that face the UK.	**Fashion Victims:** This unit explores the process of globalisation and the impact that it is having on the fashion industry. Students will be encouraged to re-evaluate their opinions on the fashion industry in light of their learning.	**Urban Change:** This unit explores how urban geographies are changing and the reasons for this. Additionally students will consider the impacts of changing urban environments and potential solutions to the problems.

FIGURE 8 Brightling KS3 planned curriculum overview, 2014

Spring 2	**The Rise and Rise of China**:	**Into Africa:**	**Hot and Bothered:**
Skills Focus: Qualitative data analysis	This unit will allow students to examine the factors that are leading to rapid changes in China in terms of their culture andeconomy. Students will be encouraged to re-evaluate their views towards a culture that in many ways contrasts the one in which they live.	Through this unit students will begin to make connections between their lives and the lives of people living in Africa and assess the perception that we and the Western world hold on Africa and challenge its accuracy.	This unit explores the causes and impacts of a changing global climate and will begin to examine the uncertainty that lies around how to mitigate against climate change as a result of the different viewpoints that exist on it.
Summer 1	**Dynamic Planet:**	**Life on the Edge:**	**Wasteful societies:**
Skills Focus: GIS	Students will investigate the tectonic processes that help to shape our world and analyse the impacts of disaster events in different places.	Students will examine a range of extreme environments in which people live. They will investigate the impacts that people are having on these landscapes and the costs and benefits of exploiting these environments. Finally theywill consider whether untouched landscapes have any intrinsic value in our society.	Students will learn about the impact that consumerist lifestyles have on water quality and availability as well as investigating the impacts on the environment of waste that is generated through mass production.
Summer 2	**Why does it always rain on me?**	**Ice Age:**	**GCSE Unit 3:**
Skills Focus: Decision Making	During this unit, students will be given the opportunity to investigate the atmospheric processes that influence both people and the environment.	During this unit, students will be given the opportunity to investigate the processes that operate in cold environments and the timescales over which they operate. Students will understand how glaciation and glaciated landscapes affect people and how people manage these environments for their benefit.	Throughout this unit students are given the opportunity to make decisions on how to make the world more sustainable. They will be required to assess sustainability in different contexts and design a sustainable urban community.

FIGURE 8 (Cont.)

rest of the world and how the rest of the world influences their lives … it allows them to become better, for want of a better phrase, I suppose global citizens. And it gives them opportunities later in life … I think it makes them employable I think it makes them a more interesting … a well-rounded person.

(Jane)

Jane places 'empowerment' in the context of the girls (who live in their 'little inner-city bubble') competing in a 'male-dominated' world. She also describes curriculum purpose as enabling action ('ability to change things'). Jane does not refer directly to 'sustainability' when she talks about the curriculum purpose. But her vision of making 'global citizens' accords with the thread of 'sustainability' running through the planned curriculum overview document and interviews.

I think that's really important for girls' education – that sense that they've got the ability to change things they've got the ability to compete in a male-dominated context and I think the geography helped them with that as of course all subjects do but I think it can be quite an empowering thing for want of a better word.

(Jane)

Engaging with the discipline to modernise the curriculum

Jane's description of curriculum work involves a 'modernisation' theme relating to the changing university discipline of geography. Jane presents a strong vision for an 'up-to-date' geography through developing the team's identity as geographers, drawing on recent developments in the discipline of geography, sharing geographical knowledge within the team and paying attention to young people's geographies.

We try to bring in our own experiences. If we don't, school geography becomes stuck. We don't bring in new ideas if we get stuck. We want to bring in cutting edge geography more from university.

We want to spend more time keeping up with subject knowledge, like going to RGS lectures.

(Jane)

Jane describes concern that her university geography is already becoming dated (she graduated 10 years ago) and wants to bring current university geography into the curriculum. She sees her young team as key to this with the geography 'filtering down' from their recent university degrees into the curriculum. Jane portrays deep interest in the school geography curriculum, explaining how she recently researched the geography national curricula of some other countries to help inform her curriculum planning. She also values the Geographical Association (GA) and the Royal Geographical Society (RGS) and she says she spends time 'reading around' including some academic texts.

> For some of the schemes of work we've looked very closely at the GA schemes of work and we've kind of taken ideas from those and we've redeveloped ideas so in some cases its (GA) had a huge influence.
>
> *(Jane)*

The GA in particular features in the department's relationship with the discipline of geography. The team are GA members and all recently attended the GA's annual conference which Jane found a very 'affirming' experience. The GA's manifesto 'a different view' (Geographical Association, 2009) and GA schemes of work had been used alongside other resources in past curriculum making. This is evident in interview data and from documents, for example in the 'moving stories' unit of work, which uses the wording from 'a different view' (ibid).

The Geography National Curriculum (GNC) and compliance

Jane downplays the Geography National Curriculum (GNC) as an influence over her curriculum planning. She portrays the department as driven by their personal understandings of geography and vision for the education of their students. But she does express a need to be compliant with the GNC as accountability to Ofsted.

> Obviously there's the whole issue around the new national curriculum ... I have made sure that everything is covered, even if it is one lesson on soils during the scheme of work on ecosystems for example. Because, obviously we work within a national framework we're going to ... we will get Ofsteded.
>
> *(Jane)*

In the KS3 curriculum planning meeting, the team referred to both the old (2008) and new (2014) GNC KS3 programme of study. Consistent with the shift in emphasis in the GNC documents, the department's planned KS3 curriculum moved from a more theme-based to more topic-based curriculum. But the 2008 GNC still influences Jane's curriculum-making. In talking about current curriculum-making, she refers to the concepts included in the 2008 GNC, such as place, space, scale, cultural diversity and sustainability. Jane's curriculum-planning is an ongoing process and she does not approach the arrival of a new GNC as the starting point of a review of her department's KS3 curriculum. As she puts it, work was done before the announcement of a new GNC. Jane portrays the GNC as playing an ambivalent role in the department's curriculum-making. On the one hand the GNC is used as principled guidance and to ensure consistency and standards of geographical education, on the other it is seen as necessary for Ofsted accountability purposes.

> It's been a bit of a tick box exercise to be honest with you, in so much as, as long as we have everything covered, that's as much time as I'd given to it.
>
> *(Jane)*

Analysis of curriculum enactment – teachers

Senior management pressure – 'building learning power'

Brightling school's senior management ask and expect all subject departments to develop strategies of 'building learning power' (Claxton 1999) in their curriculum planning and although the geography team show some resistance to this directive, the idea of building learning power is portrayed as a significant influence in teachers' curriculum making. All teaching staff attended a curriculum planning afternoon, gathering together for a whole school briefing and workshop before breaking into subject departments to plan their KS3 curriculum. The impetus for the day was the recent release of new KS3 National Curriculum programmes of study, and, although the afternoon is titled 'curriculum planning', there is no mention of using subject disciplines or how curriculum content should be chosen.

The entire focus of senior management's framing and directive for the afternoon is on learning effectiveness. The presentations to the whole staff, which set up the curriculum planning day, focus on how students can 'learn to learn'. The Assistant Headteacher, who introduces the afternoon, talks about the value of 'meta learning'. A Headteacher of a high performing local primary school, gives a keynote address explaining how she accounts for her school's success by dialogue between student and teacher and 'learnacy' (learning skills) referring to Claxton's (1999) 'building learning power', Carol Dweck's (2006) 'mindsets', marking as a dialogue between teacher and student, and the United Nations Convention on the Rights of the Child (2014) 'rights respecting teachers'. Teachers are encouraged to think about 'active learning' and the specific strategy of 'split screen planning', by which teachers think of lessons as divided between the subject content to be learned and the ways that students are learning to learn (building learning power).

The whole school workshop continues with the Assistant Head reinforcing learning skills and 'building learning power' (BLP), encouraging teachers to 'look at metacognition'. She makes clear from the example she uses that learning skills are not subject specific skills. The third speaker offers teachers a model of effectiveness drawn from his army experience he calls 'SMEAC' – Situation, Mission (aim), Executables (available resources), Actions, Check understanding. This offers a military-style clarity to curriculum work, in which the 'mission' either ends in success or failure – there is no 'grey area' in between.

The Assistant Head closes the meeting by asking staff to break into subject departments to plan how they can bring the ideas presented in the last hour into their new KS3 curriculum planning. Her final words 'Light the fire, don't just fill the bucket!' capture a view of KS3 curriculum purpose of engaging students in learning. The message the whole staff are offered is that by equipping students with skills and strategies to manage their own learning, the teacher helps students become engaged with their learning and able to make progress. Subject departments (and the heads of departments) are given a firm steer to adopt 'split-screen planning' (planning with equal attention to learning skills and subject content in lessons). There is some pressure to conform to this by being expected to share their afternoon's work with other subject departments.

When the geography team meet after the briefing, Jane (Head of department) initially ignores the SLT request to focus on 'split screen planning' and 'building learning power'. Jane has her own agenda for her department meeting, which is, geography-led KS3 curriculum planning. Jane's independent pursuit of her own vision for the geography curriculum and her department is discussed further in her own 'story' at the end of this chapter. However, the whole school briefing session is illuminative in placing Jane's work in context. The attention to skills and effectiveness, against a backdrop of erratic GCSE performance 'costing' the school an 'outstanding' Ofsted grade, is reflected in the department's planning (as well as interviews and lesson observations). Jane refers to 'learning skills' as something the department already weave into lessons.

Lesson observations provide further evidence that 'learning to learn' and building learning power is an influence in the geography department's curriculum making. In one lesson students are urged to think about working collaboratively, and (more vaguely) to 'build on previous skills acquired'. Students are asked to speculate and hypothesise about the formation of the Giant's Causeway. Such development of students' problem-solving strategies sits with the 'BLP' approach favoured by the school. In making a decision related to a geographical process, students are asked to negotiate in groups to select key words and order pictures into a sequence to show a geographical process. Students are asked to consider 'What strategies are you using? How are you selecting? How do you decide?' (Jane). This is not an entirely generic 'learning to learn' approach, however, but a blend of the 'BLP' approach with geographical data and concepts. The teacher is mediating and adapting 'BLP' for geographical thinking.

In addition to the 'soft skills' of 'BLP' (such as teamwork, resilience and reflection) the general 'learning' skill of literacy is an influential theme in the department's curriculum making and Jane (HoD) links literacy to school policy, describing literacy as 'a huge school focus for years'. The observed lessons emphasise literacy, for example with features such as a 'great word challenge' and sorting and structuring words into a paragraph to explain geographical process. In this way teachers link literacy to problem solving (learning) strategies and geographical understanding.

In department meetings, interviews and lesson observations, literacy is frequently linked to assessment and measuring outcomes (such as GCSE and A level success). Jane links literacy to her personal interests (her degree was joint honours Geography and English). She speaks positively of working with the borough literacy coordinator. She chose to focus on literacy and language, in relation to overall student performance, in her recent middle management training project called 'teaching leaders'. Skills, including literacy, are prominent in the department's curriculum making. Performance in examinations is a recurring theme in Jane's rationale for literacy skills at KS3.

The learning skill of self-assessment has affected curriculum content. A specific example showing this is the use of an assessment tool, sold to the school by the company 'Code and Pixels Interactive Technologies' which Jane describes enthusiastically. The tool provides 'ladders' in which curriculum content and learning activity progresses upward from basic to more advanced. Students select their entry point on the ladder, according to their perceived level (which may also be guided by the teacher). This means that different students may learn (and be taught) different geographical content directly as a consequence of using this self-assessment tool.

Experience, training and balanced curriculum making

Jane links the teacher's ability to balance curriculum making concerns (giving sufficient attention to the geographical content) to both the teachers' experience and the nature of their initial teacher training. She suggests that both inexperience and taking a 'Teach First' training route (rather than PGCE) are linked to over-concern for 'effective' teaching and a relative neglect for subject content.

> Katie is new and insecure in her abilities and more concerned about effective activities. But when the others in the team are talking you can see that geography is emphasised.
>
> *(Jane)*

> two of us are coming from PGCE in which we're very focused on the geographical pedagogy. One of us, just out of 'uni', is doing 'Teach First' … where it's very, you know very, very good at teaching and activities, but it was very much generic pedagogy instead … I just really want it (geographical subject knowledge) to be embedded.
>
> *(Jane)*

Favouring enquiry learning

Jane describes her preference for enquiry, or an inductive style of learning in KS3. Jane's preference for the KS3, more inductive approach reveals idealism at KS3 in contrast to pragmatism at GCSE. Jane appears to be conscious of the pressure of accountability for her students' examination performance, but she also presents a principled educational rationale for what and how the students are taught.

> We do a lot of inductive at Key Stage 3 and then it flips at Key Stage 4 because … I don't … I think at Key Stage 4 we're very aware that they need notes in their books in a logical order for revision … I think you get so panicked … you're so concerned that you've covered everything. It becomes a little bit more like: 'here is the theory, here is the case study, now let's apply to an exam question' and it's just a shame really.
>
> *(Jane)*

Teachers' enjoyment – favourite places

The teacher's enjoyment also affects curriculum decisions. Jane describes how teachers sometimes make choices about specific places based on the places they like, which in turn depends on their life experiences. The 'relevance' theme can, to an extent, be applied to teachers as well as students, as Jane illustrates when explaining how the content of part of the 'fantastic places' unit is chosen.

> So I was talking about Chatsworth Hall, it's very close to where I did lots of work from my dissertation, Derbyshire is my favourite place in the UK. I love going there, I associate it with my family ... Rhona did Crickhowell (laughs) which is where she's from. I'm not sure where Katie did, I think she did Bolivia, because she was travelling there.
>
> *(Jane)*

Jane's story – establishing a team and a progressive view of geography

Jane emphasises that curriculum making in the department is collaborative. Teachers share the curriculum materials they develop and Jane encourages them to adapt one another's work using the department intranet ('the system').

> So, all of the suggested lessons are on the system and any brand-new schemes of work etc, all the resources that are developed by the person developing them, go on the system and then any kind of differentiated materials or adaptations that teachers make for themselves, I encourage them to also put in the shared area ... I think the resources are used very collaboratively it's just the way that we work.
>
> *(Jane)*

Jane talks about many factors that can enable collaboration, including the physical space in which teachers work. She describes a historical problem of the geography team being physically split, working on different floors of the building, preparing curriculum materials separately. She has managed to arrange a shared department office, which she values as supporting collaborative curriculum work.

> We've now moved offices ... we are physically together more which is allowing us to, kind of, know what everybody is working on more.
>
> *(Jane)*

Jane's description of her curriculum work is peppered with references to collaboration, sharing and communication between the team. The collaborative curriculum making process is enacted (with the help of computer technology) through sharing, adapting and developing materials on 'the system' (the school intranet).

But Jane presents the department's collaboration as still developing and that she would like more sharing from all her team. She describes how she is trying to forge a team who work together to make the geography curriculum, how the inexperience of her team was a barrier to collaborative curriculum work and how she is encouraging the team to grow together.

> I think it's becoming much more collaborative now, I think last year it was very much led by me and Rhona working together approach. The issue has been that I have a very inexperienced department at the moment Rhona is in her third year Katie is in her second year Alan is in his first year of teaching so ... I felt that I had to be ... not so much dictatorial, but it wasn't delegated leadership it was leadership from the top ... I feel like now that they are starting to get more experience they are more confident in giving their opinions and I am having to adjust my leadership style (laughs) to accommodate that and that is good.
>
> *(Jane)*

Jane presents an image of herself leading the geography teachers (firmly when necessary) toward her vision of shared, collaborative curriculum making. Her personal strength of leadership appears to be an important influence in enabling collaborative curriculum making. 'I try to inspire others, maybe I manipulate it!' (Jane). Jane refers to Rhona's 'performance management' of using 'student voice' (ibid) to explain how some aspects of her team's work are formalised as written targets. To an extent, this allows Jane to control other teachers' curriculum making. Jane describes how the team needs to work in certain ways and she portrays her main management strategy as one of encouragement rather than coercion. She talks about 'drawing in' Katie, who she says, tends to work alone. Jane suggests that, one way or another, she will make sure the team will work collaboratively as the excerpts below illustrate.

> Rhona and I are trying to make a really big deal of everybody shares their resources. Everybody needs to work in the office for at least a percentage of your frees and blocking in time where, for example Rhona and Katie, work on year 8 together and when I work with Alan on year 10 marking, things like that ... to engage Katie with it, we've had to kind of put things in place.
>
> When I introduced that (teachers' subject knowledge audit) some people thought it was the best idea ever, others were less appreciative, but I think everybody is on board with it now. I did have to have a ... conversation with a member of the department.
>
> *(Jane)*

Jane's self-awareness of her leadership (of department and curriculum) appears to have been encouraged by the school. Jane speaks enthusiastically about the value of 'a really good middle leadership course' (Jane) funded by the school. She describes it as:

some of the best training I've ever had. It taught me how to get my own way as a leader and was very useful to how to approach underperformance.

(Jane)

The particular initiative Jane developed through the course was the use of literacy (a 'learning skill') and the language she uses to describe the training is business-like ('performance', 'blue-skies thinking', 'action plan', 'impact').

(In the 'teaching leaders' course) I had to implement an improvement initiative. That meant identifying underachieving groups and putting in an action plan this was then monitored we had training sessions and were coached ... The impact of this has been huge in some ways. A huge impact on the way we teach literacy and on the curriculum to a certain extent for example by encouraging more blue skies thinking. I learned most through the improvement initiative, the action plan and analysis. I got better at project management and curriculum design and things like that. It's about leading change.

(Jane)

Jane links the development of her management ability (supported by senior management) to curriculum change and innovation. Although she says the training is 'not prescriptive' the business-like language suggests that there may be a senior management message of performance and effectiveness influencing Jane and her department's curriculum work.

Jane's 'progressive' view of geography

Jane links three elements of curriculum making: her leadership; 'modernising' geographical content; and students' enjoyment. Through the interviews, Jane stresses how important it is to her that students are enjoying the curriculum. But she also presents a principled rationale for how enjoyment is to be achieved, which is through 'relevant' and up-to-date geography. She portrays satisfaction that she has led the curriculum away from the 'very old-fashioned geography' that she inherited in the department.

Jane further presents curriculum leadership as developing teachers' geographical knowledge by describing her use of a subject knowledge audit for teachers. (The 'red' areas mentioned are parts of geography teachers identified as weaknesses).

So this year for the first time I asked the department to carry out a subject knowledge audit at the beginning of the year ... we're taking it in turns to do kind of quick ten minutes, either activity or lead a discussion or bring in an article or something that is based on one of our 'red' areas so that we are kind of reading around the areas that we are not as familiar with and we try to build up our own subject knowledge and keep up-to-date.

(Jane)

Jane describes her actions to support geographical subject knowledge development. She reads widely (including A level and undergraduate geography textbooks and the geography curricula of other countries). She also mentions the Royal Geographical Society as a source of geography for her curriculum work. She refers to 'progress in the subject' and her curriculum making incorporates a view of geography as dynamic and progressive, not a fixed or inert content.

> We subscribe to lots of different academic journals in the library here. Our library is really good, it's been really great to the geography department and it has invested in a huge number of new books to meet the needs of our A level curriculum and a lot of them are more kind of undergraduate level, so we send people there. And we want to make more of the RGS evening lectures, that kind of thing.
>
> *(Jane)*

Jane is critical of geography curricula (like the Finnish and Singaporean examples she uses), which are too rigid. Jane talks about her curriculum 'moving forward' and she describes a 'progressive' view of geography in the curriculum in which the curriculum changes to reflect changes in geography.

> I spent time reading around, academic texts, curriculum from different countries including Finland, Singapore and two others. I found these very traditional and prescriptive. There's been progress in the subject. If something is prescriptive it is very difficult to move forwards. It's too inflexible.
>
> *(Jane)*

Navigating performance pressures

Jane describes some pressures and distractions from the expectations of the school senior leadership team (for example the 'interventions' policy to raise attainment). She also talks about the challenges of establishing a stable team of geography teachers, and the logistics of how the team communicates (such as having a department office space). Jane sometimes describes what is 'required' from senior management with a tone of resentment. But Jane's attitude to whole school policy is ambivalent. She appears enthusiastically supportive of some school policy, such as developing middle management skills for innovation and change (she valued her 'teaching leaders' course). Jane presents an acceptance of school policies on assessment as necessary and inevitable given accountability for examination results. She embraces some innovative assessment processes (such as the 'ladders' assessment tool she has used in lessons). But she implies there is a somewhat cynical culture in the school of 'too much spoon-feeding' of students driven by the pressure to achieve results.

> I'm banning intervention. The mind-set of the students is 'I don't have to do it first time round'. It gives us more time on marking. We want to spend more

time keeping up with subject knowledge … an intervention plan is required by SLT (senior leadership team) … I don't believe this benefits them in the long term. There's too much spoon-feeding.

(Jane)

Nonetheless, Jane appears to have accepted (with a slight tone of regret) the inevitability of her being accountable for results, the impact this has on her curriculum making and her impotence over some aspects of the curriculum when she says of preparation for examinations 'my feelings on that matter are fairly unimportant' (Jane).

Data analysis portrays a theme of 'learning skills' at Brightling, for example in descriptions of building learning power (BLP) in relation to curriculum work. Jane's actions and words relating to 'learning skills' are ambivalent. On the one hand she shows resistance to the school management request to include BLP in all lesson plans ('split-screen planning') and she avoids making BLP central to their KS3 curriculum planning. Jane led her team meeting by focusing on geographical content and progression. BLP was 'shelved' in this meeting. However, in interviews Jane seems convinced of the value of BLP and not at odds with the principle of developing a 'common language' of BLP across subjects. Her resistance to school management with respect to BLP, is, like her resistance to assessment pressures, a matter of degree rather than principle.

I think it (BLP) is something that we are already doing. I think we have decided that will do it (split screen planning) with year 7 and will build it up … I think we already did those kind of things like stopping the girls to talk about strategies they were using and like, meta-learning. That's something that we've been working on for a few years.

(Jane)

Jane articulates aims and purposes for her geography curriculum. She appears to be striving for a balance of three principles in her curriculum making of, 'progressive' geographical knowledge, student enjoyment, and developing skills for examination success. She describes three main challenges to achieving her aims. These are: generic approaches to 'learning'; accountability for exam performance; and an inexperienced and un-established teaching team. Jane's story is one of her working to 'navigate' these difficulties. She does not seek to remove them, and she speaks and acts with a recognition that these are part of the context of teaching at Brightling. Jane is therefore pragmatic but she also portrays a strong vision for how a 'relevant' and engaging geography can help to empower young people. Her determination and leadership abilities are directed toward this end.

Conclusion to Brightling – student voice, GCSE/A level and 'progressive geography'

Data analysis produces three prominent curriculum making themes at Brightling. The first is 'student voice'. The department portrays the enjoyment and interests of their students as strongly influencing curriculum making. The second is 'looking to GCSE and A level'. Examination courses are mentioned a great deal and are portrayed as informing KS3 curriculum making, both in terms of skill preparation and guiding geographical content. The third is engaging with a 'progressive' view of geography, which blends a view of geography as: dynamic (changing at the level of the discipline and in the popular imagination); relevant (through human issues); and enjoyable (for students).

There is conflict between Jane's drive to place geographical thinking at the forefront of her department's curriculum enactment and senior management pressure to focus on learning skills. Jane's curriculum value/belief systems are a mix of child-centred, scholar-academic and social reconstructionist. Jane is drawing on her identity as a geography teacher and working energetically to drive curriculum change and to develop a department of geography curriculum makers. Jane is exercising some control over curriculum enactment, however, use of the internet, accountability for results and expectations of enjoyment indicate wider society exerting power over the department's curriculum enactment.

6

CLAYMORE SCHOOL – TOWARD TEACHER AUTONOMY

Introduction

The analysis of curriculum making at Claymore school shows, like Arnwell and Brightling, a strong theme of student enjoyment. But the analysis also reveals two themes that are distinctive to Claymore's geography department. The first can be summarised as 'freedom'. The department portray their curriculum making as relatively autonomous and free from bureaucratic constraints and accountability pressures. This is enabled by a close-knit team, led by a charismatic Head of Department (HoD), fostering trust and respect between teachers. The second theme is the 'outside' world (beyond the school subject). This 'outside world' includes current affairs and the news, university geography departments, local area issues affecting the students and fieldwork. More than the other case study departments, Claymore makes a geography curriculum by looking 'outside' the more usual curriculum materials (of textbooks and school geography oriented websites for example).

School and geography department context

Claymore is an 11–18 girls' comprehensive school (with boys joining the sixth form) in the same inner-London borough as Arnwell High and Brightling School. Claymore is located approximately 1.5 miles away from both other schools and serves a similarly diverse socio-economic catchment. However, Claymore achieves higher GCSE and A level results. It has been rated as 'outstanding' in all areas in recent Ofsted inspections and was listed as fourth 'best' comprehensive school in England by a newspaper, based on league tables of 2013 examination results. It is heavily over-subscribed and has a more middle-class student body than other state schools in this part of the borough. However, it has an admissions policy to take a fixed proportion of lower student attainment levels at entry, students on free school meals and with SEN/disabilities. Claymore therefore retains a comprehensive ethos, although its popularity with middle class parents means the student body does not fully reflect the diverse local area.

Claymore is rather smaller than average, at 1,010 students on roll. It is housed in an imposing Victorian school building. There is an atmosphere of busy informality in the school. Unlike most other inner-city schools the main gate is left open and visitors can walk straight into the reception area where staff and students move about amidst students' artwork and some shabby furniture. There is a (whole) staff room with desks piled with papers and exercise books and teachers' belongings. There is no student uniform.

The teaching team is well established with Mat, Kay and Grant having worked together for some years (see Table 8). Laura is nearing the end of her NQT year. She spent a three month placement on teaching practice there during her PGCE. Laura was an outstanding PGCE student teacher and very keen to begin her first teaching post at the school. The teachers meet and talk informally a great deal and there is a happy and informal atmosphere in the department.

Analysis of curriculum enactment – students

Enjoyment and using students' interests and lives

Mat (HoD) frequently refers to student enjoyment in describing curriculum. He describes how he aims to excite students and to surprise them with the geography curriculum, hoping students will go home to tell parents 'you'll never guess what we did in geography today' (Mat, 11 July 2015). Mat's interview is peppered with references to student enjoyment as an influence over curriculum making and he says 'The enjoyment factor of the students, controls the way the … what's taught a lot, I would say.' (ibid). Mat describes how he encourages his department to use student enjoyment as a principle of their curriculum decisions.

> Sometimes Kay or Laura or somebody will come to me and say 'what shall I teach now, which direction should this be going in? And I often say, 'which bits are they enjoying?' and they'll say 'well, they're loving this' and I say 'well keep that running then'.
>
> *(Mat)*

TABLE 8 The geography teachers at Claymore

	School responsibilities (beyond Geography)	Age and time at the school
Mat (HoD)	Performance data management	40s 10 years
Kay	None (Part time – 0.6)	40s 8 years
Laura	None (NQT)	30 <1 year
Grant	None (Part time – 0.6)	50s 15 years
Aileen	None (Part time – 0.5)	40s 9 years

Mat describes enjoyment as the first stage of a progression through KS3. Enjoyment is presented as a way that they can engage with learning, taking risks and going beyond their existing field of knowledge and skills, feeling safe and secure.

> My number one goal in year seven is to get them to enjoy it whether we cover any material or not (laughs) ... In year eight the main ... I want them to experiment, to try new things. They can risk doing anything, the consequences are immaterial. There's nothing can go wrong, so I want them to try doing new things. In year nine I'm beginning to think 'what skills do I want them to have?'.
>
> *(Mat)*

Mat, Laura and Kay all talk about student enjoyment in department planning meetings and there is evidence of the teachers considering student fun and enjoyment in lesson planning. For example, Kay suggests 'More competitions, like "funny making food"', Laura's observed lesson uses a 'fun tray activity box' of household materials with which to design an interpretation of the demographic transition model and Mat says that a 'Docklands photo competition got them really excited'. There is a geography club, which Laura suggests should be 'fun' with an 'explorers' theme.

Student enjoyment is portrayed as influencing both how geography is taught and what geography is taught. This is particularly so in the geography club, where the teachers in a KS3 planning meeting describe using a

> newsy item, they can follow on the Internet ... tracking a friend around the world ... VIP ex-students from gap year ... making things, like volcanoes and weather stations.
>
> *(Mat)*

At the KS3 age group, the geography club is presented as an outlet for student creativity and a way to give students substantial control over curriculum making. While the geography club may be considered 'extra-curricular', it is part of the wider geography curriculum enacted during the KS3 years. Furthermore, the teachers' references to the geography club give insight into what and how the department want children to learn geography.

A student 'enjoyment' theme appears linked to the geography teachers' interest in 'student voice' because students' needs, interests and preferences are used in both curriculum planning and curriculum enactment. In all KS3 lessons observed there is dialogue between teacher and student. In Mat's year 7 lesson there is particularly prevalent use of humour and finding examples and stories that connect to students' lives. For example, in an observed lesson Mat tells the class a story of how he joked with a former student about her home as 'a dump' before reading in the local paper about inadequate council accommodation where she lived. In this example, dialogue between teacher and students becomes part of the enacted curriculum.

Another example, though referring to year 12 geography students, gives insight into how the geography department sees students as producers of curriculum arte-facts and not just as consumers of 'a curriculum'. Mat (HoD) describes how the department has curated an exhibition of students' work shown at the British Museum under the theme of 'patterns of power'. While there is no specific refer-ence to enjoyment here, students are likely to be engaged with creatively pursuing their interests to produce work of such quality. The example suggests the depart-ment see students and teachers as working together to create a curriculum.

Mat and his department want students to enjoy geography. They pay attention to what students prefer. Lesson observations show enjoyment is a feature of the enactment of the KS3 curriculum through the use of humour and students' crea-tive activity. Enjoyment is presented (by Mat) as an end in itself, though not in a 'hedonistic' sense. Evidence from interviews and curriculum documents shows how student enjoyment is linked to principles of a geographic education. The excerpt below describes how students 'love' to think about the moral questions, which arise through the geographies of inequality.

> They (geographies of inequality) are sort of moral questions which they love, those ideas about fairness and the fact that they have different ideas about fairness.
>
> *(Mat)*

Mat also connects fieldwork with enjoyment, engagement and better geographical learning.

> The other really important thing is you know, when naughty and disen-franchised students become engaged they go running around beside a river and they can't help but pick stuff up.
>
> *(Mat)*

Current 'issues' and fieldwork are prominent sub-themes in the data analysis. The evidence suggests that an 'issues' approach to geography and fieldwork are not just used as strategies to engage and enthuse students. The department portray 'issues' and fieldwork as distinctive features of curriculum making at Claymore. The data analysis shows that these features are influenced by Mat's personal preferences, the school context and the locality as the next section 'Geography' presents.

Analysis of curriculum enactment – geography

The news, 'issues' and London children

> (a theme) that the department has strongly is … making links with very topical things that are going on that week or month in the news.'
>
> *(Mat)*

Mat describes how he tries to link the news to curriculum making, and how 'anything' in the geography classroom can be connected to news and current affairs.

> So if you can find a speech that's happened in Parliament or you can find a
> Scottish vote or something, you can pin it to … anything.
>
> *(Mat)*

Mat describes a priority of connecting students' lives and the news (or current issues) to geography in his curriculum making. This is not only through the media of television, internet and newspapers. Mat describes how the department regularly hosts guest speakers, which includes journalists and politicians as well as academic geographers. He sees current affairs as a driver of curriculum making and he appears to downplay 'geography' as an influence:

> I would definitely get more inspiration for what we should be teaching from
> reading the newspaper than reading anything from the Geographical Associa-
> tion or anything remotely academic geography … I would rather use students'
> observations of (how) the built environment reflects the human activity in an
> area than looking at Hoyt's sectoral model. Yeah, that would be exactly what
> I'm trying to. So the geography would inform it but the material … may …
> be to do with an item on the news the night before or an unfair catchment
> area for a school, or something like that.
>
> *(Mat)*

Mat connects the theme of using the news and current affairs to students' own lives and the local area. He also suggests that 'issues' in the curriculum are connected to student enjoyment. He says 'they love' moral questions and ideas about fairness, referring to these particular girls who live in the highly unequal society of this part of London.

> We are in a fantastic area to look at inequalities. There are many more
> deprived areas, but I doubt there are many catchments where inequalities are
> so stark within three or four hundred metres of the school … and given the
> nature of our intake that's all reflected in the room. It's just very interesting. I
> go as far to say as I think it's important.
>
> *(Mat)*

Although he emphasises using students' lives and the news, Mat portrays a disciplined use of geography to make the curriculum. He talks of curriculum making as using students' lives and the news that is 'geography informed'. Mat and the department appear as confident, capable and committed geographers. While Mat downplays academic geography as a starting point for curriculum making (preferring to emphasise the news and students' lives) he is active in developing his own geographical knowledge. He regularly communicates with different university geography departments and he recently undertook a sabbatical at a leading university geography department to update his knowledge. The evidence presents Mat as able to draw on a deep understanding of geography while putting his energies into finding ways to connect geography to students' lives. Geography appears to be used almost subconsciously, or instinctively. So, for example, he talks of 'the news' as inspiration for his curriculum making, but in the same interview he reveals that he is able to connect the issue of inequality to the geographical concept of scale.

> I like the idea of talking about inequalities. It lends itself to different scales. Inequalities has worked very well and they end up writing what, in my view, is a really high level complex essay based on a Danny Dorling film and a Guardian article. And they had to write an essay which I'd be very happy if my year 12s wrote frankly, an essay about inequality breeds fear and prejudice in UK urban communities or something, which I think is quite a thing for a 13-year-old to write, and they do.
>
> *(Mat)*

Mat describes how topical, issues-based geography resonates with local children. He suggests that their academic performance is raised as a result. The 'high level' essay, which he'd be happy if his year 12 geographers wrote, implies that the 'issue' of inequalities has been successfully connected to the subject (or discipline) of geography. Mat appears to be successfully balancing attention to the child's life experiences with use of the discipline.

Fieldwork

Fieldwork takes place in year 7, 8 and 9 in a range of locations and is portrayed as significant to curriculum decision making in higher years, including affecting exam board selection 'GCSE may change to Edexcel (a UK examination board) in 2016, if it … lets us go to Wales.' (Mat). Mat gives several specific reasons why fieldwork is an essential part of the curriculum. He describes fieldwork as fundamental to being a geographer and he presents a role of the curriculum as inducting young people into geography fieldwork. He expresses this in comparison to how people engage with the arts.

> There's a basic reason. I see it as just like, you know, going to see the art department should be encouraging, will be encouraging people to go to galleries. The music departments will be encouraging them to go to concerts. I see the geography field trip as, in a curriculum point of view, as just the same.
>
> *(Mat)*

He describes fieldwork as: helping students to grasp concepts, describing students as 'turning to each other and going "oh I get it now!"'; giving phenomena meaning by placing them in context 'You've got to go there and see it'; engaging especially for the 'disenfranchised' students, such that they begin to take an interest in the subject; supporting geographical enquiry (by enabling the use of field data); and fieldwork as energising or 'healthy' for the department team.

An additional reason (not stated by Mat, but implicit in the wider case study evidence) is that fieldwork in KS3 supports the department's emphasis on local issues, which are part of students' lives. The local borough 'trail' and the comparison of their High Street to St Albans are part of economic geography and inequalities. They lead to assessed work and are key parts of these units of work. Mat connects fieldwork to his personal satisfaction and how he sustains his enthusiasm for geography teaching. He says, 'If I didn't do (fieldwork and other 'extra' things) I might ask myself (laughs) can I keep doing this?' (Mat).

The GNC, progression and assessment – using data

The department portrays an ambivalent relationship with accountability and regulation. The use of assessment data to support progress is taken seriously. But there is a striking theme of resistance to a perceived bureaucratic system, and the Geography National Curriculum (GNC) does not appear to exert a strong influence over curriculum making.

> I think there are things we'll not be compliant with. I think we we'll do precious little about rocks or soils. I think we'll do nothing on them. I think we'll do nothing on glaciation … and at first I thought, oh my lord! Then I thought to myself, well you know, there are so many aspects of what we do which I think are really good and I think if a man in a bowler hat comes here and says 'show me your scheme of work for rocks, soils and glaciation'. I would just fall to the ground sobbing and think all is lost, because that is just not important to me.
>
> *(Mat)*

Mat (humorously) portrays disdain, even contempt for educational regulation from outside the department in the 'man in the bowler hat' and the 'fat controller' (ibid). The image offered is of the bureaucrat being out of touch with the enacted curriculum at school level – the curriculum that Mat believes to be best for his department and their students. Though he does not clarify who that bureaucrat is, a reasonable inference is that he is talking about the Ofsted school inspector, or possibly (in the case of showing progress against levels) a manager within the school.

But Mat does describe a keen sense of accountability in his curriculum work. He describes the department as 'driven by data'. Their successful track record of results 'buys' the department relative freedom of curriculum making. The department, Mat claims, is confident to take inspectors or bureaucratic managers 'with a pinch of salt' (Mat) and confident to make their own curriculum decisions based on their own principles as geographers and teachers. However, the evidence does not portray a department in which lessons are ad hoc or outcomes uncertain. Interview, planning meetings and documentary evidence show a KS3 curriculum 'driven by data' – but (at least to an extent) on the department's own terms.

Topic assessment tasks (TATs) are discussed frequently in curriculum planning meetings and Mat describes them as 'probably central to (what and how we teach)' (ibid). There is a tension between a 'freedom' narrative constructed from Mat's interview and teachers being required to cover the same content for the TATs. Teachers are free – as long as they agree with each other over the assessed part of their KS3 curriculum.

> There is a lot of flexibility between teachers over what we teach in a topic but we all have to get to this point where students are accessing what is required of them in a TAT … everybody needs to be able to have enough knowledge to access the TAT.
>
> *(Mat)*

The strain on the 'freedom' narrative increases given that the TATs must supply data (using National Curriculum levels) to school senior management to show student progress. Furthermore, senior management (school policy) are influential, as Kathy expresses:

> The new curriculum focuses of school are differentiation, inclusion, feedback. These should all feed into the curriculum content planning. We are supposed to look at data more clearly 'laserlike'.
>
> *(Kathy)*

The department appears content to use data using NC levels. Mat describes finding the levels 'useful'.

> I think levels as an idea are useful actually. I think students understand them. I think we've finally come to understand them a bit. I think the idea of making progress independent of your age is useful.
>
> *(Mat)*

There is no evidence that other teachers in the department resent the limitation to their freedom of the TATs. Indeed, just as Mat describes TATs as 'the glue that binds the topic together' (ibid), the teachers portray the TATs as binding the team together because they are a focus of enthusiastic curriculum discussion, consensus and cooperation and part of the 'sharing' theme of the department.

The 'centrality' which Mat says that TATs have in curriculum making, and the evidence that they take up to 25 per cent of curriculum time, warrants a consideration of how they affect curriculum making. The department ensure that TATs are different 'modes' (some are written work, some are presentations for example). The TATs are often project-based involving independent study. Mat says TATs 'take two or three weeks' chunks out of the teaching' (ibid).

His words indicate that he sees these assessment 'tasks' as separate to 'teaching' geography, which implies that a requirement for data may have an effect of diminishing the 'taught' curriculum. Mat and the team do not describe TATs as a problem. His team appear to embrace the use of assessments and performance data to support students' progression. The key message from Mat is that such data use is welcomed – as long as the geography teachers feel they control how assessment data are produced and used.

GCSE and A level

Mat portrays GCSE and A level results as an indirect influence over KS3 curriculum making because a successful track record ensures the department is 'left alone' to make the curriculum. Mat claims that he does not plan KS3 geography with GCSE and A level in mind, saying:

> I don't think we've got a connection (between KS3 content and GCSE/A level). I don't consciously teach topics that we think will be useful.
>
> *(Mat)*

However, some other comments by Mat contradict this. He says that he is prepared to adapt the KS3 curriculum in response to the geographical skills required in examination courses. He gives the example of bringing statistics into KS3 should statistics be a requirement at GCSE or A level. Furthermore, enthusing students to want to take the subject further is a factor in KS3 curriculum making. Mat mentions that the introduction of the 'inequalities' topic in year 9 was

> a bit scheming, because I thought it was just an interesting topic and it was in response to wanting to have a recruiting topic in year nine.
>
> *(Mat)*

University geography departments

Mat describes how he seeks out the parts of the university discipline of geography that tend to reflect his interests, such as geopolitics and inequalities. These areas also reflect current affairs and local issues, which affect the students' own lives. The department (and particularly Mat) engage with university geography directly. Mat recently took a sabbatical to University College, London (UCL) and he describes valuing how he can bring developments in the discipline to the school curriculum.

> I looked at geopolitics ... and GIS, which we were bad on then and were now good on, that's where I tried to focus so that I brought some things back.
>
> *(Mat)*

Mat describes his engagement with university geography for his own satisfaction and keeping fresh or 'recharging the batteries' (ibid). University geography is also described in terms of relationships. Mat talks about individuals when describing how university geography has influenced the curriculum. Mat also says how he values connections with universities through former students.

> Having a big sixth form means that there are now people in all the main geography departments that have come out of school. So we've got people in Oxbridge and Manchester and Exeter and Nottingham and Edinburgh.
>
> *(Mat)*

When Mat refers to university geography, he talks about people he has worked with and built a relationship with. Mat appears to value the quality of relationships and how supportive and responsive people are in the organisations he works with – for example in valuing how SOAS Library were 'incredibly helpful'. Mat's relationship with geography is through relationships with people. He downplays the use of agencies, which act as a filter between teacher and geography (such as the RGS and GA). Mat prefers to go direct to 'geography' beyond the school subject, by building relationships with university geographers, or others (such as journalists or politicians).

Analysis of curriculum enactment – teachers – autonomy and trust

Mat describes how all subject departments in the school must account for the performance data of their students. However, he tells how a track record of successful results at A level and GCSE means he is trusted with a high degree of autonomy over the Geography Department, and curriculum.

> They (SMT) look at the data. The data are good and they don't come near me. They leave me alone (laughs). I can do what I want.
>
> *(Mat)*

Enjoyment is a prominent theme in interviews, meetings and lesson observations. The words 'fun', 'enjoy', 'like' and 'love' occur frequently in the context of both student and teacher enjoyment.

> I definitely think you can teach anything if you love it.
>
> *(Mat)*

Mat describes a department in which teachers and students enjoy geography. He makes the link between curriculum content decisions, and the enjoyment of both students and teachers.

> The feedback I get there is that people appreciate the freedom that they get given to pursue the interests that they have.
>
> *(Mat)*

Freedom and enjoyment is described so emphatically by Mat that it can be described as a curriculum making principle. Mat links the freedom he says teachers in the department enjoy, to the way teachers communicate openly and honestly, saying 'we are the only department who does 360° feedback … we are definitely a team'. Mat frequently describes the department as 'we' and portrays a close-knit team. Mat talks about his geography teaching colleagues with respect and even admiration, describing them as:

> enormously compassionate … enthusiastic and motivated and interesting people … they're all really, really good.
>
> *(Mat)*

Mat links the closeness of teamwork to curriculum making, by informal conversations about the geography they are choosing to teach, describing how 'we chat about (curriculum decisions) a lot and we see each other a lot'. The team meet frequently to talk about teaching and curriculum matters (shown by researcher observation as well as interviews). Talking about the geography curriculum might be brief and informal, but it is frequent and regular, during break times for example. There is a desk space in a corner of the (cluttered and chaotic appearing) staffroom, shared by the geographers, where they often talk about the geography they are teaching. Mat describes the team as sharing both underlying values – 'we like the kids and we want them to like geography' – and sharing curriculum approaches, such as using the news and current affairs. He also describes an advantage of the team having common backgrounds, all having worked outside the field of education before coming to teaching. He links this to his teachers gaining 'viewpoints' which they bring to geography – a point which resonates with his emphasis on current affairs and the news in the geography curriculum.

> I tell you one other influencing factor is that … none of us went from the Institute aged 21 into teaching and I suspect … no, I know for a fact that we all have views about … maybe I'm wrong (laughs), we all have views gained from working outside teaching about what are useful skills to have in the world.
>
> *(Mat)*

Mat also expresses a closeness of the team in terms of a shared philosophy of education.

> I do think we share an idea that we come to work because we like the kids and we want them to like geography. I think that's what we share.
>
> *(Mat)*

In visits to the school, humour and informality were noticeable features of the department, and particularly of Mat's manner. Transcription notes he laughed 56 times in one interview, he dresses casually and he is informal with colleagues (one planning meeting in the summer was held on a bench-table under a tree). His professional manner could be described as 'unconventional', which is consistent with his anti-bureaucracy comments about the 'man in a bowler hat'. Both enjoyment and freedom ('to teach what we like') appear to be reflected in Mat's attitude and approach. He portrays an open and unguarded management style, a high regard for his geography colleagues and valuing freedom for teachers to make their own curriculum choices. Data analysis links these aspects of the department to school management by a theme of trust. School management trusts Mat to deliver examination success and Mat trusts his team to teach (up to a point) what and how they choose.

Mat's story – the confidence for action to keep interested

Mat says he likes his job, and he links this satisfaction to his own learning, keeping his 'spark' as a teacher. To do so, he is prepared to take on 'extra things' – to seek out challenging fieldwork for example. He also describes arranging guest speakers, including journalists and academics, using the news and bringing developments from university geography departments into the geography curriculum. These challenging 'extras' affect the geography the children learn. Mat portrays curriculum making as sustaining him as a teacher.

> Yeah, that is particularly what I like about the job, is running extra things and keeping me interested. If I just taught tectonics to year eight again next year I think the spark might go. But if I can maintain those contacts, if I can learn interesting things off people who know what they're talking about … the other thing I like to do is to push it with the field trips.
> If I didn't do those (extra) things I might ask myself (laughs) can I keep doing this?
>
> *(Mat)*

Mat is modest about his achievements and downplays the time and effort of such 'extra things' as building links with universities, organising visits from journalists and politicians, and running a number of field trips. His actions show commitment both to his own development as a geographer and to curriculum development in the department. Mat portrays his own geographical knowledge development and the department's curriculum development as closely linked. He describes how the 'extra things' to develop the geography curriculum are personally motivated, with little support from outside the department.

> Do I have support? Sometimes I feel a bit unloved. It's an enormous amount of work maintaining those things and I get a lot of speakers and I tend to run … I don't know, I try in the autumn term to have maybe half a dozen external speakers. Some are university, some might be journalists or politicians or something. That's a lot of work to … I get support, maybe sometimes, someone says 'that's good' (laughs). I don't get any money (laughs).
>
> *(Mat)*

Mat portrays his motivation for the 'enormous amount of work' as job satisfaction, personal interest and keeping his 'spark'. However, Mat portrays his motivation as not entirely self-centred interest. Mat's descriptions of his work to go beyond the simpler curriculum sources (such as the internet and textbooks). He describes a connection between his own knowledge development and the needs of his students. Mat describes a view that fieldwork is an 'essential' part of geography. The 'extra work' and the 'pushing it' with the senior management to ensure field trips are plentiful and ambitious, make sense in light of how he describes the importance of fieldwork. Mat does not make the same statement explicitly about current affairs, inequalities or GIS (that they are 'essential' to geography). However, data analysis shows a pattern here, of Mat portraying commitment to the (changing) discipline of geography and to his students' needs, from which he takes personal satisfaction.

The themes of freedom, trust and informality in the department's curriculum making are also part of Mat's personal curriculum making story. Mat is well established at the school. He describes how the school senior management team (SMT) have trust and confidence to 'leave him alone' because the department maintains strong examination results in geography. He also describes how he will assert himself when he feels strongly about something (such as 'pushing it' to gain SMT agreement to field trips) and requesting a sabbatical to a university. Mat is informal to the point of being unconventional in his manner – his informal dress at school and his ever-present humour for example. He is sceptical of educational bureaucracy and he is relaxed about 'non-compliance' to outside interference.

Evidence from interviews, observing department meetings and lesson observation show Mat to be a confident Head of Geography. Mat is confident to teach content he believes is best for his students. He is confident in his geographical knowledge and understanding – so that he can focus on bringing current affairs and humour into lessons without losing the geography and Mat is confident in his team. He leads by trusting his geography teachers to make their own decisions about content.

Mat portrays a personal value of freedom to grow (for himself, his department team and his students). He describes his aim of helping to empower young women to pursue whichever future path they wish. He implies that the geography his department teaches is not aiming to steer his students in any particular direction. He advocates freedom to choose, but with 'an enlightened attitude'. 'Confidence' appears engrained in the department at different levels – Mat's personal confidence, confidence in Mat (from his team and senior management) and developing the confidence of young women by 'enlightenment'.

> I'd feel very happy if some girls went away from here feeling they could be more empowered women … we like to feel that we play a part in encouraging, yeah, creating confident women … I don't mind where they go … I like to think that if one is going to become a corporate lawyer one does it with an enlightened attitude.
>
> *(Mat)*

Mat's story is one of having built confidence, freedom and trust from which he is able to 'be himself' with an unconventional style, develop a close-knit team, which has an active engagement with geography at university, in fieldwork, politics, current affairs and local issues.

Conclusion – freedom and 'the outside world'

At Claymore, more than the other three departments, data analysis shows two distinctive curriculum making narratives. First, there is a 'freedom narrative', through winning the trust of school management, Mat leads his team to choose what to teach based on their professional judgement as individuals. Mat expresses an aversion to following a 'fixed' national curriculum content and he portrays a confidence to disregard what he sees as bureaucratic regulation. 'Freedom' also extends to the how students are encouraged to approach geography, with a sense of being able to take risks. Future examination success is downplayed (unlike Brightling). While 'freedom' (or autonomy) is not absolute for either individual or department, there is a more prominent notion of freedom of curriculum making at Claymore than the other departments. Within the freedom narrative there are themes of trust and collaboration. The teachers communicate and cooperate closely, with much humour.

Secondly, there is an 'outside world' narrative, including current affairs and the news, university geography departments, local area issues affecting the students and fieldwork. The department (in particular Mat) portrays an enactment of geography curriculum making by going 'outside' the more usual curriculum materials (of textbooks and school geography-oriented websites for example). By so doing the teachers appear to reduce their dependence on 'pre-packaged' geography lessons (geography that has been already recontextualised by others). For example, Mat downplays the RGS and GA's materials, preferring to go directly to geography 'outside' in the world, be that through the news, university geographers, local issues or fieldwork. People from 'outside' school geography are used as a resource for this, including university academics, journalists and politicians.

The department portrays a scholar academic curriculum value/belief system in commitment to engagement with geography, the university discipline and a liberal–humanist attitude in the empowerment that geographical knowledge can bring to young women. There is some tension between the autonomy for which Mat strives and the accountability for results demanded by the school and the community it serves. Curriculum change is a feature of the department, both through teachers' engagement with university geography and using the news to steer the enacted curriculum. In Claymore, the teachers take considerable control over their curriculum and they demonstrate and describe a balanced concern for geography, the student's experiences and teaching choices, as modelled by curriculum making (Lambert and Morgan 2010).

7

DERWENT SCHOOL – A KNOWLEDGE-BASED CURRICULUM

Introduction

Data analysis produces a theme of 'geographical knowledge' in curriculum making at Derwent School. The experienced Head of Department (Kathy) plays a key role in this theme through her curriculum leadership. Kathy's re-engagement with geography comes at a time when senior school staff have encouraged her to move into management. She describes actively resisting this encouragement and presents a 'renewed' enthusiasm and commitment to teaching a broad, balanced and 'deep' geographical knowledge. Her choice to study for a Master's degree in Geography Education is central in her 'renewal'. The department is distinctive by the time and commitment given to discussing the geography curriculum (both verbally and through electronic communications). High levels of collaboration, trust and respect between the geography teachers are presented. Different opinions between teachers 'come to the surface' because the department fosters a culture of open debate about the curriculum. Data analysis also shows that other sub-themes, including student enjoyment, attention to skills and the role of the internet and media, are connected to the distinctive 'geographical knowledge' narrative at Derwent.

School and geography department context

Derwent School is a large 11–18 mixed comprehensive school of 1,643 (with 430 in the sixth form). It is located two miles away from the other three case study schools. The school catchment covers both the local area, which is predominantly of expensive, private housing, and other parts of the borough, which are less privileged. There are fewer than the national average of students with SEN and disabilities and with free school meals. Academic attainment at GCSE is higher than the national average and recent Ofsted reports rate the school 'outstanding' overall. In 2014 a newspaper ranked Derwent as the '11th best' comprehensive school in England, and the school has been oversubscribed for many years. The school is housed on a compact site in a jumble of buildings and is unimposing at first impression. There is no uniform and the atmosphere, in the words of a student quoted by Ofsted, is 'informal but with high academic standards'.

The geography department consists of six geography specialists and is well established with long serving and very experienced teachers mixed with less experienced but committed geography teachers – Steve is an Advanced Skills Teacher (AST) and Said has recently taken on a role of mentoring student geography teachers (see Table 9). The department regularly mentors up to four student geography teachers on placements at Derwent each year and is an active partner of university education departments. GCSE and A level results in Geography are among the highest in the school.

Analysis of curriculum enactment – students – enjoyment and interest

Data analysis (including interviews, observations and documents) presents a theme of student enjoyment, although it is less pronounced than the other schools. Kathy says, 'We are quite child-centred in the sense that we want the kids to really enjoy their lessons' and the teachers talk about student enjoyment when describing how they make the curriculum. The teachers portray enjoyment as linked to students' engagement and interest and, to an extent, these qualities are presented as ends in themselves, or part of the purpose of the KS3 geography curriculum. Rachel describes 'curiosity' as a curriculum outcome, and the teacher's role as 'sparking' interest. Kathy and other teachers also refer to students' interest and engagement when making curriculum decisions. Christy, describing a strong commitment to fieldwork, says how she chooses 'beautiful' places for fieldwork and hopes students' reaction will be, 'Wow that's amazing!' Rachel expresses how curiosity and a 'love of learning' is part of her aim for the geography curriculum:

TABLE 9 The geography teachers at Derwent

	School responsibilities (beyond Geography)	Age and time at the school
Kathy (HoD)	Head of Humanities	late 30s 8 years
Rachel (KS3 coordinator)	None	40s 16 years
Christy	Outreach support to other schools	late 30s 10 years
Mike	Head of Year	40s 9 years
Steve	Advanced Skills Teacher (AST)	early 30s 5 years
Said	None	20s 2 years

I guess the most important thing is that we've sparked an interest to come back to at various different points in their life ... for their own sense of well-being, their own understanding, their own enjoyment of life. For me as all researchers, it's curiosity driven. I don't particularly care if later on its glaciation or development or whatever and personally, off the record, I don't particularly care how many exams they do in the subject. The central theme for me is a sort of love of learning, curiosity, yeah curiosity.

(Rachel)

The geography teachers agree that students should enjoy lessons, but there is some disagreement over how far KS3 content should reflect students' existing experience and interests. Kathy links teachers' beliefs in relation to this, to the teacher's age, suggesting that 'Not so much the older (teachers) but the younger ones that have come in' prefer what she calls a 'sensationalist' approach to topic selection (Kathy). Steve and Said express (and lesson observation corroborates) their preference for an 'issues' approach to selecting geography content. Steve says

(I prefer an) issues-based approach, partly because I think it appeals to students a bit more.

He indicates the sort of content such an approach may lead to:

We need an issue ... to get kids interested in the local area study like crime, skate-park or something ... we can let the students decide.

(Steve)

Said says he wants to choose a location to 'make it relevant to them'. Some of the team describe students choosing their own curriculum content in some circumstances. Mike also shows that students can choose topics in some circumstances saying, 'It (year 9 assessment) could be an issue of their choice like the heroin trail, crime or sport'. But Kathy, Christy and Rachel express more caution about allowing 'issues' to drive curriculum choices. Kathy says she wants a curriculum that is 'up to date ... engaging and interesting' but she disagrees with some of her team about the KS3 geography topics (such as crime and football), which are driven by students' own experiences and the 'issues' in their lives. There is debate in the team over subject knowledge, young people's issues and curriculum decisions.

Analysis of curriculum enactment – geography

Geographical knowledge

The department, in particular, Kathy, indicate a belief in the importance of 'core' knowledge and understanding, which is grounded in geographical knowledge. She refers (both directly and indirectly) to the importance of students acquiring a basic understanding of geographical concepts at KS3 such as: process 'I want them to understand why it rains'; location, 'they understand that this is a map of the world and they can, you know, know their continents'; and integration, '(students should think about) the physical environment, looking at the human environment, looking at the interaction between the two'. Kathy expresses how students' understanding should be underpinned by geographical (disciplinary) knowledge: Kathy portrays a concern that geographical knowledge may be lost or become 'superficial' when issues dominate (such as climate change or deforestation).

> If you don't know the underlying real things about the planet, so about atmospheric circulation, about soils and all the rest of it, how can you really understand about impacts of climate change or why deforestation is such a problem?
>
> *(Kathy)*

Kathy presents her aim of a broad a balanced 'core' geographical knowledge at the end of KS3, describing 'a responsibility (to teach) … all of those things that I think are at the core of geography.' Although she presents balance between physical and human geography as 'equally important to us as a department', some differences in teachers' views on how 'knowledge' in geography should inform curriculum making, are shown by data analysis. Kathy says she has had 'a tiny bit of resistance' from some of her team when she has expressed her concern that some topics (she gives examples of football and fashion) might be dropped from their curriculum.

> Christy also and Rachel are like me, and Mike as well actually … we probably lean more towards more traditional … hmm … knowledge over values I would say.
> Sometimes in the department someone wants to do the geography of football. I don't think it's right (laughs) yeah, Steve and I have disagreed sometimes about this.
>
> *(Kathy)*

There is some disagreement about curriculum content within the team. But this is not portrayed as a weakness. Kathy and others in the team describe respect for each other's opinions as geography teachers and curriculum debate (serious conversations about what to teach) is presented as a healthy and strong feature of the department.

University geography

Teachers describe university geography as an influence to a varying extent. Kathy is nearing completion of a part time MA in Geography Education, alongside her job running the department, which she links to changes in curriculum making – in particular to an emphasis on 'core' geographical knowledge. Other teachers also describe connections between their university geography and curriculum making, and make references to the department culture of open curriculum debate, as Steve illustrates by his university degree reflecting his interest in exploring environmental and development issues through the school curriculum:

> Yeah environmental. Well, I really switched the emphasis (to environmental geography) in my dissertation ... then I did a Masters in development studies after that ... Yeah environmental things ... I think I'm ... sort of more issues-based approach.
>
> *(Steve)*

Rachel describes how

> Being an archaeologist by trade, I like practical things. So if I can make a model of a volcano, I will, if I can show a river going through sand, I will.
>
> *(Rachel)*

She describes studying for an MPhil research degree with an interest in migration and the lives of diaspora in London, which she hopes to bring into the curriculum. She describes an informal process of transfer from the university to school.

> I also talk to the tutors there and I think 'oh that's interesting, so that's the bit in favour at the moment' ... then that filters down to us.
>
> *(Rachel)*

Rachel also links her own education and how she learned, to her preferred teaching style. She appears sceptical of the rationale for some popular contemporary teaching strategies.

> I think it comes from your styles of learning yourself, you know? And I guess I was quite a nerdy student. I liked learning ... I agree with a 14-year-old 'oh flipping hell, another card sort! I don't need that.' Let's face it they're control mechanisms aren't they? If you have an audience of 13-year-olds who will listen you will talk and they will enjoy that storytelling aspect.
>
> *(Rachel)*

Mike describes his university geography as formative in his 'leftward leanings' and he connects these personal views to curriculum making.

> I wouldn't consider myself a Marxist, but I definitely have leftward leanings ... anticapitalist leanings ... increasingly, globalisation is appearing ... I think it's an important message for them. All we are at the end of the day is consumers and that consumption has profound effects socially, politically and environmentally.
>
> *(Mike)*

Steve presents the influence of his degree, more as enduring values and beliefs than as tangible and specific knowledge to be imparted to students. The environmental and development issues that he advocates in the school curriculum appear to reflect the enduring impact of his university education, but he describes the specific knowledge of his degree as largely irrelevant to his curriculum making now.

> I can't say the degree takes much of an impact on what I teach now … the degree helped me find my passions in geography. But you know, being able to remember some of the stuff that I got taught back then is quite limited. So what I will think about, what I'm interested in and search the internet or read a book and find out facts and figures that start the basis of it and then create interesting lessons from that.
>
> *(Steve)*

The teachers portray their diverse university and school education as affecting curriculum making because these backgrounds influence their interests and preferences, which in turn fuel a department discussion about what geography to teach.

Skills and progression

Data analysis shows a sub-theme of 'skills', particularly geographical, and to a lesser extent generic skills (such as literacy and graphicacy) in curriculum making at Derwent. The department often refer to skills in relation to progression. The department met for a full day to focus on KS3 curriculum planning. They use the Geographical Association (GA)'s KS3 curriculum 'planning wheel' (Figure 9, below) which is a device for supporting teachers' progression in planning KS3. The three concentric circles 'growing' outward are designed to support knowledge broadening and deepening in five 'segments' (geographical topics, area of skill or concepts). The department labels five 'themes' one of which, 'investigating my world', is portrayed as geographical skills development.

At the planning meeting, the teachers combined the planning wheel with a draft curriculum map (drawn up by Kathy on the whiteboard from the meeting discussion). The curriculum map (Figure 10, below) shows much attention to skills, such as research, analysis, point-evidence-explanation paragraph writing, extended writing, annotation and decision-making. Arrows indicate a skill-progression in two assessments for each topic.

The geography team focus on skills in their KS3 curriculum planning meeting and aim for progression in geographical skills.

> We have skills running through … We need to really step back and think about the journey 7, 8, 9 and be ready for GCSE. We need to think very carefully about progression, big picture. We have a great opportunity here.
>
> *(Kathy)*

KS3 New themes and topics Sept 2014 overview

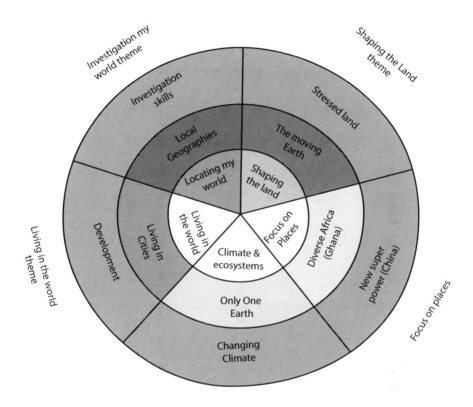

Climate & ecosystems theme

FIGURE 9 KS3 'planning wheel' used by Derwent geography department

In the meeting, Kathy led the team in a brainstorming exercise to produce a list. The list contains both specifically geographical skills (such as field sketches and OS map skills) and more generic and transferable skills (such as asking questions and extended writing).

decision–making
OS map skills
data presentation grass field sketch annotation charts and diagrams
data analysis
visual resource analysis
extended writing
fieldwork (primary data)

Seven week block	Year 7		Year 8		Year 9	
1	Investigation, research and analysis A1	----▶ A2	Climate and ecosystems PEE	Extended writing ----▶	Development PEE ----▶	DME
2	**Water** visual resource analysis	----▶ annota-tion of diagrams	**Living in cities** annotated diagram	creative solutions ----▶	GCSE style question six Mark (short answer)	
3	GCSE style question six Mark (short answer)		**Africa** energy questions	researching and presenting place ----▶	**China** collecting and describing, comparing ----▶	writing an informed conclusion ----▶
4	**Climate** Graphs A1 ----▶	A2	GCSE style question six Mark (short answer)		Stressed land defining sustainability (small task) ----▶	SDME (sustainable DME)
5	**Russia** ----▶	Tourist guide	GCSE style question six Mark (short answer)		Investigation A1 ----▶	A2

FIGURE 10 Skills and knowledge content draft curriculum map, Derwent KS3 planning meeting, 5 December 2014

all presentations
asking questions
creative solutions field sketches/annotation
Team brainstorm (written on whiteboard by Kathy) planning meeting, 12 June, 2014

Before the planning meeting, each of the team was asked to prepare a list of 'core' content and processes and core skills for the existing KS3 unit for which they have taken responsibility. The team fed back their lists in the meeting. The way this task was set up by Kathy suggests the team are steered toward prioritising geographical knowledge over skills. For example, Rachel presented her 'shaping the land' unit. Rachel's planning indicates her attention to geographical concepts (before 'issues'):

Core content and process:
process
place
interaction people and nature
issues e.g. fracking
Core skills:
fieldwork (reading the landscape)
interpreting visual sources
analysis of data (numerical)
annotated diagrams 'at GCSE is important' (Rachel)
fieldwork and reading the landscape is a key principle 'landscape literacy'
Rachel, KS3 planning meeting, 12 June 2014

The department's KS3 curriculum overview (see Figure 9) shows five themed units each year. One of these units is called 'investigating my world', which focuses on developing a wide range of geographical skills, including fieldwork and geographical enquiry. Mike has responsibility for these units and he describes the importance given to the development of students' geographical skills:

They have to learn how to research … these are really tough skills I think for year nine … We're hopefully going to teach them how to collect evidence that is relevant before they start building their report … How do you carry it out and how do you structure the writing? … methodology, results, presentation and analysis, conclusion, evaluation.

(Mike)

Mike's description of the skills the department is trying to develop includes both 'soft' transferable skills and specific geographical skills and he sees these as useful skills for future work.

I think we're quite good at giving them skills which are transferable. So teamwork, communication, research, critical thinking, critical analysis, environmental awareness, political, economic, social awareness. Amazing things to have in your toolkit which hopefully they can take to future jobs.

(Mike)

Christy, also describes how the department aims to develop transferable 'life' skills through geography.

I think the skills that we, sort of, teach through geography are almost … are life skills. So they're important things that you would carry through with you. You know, the idea of researching things and finding things out, analysing things.

(Christy)

Mike's description 'blurs' the boundary between skills and knowledge in the curriculum when he describes social, environmental, political and economic 'awareness'. Some words used by the department to describe the skills they are teaching, such as analysis, interpretation and evaluation appear influenced by Bloom's (1956) taxonomy and some of the observed lessons appear feature 'thinking' or problem solving 'skills'. In all lessons observed, teachers spent time explicitly developing skills. The department portrays attention to skills, though these tend to be geographical skills rather than wider learning skills (such as the maths being practised in geography lessons at Arnwell). For example, in a lesson to investigate the de-population of Easter Island, Steve spent time helping students develop the skill of a 'good geographical description' of location, even though this was tangential to the main lesson aim.

The Geography National Curriculum (GNC)

The GNC is one of four sub-themes, which all relate to how accountability influences teachers' curriculum making (the other three sub-themes being Ofsted, examination results and school assessment policies). The department portrays compliance with the GNC. In the planning meeting Kathy (HoD) and Rachel (KS3 coordinator) use a highlighter pen to cross reference their plans with the GNC 2014 programme of study document.

> I just play ball really. I know we've got to teach it and I know that if someone comes in and just looks at what with we're doing, it's really important that I'm doing what I should be doing.
>
> *(Kathy)*

Kathy describes GNC changes leading the team to removing valued parts of the curriculum, which suggests that GNC compliance 'trumps' concern for student enjoyment.

> (Australia) was really popular and the kids really like it but it has been removed for this September because we can't fit that in and do Russia because, as I say obviously the curriculum is dictating a bit there.
>
> *(Kathy)*

Kathy describes difficulty imagining curriculum planning without the Geography National Curriculum (GNC). This implies that the GNC is engrained in the department's curriculum thinking. But Kathy does not appear resentful of the GNC's influence, indeed she describes the GNC as important for her department and as guidance for weaker geography departments. She also appears to trust the people and organisations which produced the 'good' GNC, in particular the Geographical Association (GA).

> I think we, we're very lucky because I think what's been produced, because the GA did a lot of hard work on that, is … is a good curriculum.
>
> *(Kathy)*

There is even a tone of gratitude to the 'someone' behind the GNC, which leads to 'brilliant' ideas that her department can use. Kathy expresses a belief in the GNC as principled guidance for geography teachers.

> Adding the history of climate change, we might not have done that but actually I think now 'oh what a brilliant idea, yes of course we should do that' ... I think geography is so huge someone has to do it. Someone has to say we need to teach these things ... Now I think it's obvious, yes of course we should do that, but yeah that's interesting. I don't know what we'd do without the national curriculum.
>
> *(Kathy)*

> I think that sometimes somebody needs to sit down and guide everybody a little bit more because otherwise ... And I guess you and I might be doing it okay but I am thinking about everybody else ... I don't know.
>
> *(Kathy)*

However, Rachel is less positive than Kathy about the GNC. She feels the GNC is one of many 'constraints' or structures over curriculum-making.

> I feel we are much more constrained (in curriculum content). I feel there's constraints above us at various levels. Constraints from government and there always has been ... national curriculum.
>
> *(Rachel)*

The department therefore portrays some ambivalence towards the GNC, although it is taken seriously and is presented as an influence over curriculum decisions.

Ofsted

The analysis of interviews and planning meetings shows that Ofsted is a consideration in teachers' curriculum planning. Assessment, in particular, is an area in which teachers express anxiety that Ofsted will require evidence of student progress.

> We'll try to sort that out with assessment one having something to do with assessment two, so it's a dialogue that is occurring. Because I think if Ofsted came, for example this year, I think we'd have some difficulties in showing progress because there is a mismatch between the assessments.
>
> *(Said)*

Kathy says she believes school policy on assessment (students adding green pen comments in response to teachers' red pen marking) is driven by Ofsted. 'I think (the 'green pen' policy) is the Ofsted drive' and she feels the department must be able to provide 'evidence of student progress' (ibid). Rachel describes similar concerns and has developed a central department system of holding formal feedback sheets 'with all singing and dancing bits ... so that if your Ofsted or anyone comes, they're all there.' Kathy also describes curriculum coverage as part of her Ofsted 'worry', such as having GIS in the curriculum.

> I'm worried about how we're going to do (GIS) if Ofsted come in and ask how we do this. The plan is to put it in the 'investigating my world'.
>
> *(Kathy)*

However, like the GNC, the department presents an ambivalent attitude toward Ofsted. While Ofsted is taken seriously, progression of geographical learning is sometimes described as driven from within the department (from teachers' personal curriculum aims and beliefs) as much as from external pressures, as Mike expresses:

> For me, beyond all the stuff that is about to show they're making progress, the Ofsted jargon, that's ... I would hope that's a given. I like to see that they're developing as geographers, you know, as world citizens, as critical thinkers.
>
> *(Mike)*

Examination results

GCSE examinations are portrayed by the department as influencing KS3 curriculum decisions by guiding teachers' attention to the knowledge and skills students will need for success at GCSE. Kathy indicates concern that a knowledge base (which students are taking to GCSE from their KS3 curriculum) can be lacking:

> This (lack of geographical knowledge) is what really worries me a bit in GCSE. You can really miss what's underneath and not really understand things properly, so I guess that's where that (commitment to knowledge in KS3) comes from.
>
> *(Kathy)*

The department portrays an approach of building a knowledge and skills base at KS3 at their team planning meeting. However, there is some disagreement in the department about the relative importance of 'core knowledge' and 'relevance' for engagement. Steve, expresses uncertainty about the importance of 'building blocks' for GCSE. He relates such a strategy to the choice of a 'classic' GCSE course in the department. He lists areas of KS3 geography which are influenced by such a course.

> The GCSE, we have currently is quite classic. It's OCR B. It's rivers, coasts, hazards, population, compared to something, I don't know, like the pilot GCSE that was out, it is very classic. So yes I think we put in things like rivers

and erosion and things like that into our KS3 so they've got … it's like a building block process. I'm still undecided whether that's a good thing or a bad thing so, I don't know, to have the building blocks early on.

(Steve)

Kathy describes year 9 assessments in relation to GCSE. This could imply that the department aims to use KS3 to induct students into GCSE style questions and assessments as preparation for examination success.

The assessments at year 9 … they are almost morphing into mini-GCSEs. Like we are actually going to use GCSE questions in the year nine assessments.

(Kathy)

However, Kathy's decision to 'leave in' an assessment at KS3, even though it became redundant at GCSE, because it was 'useful' in ways other than GCSE preparation, suggests she does not see GCSE as a fundamental driver of the KS3 curriculum. Furthermore, part of the rationale presented for considering GCSE when planning the KS3 curriculum, is to avoid repetition. Such attention to progression in breadth and depth of geography is in keeping with the department's careful planning process.

So some of the case studies like China's one child policy were crossing over into KS3. We try to stop that, as … they were doing them twice. We had something in year 8 and year 10 and this was ridiculous. We had to change that.

(Kathy)

Steve, in keeping with his emphasis on student engagement, and a preference for issues in geography, is blunt in articulating how he believes students react to KS3 content being repeated at GCSE.

Is teaching the four types of erosion in year 8 important … so that they remember it more when they have to do it again in year 10? Or are we repeating ourselves so that they go 'oh no! Its bloody erosion again'.

(Steve)

Assessment policies

Kathy describes a push to spend time showing how students are acting on feedback to improve work (the 'green pen moments' in class). She indicates that the pressure to do so comes from a senior management concern to show progress, which in turn, she believes, comes from increased performance management driven by Ofsted.

So when they mark their work I have to do it in green pen. So we try to have more 'green pen moments' in lessons … it's probably more for observation, but even so it does show that we are giving them verbal feedback and verbal guidance and supporting their progression.

(Kathy)

Kathy is explicit in describing the 'green pen' marking as the department's response to accountability requirements (rather than an educational rational).

If they correct their work in their own colour pen or a green pen, yes that is accountability.

(Kathy)

Rachel, KS3 co-ordinator is sceptical about assessment policies. She describes her aim of fostering a 'love of learning' and an academic 'curiosity' and how formative learning is being superficially 'pushed' but is dominated by a more powerful drive for summative data to show student progress. She speaks with a tone of resignation about the pragmatic necessity of producing 'levelled' marks, at the expense of giving feedback to students (formative assessment). She describes 'rhetoric' coming from school management as part of a disingenuous culture, which really values performance data over providing opportunities to support learning.

There's two contradictory forces in secondary education at the moment. There's AfL (assessment for learning) being pushed … at the same time you have a much more powerful push for summative assessment … and the summative always wins over the formative, whatever rhetoric comes from schools, whatever they tell you … Level it, get the thing into the system so the management sees it … We're just a sort of summative assessment driven education system, right from the word go, from 5 to 17. The only place it begins to leave you, a little bit, is University and how sad is that?

(Rachel)

Rachel's tone of resignation to a culture of systematised assessment is added to by a nostalgia, 'Gone are the days when you can just annotate an essay' (ibid). She describes the impact of completing required assessment sheets as lost time and how the geography team had been producing high quality marking, but school management were able to tell the geography team that their practices 'had to' change to produce less detailed but more regular feedback to students, in order to follow school policy.

Rachel speaks vociferously about how assessment policies from school management (driven by Ofsted pressures) are affecting teaching.

The students have at the back of their head 'oh what's the assessment?' every couple of weeks … we want to see progress but not at the detriment of loving the subject. But again, there's constraints from above us. We have a very tight system of putting in data, as all schools do … So you've kind of always got that at the back of your mind and the kids do too. So it's a difficult balancing act trying not to overplay the influence of summative assessment.

(Rachel)

Kathy also refers to these pressures. Although little connection between changes in assessment practices and curriculum content is explicitly described, two points in teachers' descriptions indicate a connection. First, the teachers are spending more curriculum time (both in class and homework) on marking, feedback and student improvements and corrections. This implies less time available for other curriculum making work, such as introducing students to new geographical content in lessons of homework. Secondly, students come to lessons increasingly mindful of being assessed – the assessment 'at the back of their head' (Rachel) – which implies that they come to lessons with a state of mind that could affect how they think about the geography content they encounter.

The internet, new media and ICT

The geography teachers at Derwent make frequent reference to a wide range of resources informing their curriculum-making. The department presents itself as a team of skilled researchers, resourceful in their ability to find materials as they make the curriculum and always alert to new curriculum ideas or materials, often through the 'popular' geography of the media, which can be shared with the team, whether they are at home or school. Kathy describes how email and internet are used to do so:

> We will often send an email. I mean, I'll be watching TV … David Attenborough, the kids adore David Attenborough, absolutely adore him … and when I say that he's part of the optimum population trust … and go 'ooh! Are you watching this?' To the whole team. And people will find things and send it to us in a link.
>
> *(Kathy)*

Mike describes how Google is often where he begins to look for resources.

> I might sort of Google a theme or an idea, see what's returned and just go round things.
>
> *(Mike)*

The teachers refer to a number of specific websites they will use speaking enthusiastically about: 'brilliant websites' (Rachel); 'a variety of different websites which I would use … TES resources, SLN is another one' (Christy); 'I use Ed Excel Ning and Christy uses OCR Ning … you think "well I can use that".' (Kathy). Mike describes how an A level Ning was very useful as curriculum guidance when an examination board introduced new specifications 'obviously when that spec first went online, everyone was groping in the dark. I think those web-based communities are amazing' (Mike). He also mentions the RGS as an 'obvious internet location' he uses. Kathy talks about useful and reliable sites for geographical video clips, and the need for caution in using the open internet.

> BBC learning zone 'class clips' is really good because they're really short. You haven't got a whole programme and you know that they're really child friendly. There's a safeguarding issue with using YouTube. So I think yeah, Google's brilliant and YouTube is brilliant, but I use them with caution.
>
> *(Kathy)*

'Watching the news' is Steve's first response when asked where he finds curriculum ideas or materials, which is consistent with his emphasis on issues and relevance in his KS3 curriculum thinking. Kathy, despite her emphasis on geographical knowledge and care to avoid 'sensationalist' geography, recognises the news and current affairs as 'a big thing. A big thing for all of (the department)'. She also describes how popular geography through television influences her curriculum making, giving examples from natural history documentaries.

> I'll be watching TV, I mean this is another big thing, I mean watching Ian Stewart and many others ... David Attenborough.
>
> *(Kathy)*

Analysis of curriculum enactment – teachers

Pedagogy – favouring enquiry

Geographical enquiry appears frequently in the data (lesson observations, planning meetings and interviews) and is portrayed as an influential idea in the department's curriculum making. In the three lessons observed, two featured a 'mystery' activity and all three were framed by questions, requiring the students to make decisions, in part dependent on values and using a range of data sources, such as still images, video clips, maps and text. Mike, who is responsible for overseeing the 'skills' theme of the KS3 curriculum describes the curriculum as a process leading to further learning, 'They have to learn how to research' (Mike). In the planning meeting, enquiry and the use of questions as lesson titles are mentioned. 'Investigation' features twice in the draft curriculum and interview data makes frequent reference to either enquiry or investigation. For example, Said describes how he connects his students' needs with an enquiry approach, referring to Margaret Roberts' 'need to know' (Roberts 2003):

> kind of, give them a question, give them bits of information, try to piece them together, works really well here. I think that 'need to know', I think Margaret Roberts talked about.
>
> *(Said)*

Researching resources – a creative (and critical) department culture

The department portrays a creative and resourceful curriculum making culture, as the teachers' references to using the internet, discussed earlier in this chapter, show (further corroborated by lesson observations). To an extent, a critical culture is also portrayed. Kathy, in particular, makes references to the caveats and reservations she has over the materials she sources and she talks at length about how she has become a more critical curriculum maker through her own professional development and recent engagement with the GA. Interviews and lesson observations portray the teachers as evaluating resources, finding resources but being prepared to adapt them, or 'do it slightly differently' for 'our kids' (Kathy). But there is also pragmatism revealed in the teachers' descriptions of how they make the curriculum. Rachel tells how ready-made resources (either new textbooks or online materials) are helpful because they have interpreted new or unfamiliar subject content for the ease of teachers' use in the classroom.

> It'd be foolish wouldn't it, to just ignore that (GA materials and newly published textbooks) and in some schemes of work it has a bigger influence, possibly where you need more up-to-date knowledge or specific locational knowledge or something. When it's a bit trickier, like climate change which is evolving every day as a science, so there I would probably tend to lean a little bit more on new stuff coming out because I'm not a climate expert.
>
> *(Rachel)*

Teachers' enjoyment (through their preference and interests) appears to affect curriculum choices. Kathy's comment describes how one teacher's interest feeds into the curriculum taught by the whole team. Her comment also illustrates links between current issues, students own experiences and teachers' interests.

> I just thought it was really interesting and so we did a scheme of work on that. I think what happens to us is that we develop things year-on-year. Someone will say that's really interesting – that China can't access Google – so Steve will do that and that lesson will be added to the scheme of work.
>
> *(Kathy)*

The department's geography sources are a mix of more unofficial or 'informal' sources (such as Google searching, teacher sharing websites and TV documentaries) and more official or 'formal' sources, such as textbooks, exam board materials and more regulated web material (such as GA, RGS and BBC sites). GCSE and A level awarding bodies' material (including websites, 'Nings' and textbooks) are used occasionally. Different teachers describe different preferences, Mike for example, downplays the more 'official' sources (such as RGS and OCR) and emphasises more informal or unofficial shared online communities of teachers. At Derwent, data analysis produces sub-themes of 'sharing' (materials and ideas) and 'collaboration' between teachers (both in and beyond the department).

Collaboration, trust and teachers' different interests

The six geography teachers at Derwent meet regularly, and communicate informally, both in their geography office and the staffroom. They describe some differences of opinion and approach to geography (for example, Steve and Said talk about favouring 'issues' and 'relevance' in KS3, while Kathy talks about herself and the 'older' teachers as being more attentive to a balanced knowledge-based curriculum. But there is close communication, both formally through regular department meetings, and informally, by conversations and email. Curriculum making is shared and longer term planning is by consensus. Interviews, the planning meeting and documents show the process of KS3 curriculum planning at Derwent to be collaborative and thorough, with geography taken seriously.

Rachel, the longest standing geography teacher in the department, describes the importance of trust to the effectiveness of the department. She connects the trust, which Kathy gives the team, to teachers' curriculum making freedom, happiness, creativity and high quality of the curriculum ('the product' to which she refers). Rachel alludes to a view of the harm that standardisation ('McDonaldisation') can do to the curriculum.

> I think if I have to say one thing in addition to what I've said about Kathy I think it is that she does not micromanage ... It's very difficult to trust yourself and almost for us to trust the kids. I mean trust your staff to deliver quality subject ... and to allow this element of freedom ... there is a positive vibe about the subject area ... there is a positivity, there is a creativity ... there's a happiness ... If you micromanage then I think it's just not sustainable. You might deliver a fixed product. Like the McDonald's burger, it will be standard, it will be fine, it will never go below that standard but it won't go above.
>
> *(Rachel)*

Kathy portrays her leadership style as one of listening to her colleagues and trusting them to make their own curriculum choices in individual lesson content.

> I wouldn't just say 'oh we're going to do this', I would ask the department 'how do you feel about this?' and they might say 'oh yes, we want to do that' or 'no we don't'.
>
> *(Kathy)*

Kathy describes a willingness to compromise where there is disagreement and to find ways to accommodate different viewpoints in the team. For example, when there was disagreement over two possible assessments, she decided to make provision for both. Kathy's accommodating leadership style, valuing of her team and encouragement of geography-led 'curriculum conversations' are part of collaborative curriculum making portrayed by the department.

Kathy and Rachel describe an allowance and even an encouragement of teachers' individual differences in the detail of curriculum making (their 'creative thing' in Rachel's words). Where there are differences in opinion there is reference to debate. The department portrays a culture of openness, discussion and debate about geography education. The accommodating style of curriculum leadership connects to how teachers' different backgrounds influence curriculum making by allowing them to 'play to their strengths', choosing preferred areas of the curriculum for which to take responsibility and to teach in their preferred styles when planning and making the KS3 curriculum. Rachel, KS3 coordinator, says that 'certainly we chose the themes that we were most interested in'. The teachers' interviews reveal differences in geographical backgrounds, ongoing courses of study and preferences for their teaching. They connect these personal circumstances to their curriculum making. Data analysis gives a picture of the department as one of diverse curriculum approaches, fostered by the flexibility of Kathy's leadership style.

The diversity allowed by Kathy not 'micromanaging' does not mean that the teachers work in isolation. On several occasions, teachers' descriptions of their geography teaching colleagues matched closely to how those teachers described themselves. Kathy and the team know each other's styles, preferences and strengths well, and they express a trust and respect for each other's differences. The teachers' ages and levels of experience vary as do their geographical education backgrounds and their beliefs about what a curriculum is for (revealed in interviews) and therefore, what should be the content of the geography curriculum.

In marked similarity to Claymore, Kathy describes how trust from school management leads to curriculum making autonomy. Although she does not quantify the 'good job', which ensures the department are 'left alone', school management are interested in results data. The department has a record of performance in GCSE and A level results, which wins the trust and freedom Kathy describes:

> (senior management) pass what that geography is over to me. I think we're a department which is strong. We do a good job ... And I think that there is no worry about us, so we're kind of left alone.
>
> *(Kathy)*

Kathy's story – re-engagement with geography

Kathy's story is one of an ongoing and evolving relationship with geography and of strong beliefs about the importance of geography for education. She describes how, as Head of Humanities and an experienced and trusted member of staff, she has been encouraged to move away from geography leadership to take on managerial roles in the school. She describes how she has actively resisted these encouragements so that she can continue to teach and lead geography, which she prefers over having to 'deal' with management matters and being 'pulled in so many different directions' (Kathy).

> I actually like going into the classroom and just closing the door and just, teaching is just so relaxing compared to some of the things that you have to deal with when you ... because I'm a head of faculty.
>
> *(Kathy)*

Kathy's active commitment to geography is evidenced by her choosing to study for a Master's degree in Geography Education. She studies while working full time (with Head of department and Head of Faculty responsibilities), attending tutorials, and reading and writing essays during evenings, weekends and school holiday periods. She implies that her Masters is a form of resistance to a pressure to move away from geography by sending a clear signal to school management.

> I think doing my Masters was a really good way of stopping people from saying it (move into management) because I said 'I'm doing my Masters, I can't do that'. I could just sense that, because loads had come up, like ... temporary (management) for a year.
>
> *(Kathy)*

Kathy describes her Masters study and other geography professional development in a positive tone. She says the Masters has had 'a massive impact on recent thoughts' and explains how she has been stimulated to 'think' more about geography and the curriculum. She suggests something of an epiphany in her curriculum leadership. There is a sense of being refreshed in her descriptions of how she has re-engaged with geography some years since her initial teacher training.

> Everyone should do the Masters (laughs) ... I mean you do this on the PGCE but I think 14 years or 12 years down the line, I had forgotten it ... doing the (MA) course just reminded me that this is what ... I'm a geography teacher.
>
> *(Kathy)*

She links a renewed interest in geography education more widely than her Masters, including the Geographical Association, so that such 'resources' for geographical education become part of a 're-engagement with geography' narrative.

> Going back to the GA conferences and things like that, I'm actually thinking about what geography I'm actually teaching and I think that's actually having more of an impact on my department now.
>
> *(Kathy)*

Kathy describes the time and opportunity to think about geography in education through her Masters as 'a luxury, to have the time to really think about what you're doing'. Implying that in the normal course of teaching before her Masters, Kathy did not have time to 'really think about what she is doing'. However, the 'luxury' of time that Kathy portrays is something she has created for herself by giving up her own free time to 'thinking' about geography education (her Masters is additional to her teaching responsibilities, with neither time nor financial support given from the school).

Kathy talks about the importance of knowledge in the geography curriculum on several occasions and she describes seeking a broad and balanced geography curriculum (of physical and human geography) saying how 'I fight the corner of physical geography' and she talks about the importance of geographical concepts, such as integration and place. She links her concern for geographical knowledge in the curriculum to her Masters.

> (Geographical understanding) is something that comes up from my Masters. You know like 'what is geography?' You know, like, to understand what the subject is.
>
> *(Kathy)*

On occasions Kathy indicates that she uses content taken directly from the Masters to make the curriculum in her department (such as developing a 'history of geography' unit) but more typically she describes the influence as 'thinking' about what is 'important' in geography education, in particular the geographical knowledge in the curriculum.

Kathy portrays a critical approach to geography through careful use of subject knowledge. She links this to her PGCE studies (mentioning Margaret Roberts and the need for critical questioning), to her Masters and to the Geographical Association. Kathy describes how she wants to ensure her students do not have a 'superficial' understanding from issues-based 'sensationalist' geography, but rather they should 'really understand how the world works'. She describes how her Masters work, in connection with input from academic geography via the GA, has been a source of her critical approach to knowledge.

> Ian Stewart at the GA (conference) did a bit of a talk on the kinds of geography coming into the living room ... You can really miss what's underneath and not really understand things properly, so I guess that's where that comes from.
>
> *(Kathy)*

Kathy's critical approach extends to the resources she uses to make the curriculum. Kathy describes putting considerable trust in 'official' sources of knowledge, such as the GNC and the GA, which she respects and values (she says how she wants to gain the GA's 'quality mark'). She is wary of the influence of exam boards as commercially driven, asking 'Who are you trusting? You're trusting a company that's driven by profit.' (Kathy)

Kathy's personal curriculum making story is about her relationship with geography as an educational resource. She speaks passionately about learning geography herself, 'I love it. I really enjoy it' and about teaching geography and leading a geography department 'I love my job'. Her story is also about her leadership of the department.

Her leadership is portrayed as respect for the professional autonomy of her geography teaching colleagues but also of commitment to the subject. She encourages other teachers to share her vision of developing young people's geographical knowledge for a deep understanding of the world, and she counsels against distraction by a 'sensationalist' approach leading to 'superficial' geography. She describes how she tells her team (with reference to geographical knowledge) that 'you've got to try to remember what … why you're doing this.'

Derwent conclusion - taking geographical knowledge seriously

Derwent's geography curriculum making is distinctive by attention to geographical knowledge and the prominence of geography in serious curriculum discussions and thinking. The time, effort and care taken by the teachers to balance geographical content (in knowledge and skills) stands out from the other departments. Generic skills are less prominent here than at Arnwell or Brightling. There is no 'teach what we like' mantra (as at Claymore) with an emphasis on consistency between teachers by agreeing the enacted curriculum in advance. Geography as a school subject and discipline is taken seriously, and at times there is deference to the authority of some curriculum advisory and statutory bodies (including the GA and the National Curriculum). The theme of geographical knowledge appears linked to a 'renaissance' in Kathy's relationship with the discipline and the school subject of geography.

The close collaboration of teachers at Derwent contributes to a serious geography curriculum debate. Kathy and Rachel take on roles as KS3 curriculum leaders and they encourage and foster curriculum making cooperation and trust across the team. Different viewpoints are respected and to an extent valued as part of curriculum debate. The teachers hold different views about what the content of KS3 geography should be, although a pedagogy of geographical enquiry is widely adopted across the department. Student enjoyment, the news and an 'issues' approach to geography are also a secondary theme – prominent, but not distinctive to Derwent.

The context of Derwent school – a very popular and oversubscribed school with exceptionally high examination results – appears connected to the geography department's curriculum making because school management trust the geography department to deliver results, which increases their freedom. A confident and relatively autonomous geography department is portrayed, which fosters a culture of curriculum thinking.

Change (dynamism) is a feature of the department's approach to curriculum with time set aside for curriculum planning and teachers bringing their own research interests into curriculum making. There is some tension between the curriculum value/belief systems of different teachers in the department, but this feeds into curriculum discussion and there is a collegial and collaborative approach to curriculum making. There is conflict between teacher autonomy to pursue geographical curriculum making and some school policies, which are linked to teachers being accountable for results. However, the teachers take on a curriculum (making) responsibility and the department portrays considerable teacher control over the enacted curriculum. Kathy, as Head of department, plays a pivotal role in this by encouraging critical geography curriculum discussions and collaborative curriculum making while still allowing for the personal autonomy so valued by her department colleagues.

8

CURRICULUM ENACTMENT IN LATE CAPITALISM – A COMMON PROCESS AND THE SCOPE OF TEACHER AGENCY

The preceding four chapters have described, in some detail, how four geography departments enact the curriculum. I hope that readers now have a sense of the day-to-day influences on teachers' curriculum work, how the context of their department and school affects this and how personal differences, in opinions, attitudes and values for instance, come into play. In this chapter, I want to focus particularly on commonalities across the departments, connecting the earlier literature review and theoretical discussion to the empirical evidence of the four case study departments. I will put forward my argument that teachers' curriculum enactment has become 'hyper-socialised' – in all the departments to an extent. However, there are clearly differences between them, and I also discuss here the scope for teachers to act with some autonomy and agency in the face of the pervasive forces of late capitalism.

I will make three important subsidiary arguments in this chapter, the implications of which are discussed in my conclusion (Chapter 9). These are, first, that teachers' curriculum enactment is adapted to late capitalist society, in particular society's reconceptualising of the individual (as both consumer and producer). Secondly, there is a tension between the teacher's potential agency to make a geography curriculum and the controlling social-economic climate of accountability, performance pressure and technological change. The teachers are responding by a coping strategy of working together both at the school level and in wider (often virtual and unidentified) communities. Thirdly, some teachers portray a response (or form of resistance) to the pressurised and controlling climate of accountability by turning to their subject identities by seeking out and engaging with 'geography' (the discipline, popular and local geographies and subject communities). Such teachers have agency. They portray a highly personal form of subject-engaged curriculum making as a means to sustaining their identity as *geography* teachers.

In this chapter I use the same framework (of students, geography and teachers) to present the commonalities across the departments. In discussing these three broad areas, I give particular attention to the wider social and economic curriculum making influences found. These include accountability, changed conceptions of the individual as both consumer and producer, and technological changes. Enveloping all these influences is the world of late capitalism. A speeded-up, globalised world, which Friedman (2016) calls the 'age of acceleration', lies behind the curriculum enactment I have observed and describe as 'hyper-socialised'.

Students

Enjoyment and skills – post-Fordism playing out in teaching decisions

Pupil enjoyment influences teachers' curriculum planning and curriculum enactment and both generic and geographic skills are a goal in teachers' curriculum making'. This is not in itself a bad thing – who can argue that children should not enjoy learning and develop skills? But the great lengths to which the teachers go to make lessons active, often 'fun' and involving generic (as opposed to subject) learning skills becomes more controversial in light of the pressures teachers are under to simultaneously achieve strong exam results.

There is substantial evidence across the case study data that teachers are very concerned for students' enjoyment and skills development. 'Enjoyment' is portrayed consistently across the departments as a way of engaging students in geography (and learning generally) and is linked to listening to 'student voice' as part of curriculum making. Skills are portrayed as either generic 'learning skills' or as geographical skills, both of which appear in all departments to varying degrees. For example, Arnwell emphasises generic learning skills, Derwent emphasises geographical skills. There is some blurring of the boundary and overlap between geographic and generic learning skills, such as where geographical writing and graphicacy are concerned. All departments link developing student skills in KS3 to progression and performance.

The prominence of enjoyment can be interpreted 'education as therapy' (Ecclestone and Hayes 2009, Furedi 2009). A 'therapeutic turn' (Furedi 2009) is connected to late capitalist society because 'therapy' is a form of individual consumption and in late capitalism individuals are increasingly conceived as consumers (Hartley 1997). In the postmodern society, basic needs are increasingly met as war, famine and disease are in decline. The result Harari (2017) argues is a trend for societies to refocus energy from meeting basic needs to achieving greater happiness (which of course is a complex project!). But Harari's argument helps to explain a shift in education, which Furedi (2009) has criticised as 'an unhappy turn to happiness'.

Teachers describe concern that students should enjoy the geography curriculum (and that teachers should enjoy the content that they teach). Furedi (2009) argues that teachers are overly concerned that the answer to a child's well-being (and the ultimate success or failure of the curriculum) lies in how well they engage with learning. Subject content, Furedi argues, has come to be seen by 'therapeutic' educators as subservient to the development of emotional intelligence. In this line of reasoning, subject content that is perceived as dull or 'irrelevant' to students creates a problem by switching students off to learning. All departments portrayed a concern for 'relevant' curriculum content, which they connect to enjoyment. Arnwell teachers express dismay at the GNC 'forcing' them to teach soils, perceived as a threat to maintaining good behaviour because it is likely to be a 'turn off' to students and teachers alike. Enjoyment and engagement is particularly prominent at Arnwell, where behaviour is the greatest concern. However, all the departments describe a concern for student enjoyment and 'relevant' content. This can be interpreted as 'therapeutic' education (Ecclestone and Hayes 2009) playing out as 'therapeutic' curriculum making.

The 'skills' theme can be interpreted alongside 'enjoyment', through social theory, by considering the way in which the individual has been reconceptualised in late capitalism. All four departments (to varying degrees) portray part of their curriculum aim being to achieve students' teamwork, flexibility and desire to learn. The curriculum is made with concern that students enjoy their learning. Teachers are careful to listen to how students feel about the curriculum. All four departments make multiple references to 'student voice'. In the case of Brightling, students are offered choice over what and how they learn geography. Lessons are often self-consciously 'active'. Variety of tasks is prized and, in the way work is set, students are required to be flexible in how they learn.

A 'neoliberal turn' has taken place in all aspects of society, including schools. Production has shifted from Fordism to post-Fordism (see Aglietta 1979 and Morgan 2011), and from 'organised to disorganised capitalism' (see Lash and Urry 1987). This means a softening of roles. In a Fordist model of production, roles and practices are fixed and clearly defined, but in a post-Fordist world the roles of student and teacher are more flexible and less defined. Schools have re-imagined their students as part of the post-Fordist world of late capitalism. All four departments portray teachers and students frequently working together. Both students and teachers contribute to lesson content and to lesson outcomes (work produced) and technology has softened the distinction between authors and the readers.

There are differences between the schools in the way the 'outside' influence of late capitalism affects curriculum enactment. The geography teachers at Arnwell High, which (on GCSE and Ofsted measures) is the lowest performing of the four schools, describe anxiety to avoid students' misbehaving and, in the initial years of the secondary school curriculum, they prioritise 'soft' skills including cooperation, teamwork and 'learning to learn' over subject content. Soft skills and behaviour management are less prominent sub-themes in Brightling, and even less so in Claymore and Derwent, which are the highest performing schools in the research with the most privileged student body. This suggests a possible inverse relationship between performance (based on results and Ofsted grade) and the amount of attention to soft skills and behaviour in curriculum enactment.

Disorganised capitalism and Post-Fordist influence can also be seen in Brightling, where teachers are directed to use 'building learning power' strategies, and to an extent in Claymore and Derwent where variety, transferable skills and engagement in learning are portrayed as strong influences in their curriculum enactment. However, in Claymore and Derwent, there is a stronger theme of freedom in curriculum making and trust from school management than Brightling and Arnwell. The geography departments of Claymore and Derwent portray strong resistance to economic curriculum drivers and curriculum making, which prioritises 'geographical thinking' and the balancing of subject, teacher choice and students' needs. Levels of teacher autonomy and trust appear to be related to the department's capacity to resist the pressure from disorganised capitalism and Post-Fordism for 'soft' and generic learning skills to dominate geographical thinking.

Reconceptualising the individual in late capitalism

Hartley (1997) presents late capitalist society's influence as a deep-rooted tension playing out in schooling. His argument runs that there is a tension driven by two contradictory forces in the late capitalist world. One is the drive to produce, more, better, faster – an economic imperative. The other is to consume, as a self-centred individual – a cultural imperative. These forces are difficult to reconcile in many aspects of society, including schooling where they affect how the individual is being conceived. On the one hand the post-Fordist economic world is driving a technical and competitive individualism, in which there is pressure to make a highly skilled and effective workforce. On the other, postmodern culture encourages a 'self-centred and narcissistic individualism' in which the person is a consumer (Hartley, 1997: 3).

The research findings reflect Hartley's argument that, in late capitalism, there is a tension in society, playing out in schools. Students are treated as 'consumers' of the curriculum (enjoying and involved in their 'consumption' of the curriculum). The teachers describe feeling a keen sense of serving their students who expect both good exam results from their schooling and to enjoy lessons. Yet, all the departments portray curriculum making as heavily influenced by student performance, albeit sometimes as preparation or 'groundwork' for later (high stakes) GCSE and A level courses.

The 'enjoyment' narrative and seeing the student as 'consumer' (the cultural imperative) sits uneasily with the drive for efficiency, effectiveness and accountability (the economic imperative). On the one hand, teachers are trying to make a geography curriculum that is engaging, enjoyable, 'relevant' to the learner and taught with variety in stimulating ways. On the other, students (and teachers) are under pressure to 'perform'. Students must be taught (and learn) efficiently, developing skills to make rapid, demonstrable progress. The departments illustrate this tension in different ways, for example, in Derwent, teachers enact school policies for assessment, while trying to develop a stimulating geography curriculum. In Arnwell, teachers struggle to balance 'almost entertaining' students, with making progress in the subject.

Teachers' concern to support (and increase) 'student voice' in the findings can be explained through three ideas from the literature. These are first, Hartley's (1997) cultural imperative of people as consumers, secondly by a 'demotic turn', or a turn to ordinary people (Morgan 2014b, and Turner 2010), and thirdly as a 'therapeutic turn' (Ecclestone and Hayes 2009, Furedi 2009). Each of these, point to ways in which trends in wider society impinge on schooling and influence teachers' curriculum making. In my analysis, it is not possible to be sure which of the three is more applicable, each is a valid argument to explain how society's conception of the individual, their needs and how the individual operates in society have changed. Nonetheless, these three theories all point to societal shift to explain a seemingly neutral, popular practice (bringing student voice into curriculum decisions) weakening the geography teacher's control over their curriculum enactment.

But am I going too far down a road of social and economic explanation for these current teaching practices? An alternative perspective is to read the 'enjoyment' narrative as teachers applying learning theories to their teaching, such as social constructivism (Vygotsky 1962, Bruner 1966) and learner-centred theory (Dewey 1916). Enjoyment is linked to the creation of situational interest (Hidi and Ainley 2002) and to increased motivation for learning (Ryan and Deci 2000). However, my findings differ from social constructivist and learner centred theory because concern for the subject to be learned appears to have been displaced, in some of the case study departments, by enjoyment of learning for its own sake crowding out teachers' attention on subject knowledge. Such 'learnification' has been well documented (see Biesta 2013, Pring 2013 and Lambert and Hopkin 2014) so it is not enough to claim this as simply normal teaching practices. The question remains, why the intensification (the 'learnification') and why now?

Social constructivist and learner centred theories do not recognise the power of political economy within which learning is located. In teachers' descriptions, enjoyment is identified alongside an accountability and performance narrative. The degree of teachers' attention to student enjoyment, for both student satisfaction and for student engagement leading to examination performance, is neither neutral nor inevitable in curriculum making. The enjoyment theme can be interpreted as the shifting conception of the individual in late capitalism to both a more demanding (narcissistic) consumer and a more competitive producer. This societal shift to more intense individualism challenges the teacher's power to make their own curriculum decisions based on their understanding, knowledge and expertise of what makes for a good geography education.

The internet and young people

The internet is a prominent influence over teachers' curriculum making in my research. Taking account of wider societal change, this can be read in two ways. First, internet use can be seen as an enabling technology, supporting teachers to cope with the pressures to produce effective lessons in a climate of accountability. Secondly, internet use by teachers can be seen as keeping up with (or responding to) the 'demotic turn' in society (Turner 2010 and Morgan 2014b). Morgan (2014b) argues that the internet is changing the teacher-student relationship. 'Gamification of learning' is taking place (2014: 1). Teachers, willingly or not, are ceding 'power to the people' (2014: 1) and students may ask 'why do I need a teacher when I've got Google?' (2014: 1).

Hartley (1997) predicts teachers navigating an increasingly difficult situation as the 'new individualism' of late capitalist times (a tension between the individual as producer and consumer) permeates schooling. Hartley's argument (written in the 1990s) is centred on changed identities of the individual. Since then, deepening internet use among young people has changed the identity of learner and teacher, according to Kress (2006), Somekh (2006) and Moore (2015). Unlike a textbook or a teacher-led lesson, the internet has no prescribed order in which it is 'read'. Rather the internet uses a 'menu' principle so that the user chooses the content and the order in which they read. A book or teacher-led lesson has an 'author' in control, but the internet user acts as their own 'author' (Kress 2006). Therefore, as young people become accustomed to using the internet as their usual source of information at home, their culture of learning shifts away from the authority of the traditional texts, lessons and teacher.

The case study findings resonate with Kress' argument that there is a shift in the power and authority, which the teacher holds over the learner and their curriculum. The enjoyment and 'student voice' sub-themes in the findings can be seen as the increasing need for student consent when offering a curriculum to the learner.

Postman (1982) offers an explanation for the changing conception of the individual and the child in society, contending that the notion of 'childhood' (other than the biological meaning of immaturity to sexually reproduce) is entirely a social construction. Postman (1982) contends that the existence of 'childhood' is owed to books because, over time, books have communicated and reinforced the notion of childhood (such that it became embedded in society) and electronic communication and media (enabled by the internet) is allowing the blurring, and ultimately the disappearance, of the boundary between adulthood and childhood. This argument resonates with other critiques of the social shift in adult-child relationships, particularly those relating to technology such as Somekh (2006) Kress (2006) and Moore (2015) but also Furedi (2009) and Ecclestone and Hayes (20109 who argue that there is confusion about adult authority over children. Postman's arguments for 'the disappearance of childhood' (1982) and 'the end of education' (1996) are significant for my research as they offer insight into the connection of societal change, technology, the conception of children in society, and what children are taught in schools.

The world inhabited by young people and teachers has changed so that the teacher-student power relationship is unsettled. Teachers are navigating through this social-educational landscape and their curriculum enactment is influenced by an increased concern for the student as a consumer of the curriculum. However, students are also producers for the economy. The case studies show teachers under pressure to deliver 'useful' skills, 'learning to learn', enjoyment and prioritising 'relevant' content over breadth of geographical knowledge. Viewed through a social-economic lens these are also the needs of 'disorganised capitalism' (Lash and Urry 1987) and the 'post-Fordist' economy, transferred into schools.

We are experiencing a profound shift in how young people (and adults) access information and the nature of authorship. It is becoming increasingly difficult to trace the 'ownership' of ideas and the original from the recycled. The internet including social media and collaborative sites where information is posted, edited and repackaged, causes a blurring of boundaries. Some social theorists go so far as to argue the first half of the twenty-first century will see a shift in the nature of human thought, as the line between the individual's mind and artificial computation becomes unclear. It is not so difficult to imagine this when we think of young people glued to their smartphones being fed information that they are not entirely in control of. Even when the individual 'chooses' what to input to 'the cloud' they may be steered by computation and algorithms, which have access to vast amounts of information about that person. Are the questions they ask Google or the posts on Instagram of their own volition? Are our 'minds' becoming so connected and steered by computation technology that we will soon be unable to distinguish 'our own' thinking from that of computers? James Bridle (2018) calls this the dominance of 'computational thought' in his dystopian prediction of a 'New Dark Age' for humankind. Harari (2017) argues we are at the beginnings of a 'cyborg' humanity in which people and machines are becoming indistinguishable.

These ideas may seem far-fetched, but it is quite reasonable to accept that in the course of a generation, information technology has transformed people's behaviour in regard to how and what they learn (at present more obviously in informal, out of school contexts). The extension of computational 'thinking' is only set to accelerate as Freidman (2016) points out. Teachers have to navigate this aspect of the changing conception of their students as they become less inclined to learn from books and paper and increasingly immersed in virtual worlds. This realisation affects the teacher's curriculum enactment. In addition, as I found in my research, teachers are also part of the general shift to internet dependency, and I consider how they use technology themselves in their curriculum thinking in the later section of this chapter focusing on the teachers.

In summary, geography teachers are being pulled in two directions by the reconceptualising the individual in late capitalism. There is an increasing pressure to reproduce the post-Fordist economy of late capitalism through their curriculum choices (the 'useful skills', 'learning to learn' and competitive, individualistic target-setting culture). At the same time the teachers are under pressure to reproduce another aspect of late capitalist society, a postmodern individualism (excessive catering for 'relevance' to the child's life and their immediate enjoyment as they consume their geography education). Resisting these pressures (or at least coping with them) is difficult and requires teachers to draw on their identities as geography teachers to maintain the fundamental boundaries of adult/ child, teacher/student and curriculum/ pedagogy – in a world of increasingly blurred boundaries.

Geography

Recontextualised and recycled

A school curriculum is partly the result of a process of recontextualising disciplinary knowledge in an 'official recontextualising field' (ORF) involving government education departments, textbook writers, examination bodies and so forth (see Bernstein 2000). Teachers also have a role to play in the pedagogic recontextualising field (PRF) and in the field of reproduction (of disciplinary knowledge). In his examination of how the discipline of geography is recontextualised into an enacted school curriculum and building on Bernstein's ORF and PRF, Puttick (2015a) found teachers relying heavily on the internet, Google searching and shared areas of the school computer network. He finds teachers often downloading 'ready to use' materials in the form of PowerPoint presentations, worksheets and card sorts. My findings concur strongly with Puttick in this. To an extent, teachers use their knowledge of geography in personal ways, drawing on their own educational background, their interests, preferences and beliefs about the purpose of the subject. But a noticeable trait in all the cases was the extent of popular geographies and the influence of Google.

Being open to popular geography and current affairs can not only be seen as a way of teachers dealing with the volume of 'geographical' information available, but is also linked to their belief that popular geography is a valid driver of long term shifts in school geography. When Jane and Kathy (both HoDs) talked together about how the school geography curriculum changes, they described their belief that popular geography (through the media) is a subtle but powerful force, gradually shifting the focus of both the discipline and school geography. Mat is less explicit, but his enthusiasm for using the news and moulding school geography from it, shows the power of current affairs to shape geography in his department.

To examine how the case study departments recontextualised geography as they enacted the curriculum, the teaching of sustainability is a useful focus for illustration. Sustainability (or sustainable development) was a prominent theme in the case studies. A close examination of the treatment of sustainable development by the teachers illustrates how teachers' personal knowledge, beliefs and values interact with the times. Borrowing Schiro's (2008) phrase, we can ask – what are these teachers' 'curriculum ideologies' (or value-belief systems) when teaching about sustainability? Can teachers who lean toward a radical ('social-reconstructionist') geography curriculum (one leading to a better world) enact their personal value-belief system when they are teaching in late capitalism?

Sustainable development – radical geography or non-geography?

As times change so does the potential for geography teachers to make a curriculum for social change. In the 1980s education for sustainable development with an emphasis on 'futures' was established and has been consistently championed since then by a group of geography educators including Hicks (1995, 2008, 2011, 2013), Sterling (1996, 2010) and Pepper (1989). However, optimism among radical and environmental geography educators in the 1980s flowered briefly and then withered in the mainstream of geography teaching. Morgan (2011, 2012) argues that post-2008 (financial crisis), there are opportunities for 'radical' geography teachers to open up critical ways of thinking about the world in the school geography curriculum. This means teaching children to challenge a single 'taken for granted' neoliberal world view by attention to how geography affects capital performance, welfare geography, the impacts of consumption, nature in crisis and to raise alternatives to 'fast' (or late) capitalism (Morgan 2012).

Morgan (2011) drawing on Huckle (1985) and Fielding and Moss (2011) provides an account of the geography curriculum as controlled by economic forces. He argues that teachers are dominated by these wider forces through the control mechanisms of school management, state regulation (Ofsted, published league tables) and the hegemony of a neoliberal phase of capitalism.

> It seems as if geography teachers have accepted the idea that there is no alternative.
>
> *(Morgan 2011: 120)*

Morgan (ibid) also proposes that the educational landscape (post-2008 economic crisis) offers 'radical' geography teachers scope to resist these forces in their curriculum making.

> In order to realise Fielding and Moss's vision of a radical curriculum, geography teachers need to focus on introducing young people to ideas and perspectives within their subject which allow for the critical co-construction of knowledge that relates to their own lives and communities.
>
> *(Morgan 2011: 120)*

Morgan (2011) offers specific ways in which a radical geography curriculum can be realised. He raises a question of current curriculum conflict and change – can a 'radical' geography curriculum be made in these (post-2008 economic crisis) times? The findings of the four case studies substantiate Morgan's theoretical work by providing evidence of neoliberal processes influencing curriculum making, for example in the level of accountability for student performance and the consequential assessment practices and the pressure to focus on effective teaching or 'deliverology' (over geographical curriculum thinking). But the departments and some teachers also portray a resistance to the neoliberal forces of late capitalism, including a 'turning' to geographical identities. There are traces of 'radical' geography curriculum making in evidence, albeit tempered by the influence of neoliberalism embedded in the educational landscape.

Morgan (2011, 2012) suggests that in the 1980s radical geography was (relatively) thriving and a curriculum existed (in many classrooms) where the discipline was used to pose critical questions about models of economy and society and to explore alternative possibilities. This contrasts with a 'relative silence' (Morgan 2011) on issues of curriculum content, more recently, with the submission of teachers to neoliberal hegemony. Morgan (ibid) suggests three ways in which a lack of attention to alternatives are reflected – an emptying of subject content; new teacher identities focusing on teaching processes and performance; and postmodern approaches where geography is fragmented and open to multiple interpretation. These three areas are reflected in the findings to an extent, but there is also evidence that challenges Morgan's concern that teachers are 'submitting' to neoliberal hegemony. A lack of concern for (or an 'emptying' of) subject content, is particularly evident in Arnwell's portrayal of curriculum making. Skills often dominate and content is often presented as more of a vehicle for skills, values or attitudes (including simply engaging in learning). There is much concern for teacher performance and achieving students' learning objectives. Teachers are measured by, and accountable for, their effectiveness in narrow terms.

However, the geography teachers in my research (particularly the Heads of Departments) express concern that subject content is threatened by bureaucratic accountability. There is a consciousness about the 'emptying' of subject content and a concern that performativity threatens the geography curriculum work which the teachers present as their preferred professional focus. This was explicitly expressed by teachers in Derwent, and implicit in the rejection of bureaucratic control in Claymore and to a lesser extent, Brightling. Arnwell is more accepting of the shift away from geographical content. But even here, Sian, the HoD, expresses concern for 'lost' geography from the school's integrated skills approach and expresses a desire to build a team of dedicated geographers. The findings do not show the Heads of Departments identifying strongly as 'competent craftsperson', 'compliant technician' or skilled technician (see Connell 2009, Moore 2004, Weber 2007 and Goepel 2013). The findings do show the Heads of Departments identifying as geographers, and even turning toward geography, seeking to develop their 'relationship' with the discipline as 'engaged professionals' (Lambert and Morgan 2010: 38) and asserting their identity as geographers.

A 'postmodern' approach (Morgan 2011) to geography is reflected in all departments (although less so in Derwent where there is the most concern for breadth and balance and a notion of a 'core' of geographical knowledge is presented). In the other three departments and in Derwent also to an extent, there is something of a 'laissez faire' attitude to teachers' decisions about content. Content is as likely to be chosen as being of interest to students (and teachers) as driven by developments in the discipline. Multiple perspectives to subject matter include students' own viewpoints, particularly where there are matters of what the world 'ought' to be like where futures, issues and matters of sustainability are considered. The research findings show some evidence of teachers taking a 'radical geography' approach in these ways. But these are only 'traces' of radical geography curriculum making and appear dependent on the individual teacher and the school context. Nonetheless, such traces of radical geography indicate that there is (still) teacher agency in curriculum making.

All the departments pay attention to welfare geography (expressed as 'inequalities' in taught units). In particular, Mat, in Claymore school, expresses a personal interest in teaching the geographies of inequality. He introduced the unit at KS3 and has involved university geographers such as Danny Dorling (an expert in the field of the geographies of inequality) in visiting the school to speak to students. All departments teach about consuming (and producing) to excess and the consequences this has on people and nature. 'Globalisation' is taught, although teachers vary in the extent to which they describe achieving change in society as part of their curriculum aim (Mat in Claymore and Mike in Derwent being the most overtly 'radical' in their intentions to change society through geography education). The 'traces' of Morgan's version of a 'radical' geography in the findings is significant for the research as it shows teachers' agency to make the curriculum and shows that teachers' value-belief systems are influencing curriculum making. Some teachers appear to be resisting the emptying of geographical knowledge in a performativity climate (Pring 2013, Mitchell and Lambert 2015) by curriculum making that is motivated by changing society through geographical education. This suggests that teaching geography 'as if the planet mattered' (Morgan 2012) and 'teaching geography for a better world' (Fien and Gerber 1988) are pursued in some geography departments, even in neoliberal times. However, such an attitude is balanced by evidence that curriculum making with a critical economic lens is limited. A 'radical' and critical geography education is somewhat controversial. In geography education, there is debate about whether school geography should aim for societal change or be confined to passing disciplinary knowledge to the next generation (Standish 2009, 2012).

All departments show some 'critical co-construction of knowledge' that relates to students' own lives and communities Morgan (2011: 120). Local studies feature in all departments' descriptions of curriculum making, particularly in Claymore, where inequalities are starkly visible, the students come from very different socio-economic home lives and the Head of Department describes a keen interest in teaching 'inequalities'. Lesson observations show students encouraged to think about issues in the context of their own experiences and to offer their ideas about what 'ought' to happen in the future.

Sustainability features frequently as a concept to be explored by students. However, the extent to which students are encouraged to question political economy and to explore alternatives to fast capitalism is difficult to judge from the research. The findings reveal teachers' different perspectives about geography and geography education, even within the same department. In Derwent, Mike describes his students as being aware of his 'ant-capitalist tendencies'. He talks about wanting students to be critically aware of the impacts of contemporary capitalism and consumption on social justice. While there are some signs of the critical approach (teaching geography that reveals the economic forces at work) called for by Morgan (2011, 2012), there is insufficient evidence to claim that the narrative of 'ecological modernisation' and the inevitability of a single model of capitalism (Morgan 2012) is being widely challenged, indeed there is some evidence that it is being reinforced.

A 'sustainability' lesson, at Arnwell (which I presented at the beginning of this book) was taught very effectively to engage students and develop 'learning skills' illustrating both the 'ecological modernisation' and a therapeutic notion of curriculum purpose. The lesson is part of a weather and climate unit, but is about exploring the issue of 'sustainability' with little connection made to weather or climate. 'Sustainability' is explored in two ways, first the roles and responsibilities of state, international community and individual are explored in the context of finding ways to manage scarce resources and limit environmental impacts of high levels of production and consumption around the world. The emphasis is on technological solutions – finding ways to increase efficiency, minimise waste and modify individual behaviour. There is no exploration of the economic system causing the problem – the capitalism, which drives production and consumption to excess. This view of geography presented to students is a world within the 'ecological modernisation' narrative (Morgan 2012). Secondly, students are taught that they have a responsibility to act in sustainable ways (like travelling by bicycle more often), reflecting the concern that a knowledge-based education is being replaced by an education in 'ethics' (Furedi 2009, Marsden 1997, Standish 2009).

However, there is other evidence, from all the departments to challenge the assertion that geography teachers' curriculum making is 'submitting' to wider societal narratives of ecological modernisation and therapeutic education. For example, lessons were observed that touched on the underlying (systemic) economic causes of marginalised groups and unfair trade (Derwent). Other lessons took a critical approach to development, for example looking at alternatives to GDP as measures of development (Claymore). Interviews and curriculum plans also revealed teachers' looking to explore alternative worldviews through curriculum making. Teachers expressed much in common in their vision of the purpose of the geography curriculum. All the Heads of Department described a desire to open up alternative ways of seeing the world to empower young people, and some went as far as saying they hoped this would lead to responsible action for change. But the teachers' freedom to follow their personal aims for geography education is restricted, and viewing curriculum enactment through the lens of teachers helps to explain why, as I now explore.

Teachers

Accountability and surveillance

The departments portray three areas that indicate the influence of accountability on curriculum making. These are: producing data on student progress; following policies on teaching and assessment practice; and GCSE and A level results. In each department, the senior management team (SMT) require data from regular assessments at KS3, to track student progress. Three of the departments (Claymore being the exception) indicate pressure from senior management to teach in certain ways, such as 'green pen' dialogic marking (Derwent), the expectation for teacher talk to be limited to a specific amount of time, so that lessons are 'active' for students (Arnwell), and 'split screen' planning (Brightling).

Arnwell and Brightling explicitly show how school management policies have affected the enactment of the KS3 curriculum. At Arnwell the integrated skills curriculum breaks up geography in year 7 into units, so that other humanities subjects or cross curricular units are taught to the exclusion of geography at times. Sian, HoD describes the impact of this on geography when she says 'year 7 is lost'. Arnwell also presents curriculum making as influenced by SMT expectations (and some specific guidelines) for 'active' learning. The Deputy Head talks of avoiding 'lily pad' learning and more child-centred approaches, coupled to a generic 'learning skills' agenda, dominate. Of the four schools, Arnwell shows the most direct senior management control over the KS3 curriculum.

Brightling also shows substantial SMT 'interference' in curriculum making, illustrated by the whole school drive to introduce 'building learning power' (Claxton 1999) to subject departments' curriculum making. This is resisted to an extent by Jane (HoD) who asserts a geography-led approach in her department. But the 'split-screen planning' expected by senior management 'is there' Jane says, and despite her commitment to geography, she is enthusiastic about managerial interventions to improve performance by focusing on pedagogy, assessment and skills.

Whole school senior management team (SMT) influence is not always made explicit. Some practices, such as the consistent use of learning objectives (both in the classroom and in curriculum planning) and the use of starters in lessons, are embedded to such a degree that the teachers appear to use them 'automatically', which makes a 'process' model of curriculum less likely, and inclines curriculum making toward the 'rational' curriculum planning model (Kelly 2008 and Graves 1979). In this way, all departments portray the lingering influence of the national strategies of the 1990s (Rawling 2001).

At times, teachers explicitly suggest that school policies, which they are required to follow, are driven by Ofsted anxiety. All departments indicate that Ofsted inspections and GCSE and A level (external, 'high stakes' examinations later in the school) have an influence over KS3 curriculum making. The departments (and the teachers within the department) vary in the extent to which they describe the influence of these forms of accountability. There is also a 'smaller scale' form of accountability to one another within the geography teaching team (and particularly to the Head of Department) in the requirement to cover the same learning objectives. This is portrayed as being for students' equal access to the regular KS3 assessments, which provide the data needed by SMT. There is no scope for the teacher to be an entirely 'free agent' in their curriculum making.

Descriptions of curriculum making show that regular assessments and marking policies influence the KS3 curriculum making in two ways. First, they influence teaching and learning styles. Secondly, they take time. Teachers portray the requirement to have regular assessments (to produce data for SMT) as a largely positive influence in their curriculum making. Teachers tend to speak positively about designing assessments. As long as the teachers are able to give a mark (GNC levels were used in all departments) the design of the assessment is left to the department's judgement. In planning meetings and interviews, teachers appear to enjoy designing assessments. Assessments form a key part of the geographical 'progression' theme in Derwent for example. At Claymore, the team speak enthusiastically (and rather fondly) about their KS3 'TATs' (topic assessment tasks). The Head of Department describes them as 'central' to what and how they teach at KS3.

Assessments appear to be a stimulus to the departments to think about the way students are learning geography. Teachers (and the evidence of documents) indicate that assessments are a focus for: steering geographical content; ensuring variety in learning styles; and balance in the geographical (and generic) skills. So, for example, students will produce extended writing in a variety of forms, make presentations, interpret graphs and other forms of data and so forth. The research cannot show conclusively how far assessment as a stimulus for curriculum thinking is caused by the pressure from SMT to produce data. All departments present assessment as central to their KS3 curriculum making. When asked if they would plan differently without the requirement for regular data from SMT, the teachers find it difficult to say. GNC levels (used to produce statistical data) are accepted and none of the teachers indicate they have any problem or issue with using them. The design and marking of regular assessments are presented as unproblematic and even as an incentive to creative geographical curriculum making. More 'micromanaged' aspects of assessment are a different matter. The departments portray some resentment to controls they perceive as excessive interference. Two department heads express how they value being 'left alone'. Data analysis shows both overt and more subtle management control to be influential in curriculum making in all four departments. This can be interpreted through social theory.

Hartley (1997) argues that a 'postmodern' society and 'post-Fordist' economy has led to schools emphasising 'performativity' (Hartley 1997: 125) with 'total quality management' (ibid: 132) the mantra of the school. A managerial culture in school, driven by the dominance of neoliberalism in society has been widely accepted in curriculum literature (Apple 2004, Fielding and Moss 2011, Pring 2013, Huckle 1985 and Morgan 2011) presenting a picture of teachers' curriculum making as curtailed by school management exerting increasing control over teachers' day to day practices.

Foucault (1977) contends that people follow the rules of their masters (to discipline themselves) through a sense that they are under surveillance at all times. Teachers appear to be responding to surveillance in the Foucauldian sense, which Hartley (1997: 113) describes as part of how society changes schooling. School managers sense they are being constantly watched by Ofsted, the Head of Department senses they are being constantly watched by the school managers, and although they are not literally being watched at all times, the sense is sufficient to ensure that the department 'self-manages' to the wishes of those 'above'.

All the geography departments describe a keen awareness that school senior management monitors their effectiveness (measured chiefly by examination results). The teachers' curriculum work takes place in such a climate of 'surveillance'. When results are good, departments have relative autonomy over curriculum making, for example Claymore and Derwent. Teachers indicate that they are aware of the teaching and assessment policies and expectations of SMT and these expectations directly influence curriculum making, for example in Arnwell, Brightling and Derwent. But this influence is rarely described as heavy handed, dogmatic or even prescriptive. Rather the departments know what is expected and they self-manage to ensure that, should they be called to account, or their practice observed, they can show that they are in line with policy. This appears to be the increased 'self-regulation' which, Hartley (1997) argues, is part of postmodern life, with performativity (of teacher and student) increasingly the focus of schools. School managers exert a control over teachers' curriculum work – but that control is often implicit, or 'at arm's length' rather than being enforced systems. The flexibility with which the departments design their assessments to produce student performance data are an example. The Derwent 'green pen' procedure is a somewhat more explicit control. But the Foucauldian image fits well – of the 'self-disciplined' (teachers) who are watched, but 'left alone' so long as they are seen to be performing suitably (Foucault 1977).

Pring (2013) calls for trust in teachers so that teachers can be engaged in 'curriculum thinking' rather than 'deliverology', assessment for learning rather than 'assessment for accountability' and for teachers to work collaboratively. Goepel (2013) argues for a professionalism borne of public trust in teachers, suggesting that this comes through 'accountability which is volunteered and maintained through relationships of trust' (Goepel 2013: 502). 'Public' accountability of teachers can be seen as mediated by the school senior management. Ofsted reports, published examination results and the outward 'face' of each school falls to the responsibility of school senior management (SMT). But the SMT pass this accountability down to their subject heads of department, who in turn pass it on to (or share the accountability with) their teaching team. The departments portray teachers accepting and volunteering their public accountability to an extent. But they present the 'trust' of their SMT as 'hard won' though a proven record of success. The trust is contingent, on strong performance, and it is relative – with insecurity comes interference. The extent to which teachers are engaged in 'curriculum thinking' (over 'deliverology') and the level of teacher collaboration in curriculum varies between departments. The two departments in schools with less 'performance security' (Arnwell and Brightling) are those with the less 'ideal' situation, having less collaborative geography curriculum making than Claymore and Derwent.

The level of 'privilege' in school context (in terms of popularity with parents, a positive reputation and strong whole school performance) appears to play a part in how far trust and collaboration extend into curriculum making. Claymore and Derwent have the most privileged context by these measures. The 'trust' narrative coming from these two schools supports the assertion that relative 'freedom' to exercise professional judgement (with the trust, collaboration and 'curriculum thinking' that this entails) is located in the 'confidence' and 'security' of the school context – a context that is passed on to subject teachers. However, none of the departments appear immune from the influence (and to an extent the control) of accountability, passed down through the SMT.

The departments portray SMT assessment policies as influencing curriculum making in specific ways. Derwent School by the marking and assessment policies from school management to 'raise achievement levels', which take up teachers' time. By dwelling on the performance of students, or 'going over' their work for longer, the geographical context of that work is, necessarily, also dwelled upon for longer, giving less time to cover new geographical content. Dialogic marking has been recently introduced at Derwent. Students are expected to show their own responses to marked work or lesson feedback in green pen. SMT have provided all classrooms with green pens. The significance of the green ink can be thought of as helping the teacher and student to see that students are reflecting on 'targets' and improving their work. But the green ink is also helpful for senior managers to easily monitor their teachers' classroom assessment practices. This latter purpose is suggested by the way teachers describe looking for 'more green pen moments' to placate senior management. Kathy (Head of Geography) explicitly says that the 'green pen' policy is driven by accountability, because, she says, her SMT believe that Ofsted will require evidence of Derwent's assessment for learning practices.

The formal 'assessments' about which the teachers speak positively, also take time. Up to a quarter of KS3 curriculum lesson and homework time was described as spent on the assessment work (either producing the assessment or making corrections when marked work is given back). Time is spent by both students and teachers. While this can be considered all part of 'teaching' the curriculum, there are indications that some teachers may see assessments as separate to the taught curriculum by taking a 'chunk out of the teaching'.

Performance is measured (mainly) by the high stakes examinations of GCSE and A level. The description by Brightling's Head of Geography of GCSE and A level 'driving' KS3, seems unlikely to be coincidental to the school's 'fragile' Ofsted position (there is a concern raised by Ofsted over consistency of examination results). All the departments describe GCSE and A level as influential in their KS3 curriculum making, albeit in different ways and not always explicitly.

Puttick (2015) finds GCSE and A level examination boards are highly influential in the construction of school geography. He argues that the trust placed in examination boards by teachers may limit students' access to the 'powerful knowledge' of geography.

> Examination grades are an important aspect of a culture of performativity, with implications for the power and status attributed to materials from examination boards. Legitimacy and trust are given to examination board approved resources, which reduces the potential for questioning them.
>
> *(Puttick 2015: 216)*

My research findings reflect Puttick's (2015) finding that teachers look to GCSE and A level as guidance for curriculum making. This is so, even at KS3 where there is no formal examination. Jane at Brightling is the most explicit of the Heads of Department in her descriptions of laying 'the foundations' of skills in particular (but knowledge to an extent) for GCSE and A level. Claymore presents their KS3 curriculum as the least influenced by GSCE and A level geography. But even Mat (Claymore) indicates a relationship. He appears to contradict himself when he initially says that there is no connection between curriculum making at KS3 and GCSE and A level requirements, but he goes on to say that he will change KS3 if there are certain changes at GCSE. He also says that his choice of what to teach and when is, in part, a conscious strategy for recruitment to GCSE. Mat's 'freedom' narrative seems strong enough to skew his perception (or at least how he describes his perception) of KS3 curriculum making. Curriculum enactment is strongly influenced by pressure to perform for high stakes public examinations.

Curriculum inertia

By focusing on curriculum *making*, there is a risk of over-emphasising curriculum change. The findings show much curriculum inertia as Mat's comment indicates:

> It's been a story of very gentle organic change (laughs). I suppose lots of the themes may have been themes that have been there for quite a long time.
>
> *(Mat)*

All the heads of departments portray a keen desire to change and develop the geography curriculum. However, evidence (from curriculum documents in particular but also interviews) shows much curriculum inertia – topics, lessons and materials, which remain for many years. This inertia can be linked to accountability. Teachers portray change as risk. The drivers of the most marked and rapid KS3 curriculum change are linked to accountability: anxiety over compliance to the GNC; Ofsted and preparing students for GCSE and A level; and to a lesser extent, SMT policies. Even when the department planning meetings discuss the curriculum from 'first principles', for example the 'finished geographer', and working backwards to KS3, the process is one of making adjustments to the existing curriculum plans rather than 'wholesale' re-writing. While planning meetings draw attention to curriculum change, the enactment of the curriculum indicates inertia. This can be understood through the wider social-economic landscape in which the curriculum is made, as I now discuss.

Each department portrays themselves as busy and under increasing pressure of time. While all the HoDs indicate that they value and enjoy time to think, discuss and plan curriculum change, data analysis portrays inertia, as built into the KS3 curriculum making process, as a response to the accountability pressure and the risk of change. The shared department network ensures that curriculum materials are easily stored and reused. The collaborative curriculum making process encourages teachers to 'defend' their part of the shared curriculum because they have invested their time preparing plans and materials (which tend to be parts of geography in which they have personal interest). The pressures of assessment and accountability and the priority of high stakes examination courses (GCSE and A Levels) conspire against spending time making substantial changes to the KS3 curriculum. Teacher strategies to maximise curriculum recycling that avoid change, can be interpreted as a response to the social tensions of late capitalism (Hartley 1997), which play out as increasingly time-pressurised teachers.

Sharing and collaboration

All the departments follow a common curriculum making process of steps:

1. Department team discuss and agree overall content and assessment principles (consensus planning).
2. The Head of Department (HoD) delegates (across the team) responsibility for planning the lesson objectives (LOs) of specific units of work.
3. The team share their planned unit LOs via a shared intranet. HoD encourages the team to post feedback comments.
4. HoD confirms final LOs and assignment guidelines for each unit.
5. HoD delegates (across the team) the production of lesson materials.
6. Lesson materials are shared on the department intranet.
7. HoD encourages team to add and amend materials as they are taught.

Curriculum making is a collaborative process, though there is not always consensus between all the teachers about what should be taught and how. 'Collaborative' is used here in its common definition as 'working together toward a shared goal'. So, while teachers may debate and disagree about some curriculum content (as in Derwent school) the curriculum made is the result of collaboration between teachers. The sharing process is strikingly intense. There is a carefully managed division of labour in curriculum planning and at the point of enactment. Teachers download or 'pull off' lesson plans from 'the system', sometimes at the point of their entry to the classroom to teach the lesson. The teachers in each department work in close cooperation, even when there are some different teaching styles and opinions about what and how to teach. Learning objectives and assessments are agreed and adhered to, and through 'the system' (shared intranet) teachers rely on one another to ensure curriculum materials are there when they need them. The teachers portray this process of close cooperation as inevitable – embedded in their normal working practices. The intensity of sharing and cooperation between teachers at the department can be interpreted as a response to and a coping mechanism for the pressure that teachers are under in late capitalist times. This is the pressure to meet the needs of individuals who are increasingly demanding as consumers and expected to be ever more competitive as producers (Hartley 1997).

There is also an intensity in how teachers work in networks with teachers (and people interested in the geography curriculum) beyond school. These people are unseen and often anonymous, appearing as contributors to sharing websites such as 'Geography Pods' or 'Geography all way', or rather more official community sites, such as the GA or RGS. They have developed (or re-purposed and recycled) ideas and materials, and uploaded them to such websites for teachers to use. The 'social' nature of curriculum making is again striking by the level of sharing through wider communities, enabled by the internet. This is Castells' (2004) version of globalisation (the network society) reflected in curriculum enactment. The use of internet communities can, like the collaboration within the department, be interpreted as teachers' response to pressures of late capitalism. A society-curriculum dialectic is not a new phenomenon (Bourdieu and Passeron 1977 and Huckle 1985). However, there is an 'accelerated intensification of activity' (Lambert and Morgan 2010: 31) in teachers' work. An intensification or 'speed up' of life in late capitalism changes the way society influences curriculum making, and how teachers respond to the times.

Late capitalism is driving a shift in the way the individual is conceived in society. There are notions of a 'new individualism' creating a tension between the drive to produce and to consume (Hartley 1997, Morgan 2011) and the notion of teacher-student identities shifting as a globalised society becomes 'networked' through the internet (Castells 2004, Herod 2011, Kress 2006, Somekh 2006 and Moore 2015). These accounts of a shift in how the individual is conceived are all part of an intensification of life and explained by the technological, economic and social climate.

Intensely collaborative processes of curriculum enactment are adopted by teachers as a way of coping with 'performance' pressure, which threatens to 'squeeze out' time and space to think about geography in the curriculum. This is somewhat alienating for the individual, who might ask 'where do I fit in?' or a step further 'who am I in all this?' The research finds that committed geography teachers are indeed asking these questions (albeit implicitly) and turning to their personal identities as geography teachers as a form of resistance to the threat of overwhelming power from society 'outside' controlling their lives and work as geography teachers.

Teacher identities and resistance

Easy access to information in the internet age, combined with a 'demotic turn' (toward ordinary people) threatens to make teacher and learner roles interchangeable, undermining the authority and status of the subject teacher as 'expert' and throwing into question the status of curriculum (subject) knowledge. It is true that teachers are at pains to listen to 'student voice' and the internet is prominent in teachers' curriculum thinking. However, the teachers' stories I have presented produce a rather different narrative to that of teachers relinquishing their curriculum responsibility and learners calling the shots. Rather, the narrative presented is one of a 'turning toward' a distinctive identity – of geography teacher. This seems a perfectly rational response to the threat of losing that identity, posed by the internet and the demotic turn.

A 'turning toward' the teachers' professional identity found in the case studies (in particular the Heads of Department in Brightling, Claymore and Derwent) is consistent with Brooks' argument that geography teachers are 'reforming and remaking their professional practice in the light of their changing contexts' (2012: 305). A turning to professional identity also resonates with Brooks' (2016) contention that teachers use their subject-teacher identity (geography) as a 'professional compass' to navigate changing times.

Puttick's (2016) finding that teachers are 'sustained' in their work by the geography department developing 'shared narratives' (2016: 15) is reflected in the research findings in two ways. First, the research finds teachers (especially the Heads of Geography) turning to their geography teacher identity as a means to sustain their energy and enthusiasm for curriculum making in pressurised times. Secondly, Puttick's (2016) emphasis on sharing in the department (connected to teachers' ability to sustain their work) is reflected in the theme of teacher sharing in the research findings. The geography teachers are 'banding together' – collaborating and sharing their curriculum making to sustain themselves in pressurised times.

All the Heads of Departments (HoDs) and some of the teachers portray an enthusiasm for geography in their work. The teachers are drawing on geography as a 'curriculum resource' (Lambert 2011: 258), which helps to explain teachers' response to the late capitalist times. Three of the HoDs in particular, describe and present attitudes and actions that indicate a 'turning toward geography' in their identities. They do so faced by the heightened managerialism and accountability pressure of schooling in late capitalism (a condition which has been widely analysed) – see Hartley 1997, Apple 2004, Fielding and Moss 2011, Pring 2013, Huckle 1985 and Morgan 2011).

A 'turning' to personal identity can also be interpreted through the lens of social theory. Postmodernity is a bewildering time for society with a shifting 'outside' world. Beck (1992) shows there is greater individualisation and choice – but accompanied by heightened sense of risk. Giddens (2000) provides the image of society progressing like a juggernaut, careering out of control and a blurring of the roles of individual and society as agents shaping human actions. Castells (2004) draws attention to 'globalisation' and a 'network' society. Baudrillard (1994) conjures the image of an 'information-blizzard' where reality and simulation become inseparable. Bauman (2005 describes a fluidity to society where all at once 'solid' becomes 'liquid', Friedman (2016) presents a dizzying 'age of acceleration' and Harari (2017) as a power shift from human minds to computer algorithms. Such times, these social theorists contend, 'feel' dangerous and somewhat out of control. Such an interpretation of society can explain the actions of teachers to reassert a sense of personal control by strengthening a sense of identity.

Kathy's story (Derwent School) is perhaps most explicitly one of restating her identity as a geography teacher in response to pressure (from her school management) to move from the classroom to school management herself. Indeed, she speaks of this action as not only for personal development, but as sending a message to her school management, that she is committed to being and remaining a geography teacher. She is studying for a Master's degree in Geography Education and she describes her increased engagement with the GA. She relates much of her curriculum thinking to ideas to which she has been introduced on her Masters course and her subsequent reflections on these ideas – for example on the role of knowledge in the curriculum. Kathy describes her rigorous attention to broad subject knowledge in the curriculum in the context of her concern that 'relevant' or child-centred approaches may undermine a geographical education. 'Turning' to her subject identity can be read, therefore, not only as a response to the technical (economic) pressure for performativity, but also as her response to the therapeutic (cultural) pressure for children to 'consume' their schooling. In both ways, Kathy appears as asserting herself – taking a strong position in the late capitalism schooling landscape – by turning to her identity as a geographer.

Mat's story (Claymore School) is one of pursuing the 'leading edge' (or boundaries) of geography, both through bringing the news, current affairs and political debates into the curriculum, and by personal communication with university departments. Mat portrays himself as 'pushing' those boundaries, for example in how he downplays the use of established academic texts over using 'the news'. Mat comes across as something of a rebel and a free thinker. He wants his students to be free thinking and risk taking too. He makes the curriculum to 'break free' of the restriction that performance management and bureaucracy threaten – as a way of 'resisting' these pressures. But he does so by 'playing the game'. He ensures that 'the data are good' so that he and his department are left alone to get on with the curriculum work as they decide. Being a geographer, a teacher and relating to young people's lives, are three resources for curriculum making held in balance by Mat. As such, he personifies the curriculum making model (Lambert and Morgan 2010). Mat describes driving these personal resources forward for his own professional sustenance. He seeks out personal challenges such as organising fieldwork, visiting speakers and his own study at university. He says this is to keep himself interested. Mat thus appears to sustain himself by rising above the bureaucratic pressures around him through focusing on his own growth as a geography teacher.

Jane (Brightling School) also portrays a determination to engage with geography. She describes wanting to lead her team to develop a culture of bringing 'up-to-date' geography into the curriculum. She reads some academic (university) geography and undertakes some background personal research, such as into the school curricula of some other countries. The Geographical Association (GA) and the Royal Geographical Society (RGA) are influences and she says she wants her department to have more interaction with them. Like Mat, Jane shows something of a free-mindedness and a resistance to bureaucracy – such as when she rejects the school management's request to focus curriculum planning time on 'building learning power' (Claxton 1999) and follows her own, geography-focused agenda.

Sian (HoD at Arnwell) is less clearly 'resisting' managerial pressures. Her situation makes such resistance rather more difficult than the other Heads of Geography. Her case reinforces the point that the school culture and leadership priorities has a huge effect on the capacity for teachers to be curriculum makers.

She is more isolated and working in a school who demonstrably value subject departments less (there is no recognised geography department, nor is geography taught discretely in year 7). Nonetheless, Sian has aspirations to develop a curriculum making team of teachers. She describes trying to build her geography department and she would like more (personal) interaction with the geography teaching community.

I cannot 'prove' a causal link between the educational landscape of the time and teachers' actions and attitudes (which indicate their identities as geographers and teachers), nor has it been my intention to make such a claim. We cannot be sure these teachers are 'turning' to geography as a response to the pressures of the times, rather than these being attitudes that are simply part of the 'nature' of these particular teachers. But what I can offer is a justified interpretation based on the case study evidence and literature examining the societal context in which the teachers are acting, the school and the wider 'climate' (of accountability, performativity and students as consumers). The teachers' actions, their descriptions and their narratives should be understood in this wider context. When human stories are examined in the wider contexts (of society, economy or policy) powerful meanings can be drawn. And so, I argue, a 'turning' to professional identity (as geography teacher) can be interpreted as a response to the pressures of schooling in times of late capitalism.

Teachers' values and beliefs

These are all comprehensive schools in the same city at the same time, with a statutory requirement to teach the national curriculum – but a different geography curriculum is enacted at each school. The application of these curriculum models shows that each department has a different mix of curriculum 'value-belief systems' among the teachers, which influences the enacted curriculum. The descriptions of each department's curriculum enactment show that the school's history and management, the local area, the students and the teachers' educational and life experiences affect which value-belief systems influence curriculum making.

None of the departments can be neatly classified into a single value-belief system. Each is something of a 'hybrid', or mix of value-belief systems. The neoliberal domination of schooling necessitates teachers' attention to examination success. Accountability and performance management is fully accepted as inevitable (if not fully welcomed) by all the departments and the different 'leanings' of teachers are framed within the 'social-efficiency' or 'utilitarian' value-belief system dominant in society (see Schiro 2008, Rawling 2001, Pring 2013 and Fielding and Moss 2011). Each school in this study shows a prominent concern for examination grades (accepted as currency for progression into further study, for accessing jobs and as the key measure of a school's success). Furthermore, the geography department is performance managed (albeit to varying degrees) in each school and regular assessment data are required by the management of each school.

A team of different teachers enhances the hybridity of each department. Each teacher brings their own value-belief systems into the mix. But, as Schiro (2008) recognises, individuals can hold different 'curriculum-ideologies' simultaneously, and cannot be easily compartmentalised into a single 'ideology' or value-belief system. This appears in the Head of each department, for example, Mat's (Claymore) mix of the child-centred and the scholar-academic curriculum value-belief systems. Competing value-belief systems play out in curriculum enactment. There are tensions between the competing value-belief systems, which pull teachers in different directions as they make curriculum choices. This includes the values and beliefs held personally and those which permeate schooling from wider society (so far as these are distinguishable). Accountability (driven by a dominant social-efficiency value-belief system) is influencing and threatening geography teachers' balanced curriculum making. Departments and individual teachers are navigating their way through a landscape of management surveillance and accountability so that they can enact a curriculum with personal integrity.

Technology

Technology is a prominent theme in the department descriptions of curriculum enactment, which does not fit easily into the categories of students, geography or teachers, and so it is given a separate section, here. Just as Puttick (2015a, 2015b) found, my research shows a substantial role played by technology as teachers make the curriculum. When technology is described by the four departments, it is mainly in two ways. The first is a departmental context of sharing ideas and materials with colleagues. The second is finding lesson materials and plans, 'ready-made' by other geography teachers (or people who support geography teachers). The teachers do not say so much about how their students use technology, but it goes without saying, that young people are spending increasing amounts of time online (particularly outside school). Technology is used to support the sharing of curriculum ideas and materials within a group of teachers – 'the group' being either the department or a wider geography teacher community.

A secondary context of technology use is searching for or 'coming across' material and ideas serendipitously from outside the geography teaching community. Such material needs to be re-contextualised for use in the classroom, for example, news items. The third (rather less prominent) context of technology, is as a technique of students' learning geography, such as GIS or using an excel spreadsheet.

Computer technology is embedded in the curriculum making process, such that teachers rely on the technology. Teachers describe difficulty imagining curriculum making without a shared network drive at school, the internet and the software (like PowerPoint), which allows quick and easy sharing of 'ready-made' lesson materials. There is nothing new (or technology-dependent) about a department dividing curriculum making responsibilities and sharing their materials. However, the 'network' (both in school and the open internet) have accelerated the speed of sharing and the volume of material that can be accessed. Technology is used to enable the sharing of complex curriculum material and ideas, which would otherwise take up more of the teacher's time. Often, lessons, sourced on the internet and shared on the school network, are very visual (containing images and

embedded video clips) and with varied activity materials – card sorts, map annotation, role plays and 'treasure hunts' for example, as in Sian's (Arnwell) lesson,
which she downloaded from the Royal Geographical Website school geography
website, which in turn sourced the materials from another agency.

The 'speed up' and intensification of teachers and other interest groups sharing
curriculum material can be read alongside the other sub-themes constructed in the
research and supported by the literature. Hartley's (1997) argument that schools and
teachers must manage a conflict between an economic driver (producer/efficiency)
and a cultural driver (consumer/therapy) of curriculum making is connected to the
use of network technology. Teachers are using the technology to support active and
engaging lessons with exciting visuals and plenty of ideas for a variety of activities to
be found online (the therapeutic driver). But the technology also 'frees up' teachers
from the time consuming task of creating original geographical content themselves.
They are able to spend more time on other matters of practice, much of which is
driven by performance pressure, including producing attainment data and carrying
out student interventions for example. There is a downside to this. Teachers
appear less inclined to use their own geographical knowledge to make teaching
resources and more inclined (as expert 'resource finders') to pass that role to
another person or organisation. The research thus concurs with Puttick (2015a,
2015b) that some teachers are passing on and entrusting the recontextualising of
geography (into a school curriculum) to others.

A 'technological turn' in curriculum making can also be interpreted through the
'network society'. The saturation of technology use in society helps to understand
the significance of technology portrayed by the departments. Castells' (2004) 'network society' appears to be realised in the findings. Curriculum enactment in the
case studies is a process of using social and information networks – online and local
communities to access and share material. Popular ideas and materials are rapidly
picked up, shared, edited, added to or repackaged for a particular class or for the
teacher's personal preference. This 'recycling' or re-purposing of material is such
that it can become difficult (sometimes impossible) to know the origin or the
author of a part of the geography curriculum (and there is little capacity to find out
about these origins among the busy teachers).

An example of such 'recycling' of geography, whereby 'recontextualisation'
(Bernstein 2000 and Puttick 2015a, 2015b) is already done for the teacher from the
case studies is Steve's Easter Island mystery lesson at Derwent School. The lesson
plan and materials, complete with card sort activities, images and video clips has
been in the department 'system' for some years. Steve sourced the materials from
the internet, but from whom or where the idea for this case study of over-
population originated, he cannot say. Sian's 'sustainability' lesson at Arnwell is
another example. In this case, she downloaded the lesson from a trusted website
(and a community of geography teachers and educators – the RGS, schools' section). She taught the lesson largely unchanged from the downloaded material
(although the skill with which she taught the lesson gives the impression that this is
her lesson, with no sense of the ideas coming from someone else). A third example

is Jane's 'trading game' lesson. She was first introduced to this idea during her PGCE teacher education, but again she uses a trusted website to access the material and then stores it for reuse and sharing on the department computer network.

Teachers describe using a range of sources, with some favourite sites. But their curriculum decisions are made quickly (they have to be). The teachers describe having little time for (in Kathy's words) 'the luxury' of thinking deeply or critically about how resources interpret or represent geography. Teachers' work has accelerated under pressure of increased accountability and expectations of a curriculum of both engagement and productivity. They are forced to become hyper-efficient curriculum enactors. So, teachers put their trust in the curriculum thinking of others. This can be seen as a good thing – collaborative curriculum planning, but it also makes it more difficult for the teacher to think deeply about the curriculum. In one of my case studies, the trading game is an example. It is part of Christian Aid's education section. Christian Aid has a stated purpose of eradicating global poverty, education is not a primary purpose, but a part of a strategy to another end. Bringing organisations such as charities into school geography can be enriching. But it can also reflect 'education for a good cause' (Marsden 1997: 241) and the concern that geography education can sometimes be at risk of being influenced by pressure groups (see Standish 2009 and Furedi 2009). In the 'hyper-socialised' teacher's world, it becomes difficult to stay on top of curriculum thinking, this work can become, almost unwittingly, contracted out to others.

There are two significant wider points here. First, teachers, under pressure to make the geography curriculum engaging for an ever more 'consumer-oriented' student (Hartley 1997, Furedi 2009 and Morgan 2014b) and with limited time, turn to shared material and ideas on the internet. In doing so teachers place much trust in other people's curriculum thinking, which feeds into the final enactment of the curriculum. Secondly, the reuse and recycling of ideas and materials is such that sources and origins are lost. These are significant points because they connect the two wider societal trends of consumerisation (Naidoo, Shankar and Veer 2011 and Postman 1996) and a 'technological turn'. These trends are in turn linked to the way teachers work with one another. The connection between wider societal trends (of higher 'consumer' expectations and 'speed up' of communications) and teachers' curriculum making response by turning to others to 'deliver' in an intensified climate of performativity is part of the 'hyper-socialisation' of curriculum enactment.

Baudrillard (1994) argues that society will increasingly face an 'information-blizzard' in which the original and the reproduced become indistinct. In such a society, the real and the simulated become inseparable and the world becomes increasingly superficial, where everything is encountered at surface level. Baudrillard portrays an extreme world, which is hard to fully apply to my research findings. But there is a ring of truth to his imagery in how the four departments are using digital technology. Children spend much of their school geography lessons offered images on PowerPoint, and video clips, rarely lingering for long on any piece of geographical data. In the spirit of 'engagement' they move on at high pace through the lesson. There is a risk of the world presented superficially through visual media. Teachers are faced with vast resources on the internet (an opportunity, but also a threat). In the 'information blizzard', they often turn to Google to make decisions, as Jane (Brightling) does for example in deferring to Google to suggest which 'fantastic places' should be offered to students. The unplaced, generic example of a geographical feature has become commonplace in geography lessons, particularly the less experienced or non-specialist teachers – the result of Googling 'meander' or 'glacier', and choosing the most appealing image. Though this particular issue is not common in the four 'strong' departments, there is evidence of both a reliance (and trust) to delegate some curriculum 'thinking' to Google in order to handle information overload.

The work of recontextualising knowledge becomes obscured by the internet, lying somewhere between the official recontextualising field and the pedagogical recontextualising field (Bernstein 2000, Puttick 2016). The recycling of ideas and materials is such that the authorship of the curriculum is uncertain. Baudrillard (1994) argues that society is becoming 'simulcara', meaning the origins of things are lost, the 'real' becomes uncertain and there is a trend toward imitation and simulation of the original. I found that teachers rapidly both source and share a great deal of material through the internet. Teachers' curriculum enactment seems to reflect the trend toward 'simulcara' and 'simulation' in life.

The teachers show different ways of dealing with the problem of the 'information blizzard' and the obfuscation of original sources of geography. Only Kathy, at Derwent, is explicit about the need to ask critical questions of sources. But all the teachers describe their use of a personal 'bank' of their preferred sources from the web. They appear to be using a strategy of turning to 'ready-made' materials and placing trust in the community of teachers or broadly speaking 'educators' who upload content to their websites. The websites vary in how far they are perceived as 'official' sources of the geography curriculum. Exam boards' websites and 'Nings' are used as an authoritative, or 'official' source of material, so too are organisations on which web-based content is filtered by geography educators (such the GA and RGS). Other sources are presented by the teachers as trusted or reliable, such as the BBC 'learning zone' and the Times Educational Supplement curriculum site 'TES connect'. These are managed and content is filtered, though not necessarily by specialist geography educators, and so can be thought of as 'semi-official' sources. Other websites mentioned are essentially open and unregulated sharing sites such as 'Geography all the way', 'Geography pods' and 'Geography at the movies'. These have no 'official' status and sit outside large organisations. How and by whom their content is managed is unclear, therefore they hold less 'authority' of content. Nonetheless, teachers portray these 'unofficial' sources as trusted, used regularly and speaking to the geography teacher community in practical ways.

Giddens' (2000) ideas are pertinent here. He argues that there is a blurring of boundaries between society and individual. Giddens (ibid) explores the question of whether the individual has agency and power to shape society, or whether society shapes the individual's actions. The intense sharing and recycling of curriculum materials – or to extrapolate further, of the curriculum itself, 'blurs' the individual-society boundary. My research findings indicate a curriculum where (in terms of curriculum materials) little is 'original', but is borrowed, shared, recycled or revised. Computer technology exacerbates this.

Another way that the 'information blizzard' is handled, is by teachers letting new information 'wash over' them while being constantly 'on the lookout' for turning current affairs or popular geography into new or adapted geography lessons. Kathy's description of sitting at home, inspired by David Attenborough in a television programme and emailing her team, illustrates the serendipitous power of 'popular geography'. Mat's descriptions of looking to the news as inspiration illustrates the influence of current affairs over curriculum making. Such strategies tend to move away from the 'ready-made' curriculum resource (such as the PowerPoint lesson or activity) – using the news or popular geographies as a starting point requires the teacher to do much recontextualising to turn such sources into a geography curriculum.

Harari (2017) and Bridle (2018) take the notion of technology blurring the boundaries of individual-society further. The internet and computational power is now a key aspect of wider society. Both Harari and Bridle suggest that computer algorithms have become so pervasive, influential and closely connected to human thought (what Harari argues is akin to the new religion of 'dataism') that the human mind and machines (computers) have actually begun to merge. I am not arguing that this is yet the case for teachers or their students, but the algorithms controlling the search results when a busy teacher searches for information have a significant influence over the enacted curriculum. Too frequently, I have observed geography trainee teachers show their class an image of a striking landscape (a natural feature or an urban landscape for example) and the teacher does not know *where* that landscape is, so it cannot be taught or studied in context. They have sourced the image by a hurried Google search, forgetting that 'real' world, including place and location is the very substance of their subject. In an age of internet dependency, it becomes all the more important for the teacher to keep a critical eye on their sources and to keep their educational aims and purposes (the powerful subject knowledge they want to teach) clearly in mind.

It is still possible for teachers to have agency and to be curriculum makers. Mat (Claymore) and Kathy (Brightling) are confident and committed geography teachers (both have recently given time to study at universities, re-energising their relationship with geography). Jane (Brightling) also portrays a willingness to engage in the hard work of recontextualising geography, for example by attending lectures at the Royal Geographical Society and reading some academic geography. Sian (Arnwell) portrays a Head of Department more restricted in such engagement with geography.

Teachers can be curriculum makers in late capitalist society but the role is hard-won. There is a tension between the teacher's agency needed for curriculum making and the controlling social-economic climate of accountability, performance pressure and technological change. Some teachers are responding this 'climate' by turning to their subject (geography) identities. Such a form of teacher 'resistance' to the pressure, which threatens their professional role as curriculum maker, has implications for teacher education and professional development as I will discuss in the final chapter, but at this point I would like to recap to clarify my meaning of 'hyper-socialisation'.

'Hyper-Socialised' curriculum enactment

In my research I found that an idealised praxis of curriculum *making* does not always happen. The reality of curriculum *enactment* is a complex and nuanced process, in which the teacher is subject to pressures and tensions, through which they must navigate. Much of the pressure is a product of late capitalist times affecting students, teaching and school geography. My research produced a complex picture of many influences upon teachers' curriculum work in 2014. This can appear to be an intractable web of interconnections. However, my interpretation of findings using four dimensions: the lens of late capitalism and contemporary social theory; the historical analysis of literature; inductive coding of case study data; and department narratives, intersect at a common 'thread' of 'hyper-socialised' curriculum enactment (see Figure 11).

The phrase 'hyper-socialised' articulates the process of curriculum enactment found in the case studies. I use this phrase to capture an explanation for how far (the idealised praxis of) curriculum making is happening (and can happen) in contemporary society. Late capitalist society has changed the way teachers are enacting the curriculum. Young people are increasingly sophisticated consumers while also being future producers for economic growth. The internet and mobile technologyhas changed the way teachers construct geographical knowledge. Under pressure to perform in these times, and in order to cope with heightened demands, teachers are 'contracting out' curriculum work to others. Curriculum enactment has become 'hyper-socialised' in a 'speeded-up' world.

The original Greek meaning of 'hyper' is 'excessive' or 'exaggerated' – qualities which describe the heightened level to which curriculum enactment has become 'socialised' (involving people other than the teacher themselves). The crucial aspect of the late capitalist analysis leading to a 'hyper-socialised' description of curriculum enactment is the changed way the individual has become conceived in society. Social and economic forces have intensified the tension of a 'dual individualism' driven simultaneously by postmodern culture creating a narcissistic individualism and post-Fordist economy creating a competitive individualism (Jameson 1992, Hartley 1997). This tension plays out as pressure on teachers to achieve both student 'happiness' and technical performance through the curriculum. Furthermore, there are endless and bewildering possibilities opened up by the internet and computers – an 'information blizzard' (Baudrillard 1994) – both for making an 'exciting' curriculum and tracking and measuring students' performance with ever more data.

These pressures *exceed* the teacher's individual curriculum making resources (time, knowledge and creativity) forcing them to use the coping strategy of turning to other people and devolving curriculum making, particularly by using

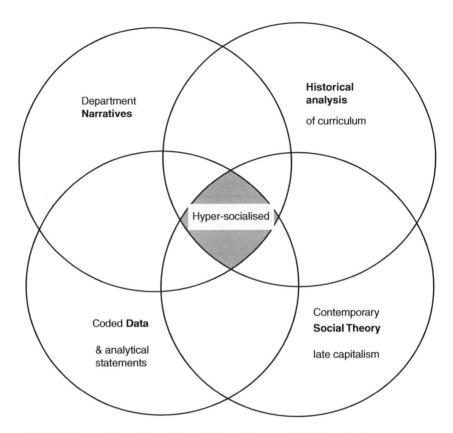

FIGURE 11 Construction of research conclusion: 'hyper-socialised' curriculum enactment

technology, to communities that can help them. The extent to which the teacher's individual curriculum making resources is exceeded is such that, alone, the teacher in the late capitalist schooling landscape, is 'out of control' – reflecting Giddens' (2000) image of the 'runaway world'. Only by passing on (or sharing) excessive pressure, can the geography teacher manage and make sense of their curriculum making task. 'Hyper-Socialised' curriculum enactment captures the intensity of the pressure on teachers from a changed individualism in society and the response of intense sharing and delegation of curriculum decisions to communities, enabled by the 'network society' (Castells 2004).

Hyper-Socialised curriculum enactment should not be mistaken for hyper-*sociable* curriculum making. Lambert and Morgan (2010) drawing on Gewirtz (2001) link the intensified pressure of teachers' work to a 'decline in the sociability of teaching' (2010: 31). My research findings concur to an extent. Teachers spend much time at computers and limited time in face to face conversations with other teachers, as they are under pressure to perform (for example to produce data for senior management to report pupil progression and to show evidence that whole school initiatives, such as the use of dialogic marking, are being implemented). Teachers' social contact with peers (in terms of curriculum work) is increasingly virtual – my research findings show that teachers are working together and sharing their curriculum making, but at an intense pace and with wide-ranging communities through the internet.

Nor should hyper-socialised curriculum enactment be conflated with Young and Muller's (2010) notion of an 'over-socialised' curriculum future (their 'future 2' curriculum), which privileges the learner and societal needs over the discipline. Hyper-Socialisation differs in its emphasis on *the process* teachers follow as they prepare their sequences of lessons in particular, how they are pressured into intense sharing and delegating to cope with the demands of the new individualism of late capitalism. While there is certainly a connection between a future 2 curriculum and the 'hyper-socialised' situation I have described – in the pressure to focus on enjoyment and soft skills over disciplinary knowledge, it is possible for a hyper-socialisation to produce either a future 2, or the more desirable future 3 curriculum. Future 3 takes a balanced, social-realist view of knowledge, and depending on how a department approaches their recontextualisation of disciplinary knowledge into a curriculum, they may be able to achieve a future 3 for the curriculum, even within a hyper-socialised process of curriculum enactment.

Finally, the notion of 'hyper-normalisation' (Curtis 2016) is worthy of consideration here, for its resonance with my term 'hyper-socialisation'. The two are not the same and used in different contexts. Hyper-normalisation refers to the acceptance of an over-simplified 'fake' reality presented by governments and corporations and readily accepted by the people. But it is significant that Curtis has used his term to express the nature of the way people 'normalise' under pressure to accept systems, which rationally they may know to be false, oversimplified or leading in the wrong direction. Curtis captures the 'speeded up' and hyper-connected world in which people are easily manipulated, and, perhaps for a sense of safety or perceived necessity they will accept 'group-think' even when rationally or individually they may believe there is a better way of doing things. While I do not suggest teachers are an easily led group (quite the opposite in fact) this has some parallels with my finding that teachers are compelled to adopt coping strategies under the pressure of late capitalism by 'banding together' in what I call 'hyper-socialisation'.

The curriculum making model offers an ideal of balanced attention to geography, teaching and the student's needs. This provides a professional model toward which the geography teacher may strive, and so curriculum making can be interpreted as a response to threats to the 'health' of the geography curriculum and to school geography itself, posed by the drive to school efficiency and the academisation (privatisation) of schooling in England in recent times. Furthermore, the (idealised) curriculum making model can be understood as contingent on a high level of teacher autonomy and teacher agency. My research finds that such a level of autonomy cannot be assumed, and at best is a hard-won situation. The contingency of curriculum making can be illustrated

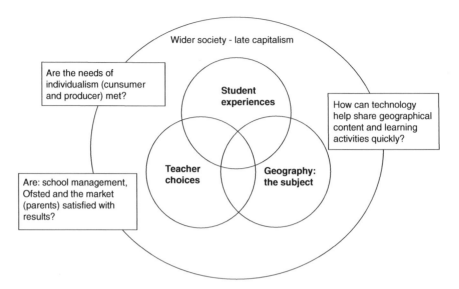

FIGURE 12 Curriculum making located within a societal context (late capitalism)

by its location within a societal context (Figure 12). This diagram represents 'hyper-socialised' curriculum enactment.

'Late capitalism thinking'

The 'contextualised' curriculum making model (Figure 12) illustrates how late capitalist society affects teachers' curriculum work, such that the balanced 'curriculum thinking' called for by the original model of the Geographical Association and Lambert and Morgan (2010) can be obscured by other pressures. The diagram (Figure 12) deliberately omits the four 'thought bubbles' (questions and prompts for the teacher's 'curriculum thinking') present in Lambert and Morgan's model (Figure 2). This omission is to show that such curriculum thinking may be obscured by a type of thinking driven my current society, represented by the questions in Figure 12. The 'curriculum thinking' questions are pushed into the background or hidden but they have not been completely lost. I have found that some departments and teachers are able to maintain 'curriculum thinking', but they must do so while also being giving sufficient attention to the 'late capitalism thinking', to cope in the current times.

The level of 'late capitalism thinking' varies between teachers to play a greater or lesser role in their curriculum enactment. Some teachers and departments are able to pay sufficient attention to satisfying the demands of a changed individualism, accountability and new globalised technologies, while still being deeply motivated by curriculum thinking and holding on to questions of how to achieve progression in the student's geographical thinking.

However, curriculum making in late capitalist times is contingent on teachers effectively navigating the pressures that threaten to distract from, and obscure, curriculum thinking. There is, therefore, something of a disjuncture between the current society/curriculum/teacher formation and the scope for curriculum making to become common practice for teachers.

9

CONCLUSION – PREPARING TEACHERS TO BE RESILIENT 'CURRICULUM MAKERS'

In this book, I have explored how the late capitalist times are reflected in curriculum enactment, through a process that I have called 'hyper-socialisation'. It is only teachers who can enact the curriculum (in the classroom at least), and I conclude by asking – what are the implications of 'hyper-socialisation' for teachers and educators? Particularly important in this are the Heads of subject department, but so too are headteachers, teacher educators and educational researchers.

But, before concluding with what needs to be done to better prepare teachers as curriculum makers, it is helpful to look at subject teachers as not so much passively influenced by changing times, but as more actively responding to them. This perspective puts us in a better position to consider the education and support that teachers need.

Understanding teachers' responses to the times

'Hyper-socialised' curriculum enactment is the result of pressure brought to bear on teachers by the structures, norms and expectations of late capitalist society. Many teachers share, borrow and 'contract out' their curriculum making (relying heavily on the internet) by necessity, to cope. So, while the drivers of hyper-socialisation can be seen in late capitalist society (a heightened consumer/producer individualism, more open and rapid data flows, a pervasive internet and increased accountability) so the response of teachers can unwittingly collude with and exacerbate hyper-socialisation. Teachers' curriculum work therefore both reflects and constitutes the society of these times – giving further credence to the theory of a curriculum-society dialectic (Huckle 1985, Bourdieu and Passeron 1977).

Paradoxically, hyper-socialised curriculum enactment can be alienating for the individual, because the intensely 'socialised' nature of curriculum making removes the time and space for geographical curriculum making – described by one teacher in the study as a 'luxury'. Should this not be the core work of a subject teacher? Nonetheless, some (and perhaps a great many) committed geography teachers are turning to their identities as *geography* teachers as a form of resistance to the threat of overwhelming power of society 'outside' controlling their lives and work. In doing so, these geography teachers are asserting their personal values and beliefs. Some are adopting the radical geography stance called for by Huckle (1985) and Morgan (2011) by making a geography curriculum that challenges the neoliberal status quo.

However, the capacity of teachers to lead the subject curriculum development and to be curriculum makers is limited. Teachers must navigate through very challenging late capitalist times and in my research, I found teachers somewhat ambivalent with respect to handling change. While innovation and actively seeking to bring new geographies to the curriculum is prevalent in some teachers' curriculum narratives (in particular the Heads of Departments) there is also some curriculum inertia as teachers manage pressurised times by limiting the changes over which they have control. This is perfectly rational given the huge demands on teachers to 'perform' and produce exam results. Much of the geography curriculum in departments is recycled, shared and re-used, even when the Head of Department is trying to make curriculum changes. The geography teacher's identity gives a steadiness to their focus on geography in changing times but this does not always translate to driving curriculum change.

My findings build on previous research into geography teachers' identities by Brooks (2012, 2016) and Puttick (2016) both of whom found that geography teachers use their identities as geographers to navigate and sustain their work through changing times. Puttick (2016) found collaboration between teachers in the geography department to be an important influence on curriculum enactment because individual curriculum values and beliefs are shaped by the construction of a shared department narrative. However, using the lens of late capitalist society I argue that collaboration is intensifying as a coping strategy and teacher identities are (in some cases) being turned to, to sustain geographical curriculum making in a 'hyper-socialised' situation.

Teachers – becoming self-aware as curriculum makers in changing times

Teachers are better equipped to produce a curriculum of 'powerful knowledge' when they develop critical self-awareness of their role and responsibility as curriculum makers. If teachers are able to recognise the hyper-socialised situation of their work, they are better placed to make sound curriculum making decisions based on independent professional judgements as subject specialists. But recognising hyper-socialisation is not intuitive. The pace of life sweeps us all along and it is hard to step back to reflect. Busy teachers are unlikely to analyse their own curriculum work with a social-economic lens (the lens of late capitalism), unless prompted and supported to do so. There is a key role here for teacher trainers and educators. Universities are particularly well-placed to help teachers look at the wider picture of schools, society and curriculum, and so to equip them with a critical lens to think about the possible controls and influences over their own curriculum enactment. This helps them become curriculum leaders and 'makers'. Such curriculum leadership should be largely autonomous and driven by teachers' own professional (subject teaching) expertise. It can also be collaborative in positive ways – drawing on communities in critical and developmental ways, rather than as a survival strategy.

Hyper-socialisation is a threat to the enactment of a 'quality' subject curriculum, but there is also optimism here and a way forward. The case studies I have presented in this book show the importance of the subject teacher self-identifying as *geography* teacher, and as a 'curriculum maker' (although most teachers probably only tacitly acknowledge the latter). Curriculum leadership flourishes through good communication within the department in a critical and open culture, with a shared commitment to curriculum making. In both their initial training and ongoing professional development, teachers can reflect critically on the influences over their own curriculum *enactment* to develop attitudes, values and beliefs, which support them toward becoming curriculum *makers* (and leaders). One way to do this is for trainers and educators to give teachers the conceptual tools to compare a 'hyper-socialised' model of curriculum enactment, with the aspirational model of 'curriculum making'. Doing so could lead to adjustments in teachers' attitudes and practices.

The future – how could (and how should) curriculum making happen?

Resilient curriculum making teachers

'Hyper-Socialised' curriculum enactment aims to articulate neither a utopian nor a dystopian future for geography teaching, but rather to describe the current situation. Nonetheless, the analysis of curriculum enactment in late capitalist times brings to light both problems and opportunities for geography teachers. My research shows that the praxis of curriculum making is 'hard won' by teachers who must also 'perform' to meet changed expectations and demands of school managers, inspectors, students and parents. These demands are not always clearly stated, and they are rarely overtly coercive. Rather, teachers self-manage according to their perceptions of the expectations of those 'watching' them. Late capitalist times bring a heightened sense of accountability and pressure to perform.

Some of the teachers and departments in the study offer a model of resilience to 'outside' pressure by their turning to identities as geography teachers and showing curriculum leadership. They do so by adopting an attitude of curriculum thinking and encouraging colleagues in the department to do the same. The resilience to keep curriculum thinking central to their work is supported in different ways, some highly personal and some context dependent (such as the school context). Individual attitudes, values and beliefs about geographical education sustain teachers. Some teachers show courage in choosing to resist 'higher' directives and expectations (from school management, or the perception of Ofsted requirements) when they are at odds with the teacher's personal commitment to geography curriculum making. However, the school context matters. In my research, I found the Heads of Department all trying to develop their curriculum, but in the schools with greater 'security' (in terms of higher results and more popularity with parents) there is more freedom to be curriculum makers than those with less security who are more tightly controlled and restricted by school management structures.

The role of teacher education and professional development

Hyper-socialisation has particular implications for both initial teacher education and ongoing professional development. Curriculum making is a theory now taught to many geography teachers entering the profession (see Biddulph, Lambert and Balderstone 2015). However, in the speeded-up world of late capitalism, 'what works' has immediate traction with teachers. Across society at all levels a 'demotic turn' (to ordinary people) and a suspicion, a rejection even, of 'expert' authority can leave doubt over the value of theory being taught – this doubt can extend to new teachers and their school colleagues. This is a real danger for teacher education. The issue is not usually with flaws in the theories, but in unrealistic expectations of what the theory will do for the teacher. Furthermore, unrealistic expectations of quick fixes are linked to the speeded-up world of late capitalism and so this problem is exacerbated. Morgan (2010) explains this rejection of theory well. He argues that new teachers may reject theory when it seems 'far removed from their experience of actual classrooms' (2010: 30). He explains that theory suffers from an 'idealist legacy in geography teaching' (2010: 29), which fails to locate theory in historical (social, economic and political) contexts. This is all the more reason to help teachers to understand that how their practice 'feels' can be explained by their location in late capitalism and hyper-socialised curriculum enactment.

Teacher education can support teachers' understanding of the social contexts in which they enact the curriculum and how they may become curriculum makers. Today there are changing influences over curriculum enactment, including the internet, the changing way in which the young person is conceived as consumer-producer and how intense accountability can distract from 'curriculum thinking'. Resilience increases when the geography teacher self-identifies as curriculum maker. Their curriculum leadership flourishes through good communication within the department in a critical and open culture with a shared commitment to geography curriculum making. Teacher education can help this critical stance by using curriculum making as a conceptual model for reflection on what and how to teach. In both their initial education and ongoing professional development, teachers can reflect critically on the influences over their own curriculum enactment to develop attitudes, values and beliefs that support them becoming curriculum makers. For example, the teacher could compare the curriculum making model (Figure 2) with the socially contextualised curriculum making model (Figure 12) to examine her practice, or that of other teachers that they observe in a geography department.

Teacher education and continuing professional development can help geography teachers to understand that curriculum making is contingent on the power and control of society at that time. With such understanding the teacher in late capitalist times can recognise that their agency to make the curriculum requires them to identify as 'curriculum maker' (Mitchell and Lambert 2015). By recognising that curriculum enactment has become 'hyper-socialised' both new and experienced geography teachers are better prepared to resist the pressures of late capitalism, which threaten geography curriculum making.

The importance of a curriculum rationale – why does subject knowledge matter?

Hyper-socialisation, which influences the enacted curriculum, is countered by encouraging the teacher to see the 'bigger picture' beyond the dominant performativity and results culture in education. The curriculum making model encourages the teacher to focus on three things: the child; the subject; their teaching. At an even more fundamental level, the focus can be on aims and purposes – what should this curriculum lead to? One way to answer this is by using a human 'capability' approach to education. We can ask: in what ways should the curriculum (and the powerful knowledge within it) transform a person, giving them capabilities, of which they would otherwise be deprived? Some geography educators have embraced this by linking human capabilities theory (see Sen 1995 and Nussbaum 2011) to geography in a notion of 'Geocapabilities' (Lambert, Solem and Tani 2015). At the time of writing a project is underway to explore how far a 'Geocapabilities' approach can support the curriculum making of teachers working under pressure in challenging schools (not unlike some in the case study schools presented here) so that children gain better access to powerful disciplinary knowledge (PDK). It is possible to describe the transformative potential of PDK. With the PDK of geography, children can: analyse the experiences and events they will encounter using geographical concepts (such as scale, inter-connection and environment); be empowered with critical awareness of knowledge claims (understand *how* they know); and able to participate in important debates that shape the future (see Maude 2016).

Going back to the fundamentals of *why* we are teaching a subject has to underpin the curriculum question – *what* shall we teach (these young people)? Teachers must be encouraged to return constantly to the curriculum question if we are to avoid hyper-socialisation drawing curriculum thinking away from the teacher to … somewhere else. That 'somewhere' is difficult to identify, let alone to control or regulate for quality. The subject teacher is best placed to be the curriculum maker and they should be encouraged and supported to take on this role and responsibility.

Suggestions for further research

Curriculum continues to be a 'significant gap in geography education research' (Roberts 2015: 49). My research findings contribute to the sub-field of geography curriculum research and to the wider field of curriculum studies. The idea of curriculum making (Lambert and Morgan 2010) is a powerful one, which has gained considerable purchase in geography education, being a common feature of many initial teacher education programmes and it has informed debates about curriculum, knowledge and the teacher's role across subjects. By offering a social-economic explanation for the influences over teachers' curriculum work, I have sought to develop the understanding of curriculum making in the real-world contexts of curriculum enactment.

I have described the key finding in my research as 'hyper-socialised' curriculum enactment to capture the society-curriculum-teacher relationship in recent times. I hope that this contributes to the ongoing debate about what it means to be a subject teacher (in late capitalism) and the teacher's relationship to subject knowledge in the curriculum. Better understanding of how the curriculum is enacted in challenging circumstances (the current times) can allow geography teachers and educators to identify the barriers and threats to curriculum making. In doing so, teachers and educators can become better equipped to 'navigate' their way toward the process of curriculum making called for by Lambert and Morgan (2010).

However, there is more to be done. The world continues to change. The future feels fluid and uncertain as late capitalism deepens and technology extends its reach into our lives and work. This context of change alone invites ongoing research in the long term as the question 'How are teachers enacting the curriculum in this day and age?' will remain pertinent and is always likely to throw up new insights. More immediately, we can 'test' and explore the notion of hyper-socialised curriculum enactment in different contexts (internationally and across subjects), we can examine the role and potential of teacher education for developing teachers as curriculum makers in challenging circumstances and we can look closely at how teachers under pressure develop their resilience as curriculum makers. I suggest research questions and a possible approach for this agenda as follows:

What role does teacher education play in developing curriculum makers?

I found that individual teachers can be geography curriculum makers when they have strong geography teacher identities and the confidence to resist the pressures of the times, which threaten to turn attention away from curriculum thinking. This implies that teacher education, both as initial preparation and as continuing professional development, can play a key role in nurturing the teacher's curriculum leadership and identity as curriculum maker. However, it is not yet clear how (and how effectively) this happens. Further research could illuminate the relationship of teacher education to curriculum making, including the effectiveness and impact of particular approaches. A case study approach, exploring in depth the experiences of teachers with a range of professional development experiences would be a suitable methodology.

How does an identity as geography curriculum maker develop?

Linked to the first question is research that could lead to better understanding of how teachers develop an identity as curriculum maker. This could help to develop effective programmes of initial teacher education and further professional development, as well as potentially influencing whole school approaches to curriculum development and system wide policy (for example, on how national curricula are developed and implemented). My research question is challenging, involving a highly complex process that is difficult to 'surface' and invites a range of possible methodologies. Case study, narrative and life history approaches might each be adopted for such research. Ethnography could also be a valid methodology to explore the nuance of teacher identity development. A longitudinal study, for example tracking teachers from their decision to train as geography teachers through their early career, might also be illuminative.

How far is 'hyper-socialised' curriculum enactment reflected in other contexts?

My research was limited to a small scale of four case studies in London in 2014. While 'late capitalist society' is a global phenomenon, I found that the national and local context influences curriculum enactment. The society/curriculum making (and enactment) relationship should be explored in a range of school types (including academies and the independent sector) in England and in other countries with a range of approaches to education and contrasting curriculum value/belief system histories, for example Finland, Singapore and particular states of the USA. Comparative methodology is appropriate for such research across cultures. Some quantitative approaches, such as the use of questionnaire data, could be used to research the influences over teachers' curriculum enactment across a large sample of schools, for example, to compare curriculum enactment between state and independent schools in England.

Is hyper-socialised curriculum enactment reflected by other subjects?

I have described curriculum enactment in the context of geography. Geography is distinctive in its breadth of content, tendency to change as a discipline and association with the concept of 'curriculum making', giving geography a particular openness to the curriculum question of what to teach and therefore a particularly significant role for the teacher as curriculum maker. However, this leaves a question of how other subject curricula are enacted (and 'made') by teachers. The key findings of my research may apply to a greater or lesser extent to other school subjects and their teachers.

Research into other subjects building on this book could give wider reach and currency to 'hyper-socialised' curriculum enactment and its implications for teacher education. Such research could also help to identify how far geography is a 'special' subject in terms of the significance of curriculum making. Such research could be approached by a mixed methods approach. Comparative research could be used with large samples, for example using questionnaire data, to give broad differences between subjects and this could be followed by case studies to explore a small number of teachers' curriculum enactment, in depth.

REFERENCES

Aglietta, M. (1979) *A Theory of Capitalist Regulation: The US experience*. London: Verso.

Alexander, R. (2009) *Culture and Pedagogy: International Comparisons in Primary Education*. Oxford: Blackwell.

Apple, M. (2000) *Teachers and Texts*. London: Routledge.

Apple, M. (2004) *Ideology and Curriculum*, 3rd Edition. New York: RoutledgeFalmer.

Austin, J.L. (1962) *How to Do Things with Words*. Oxford: Clarendon Press.

Ball, S. (2000) *Sociology of Education: Major Themes*. Abingdon, UK: Routledge.

Ball, S. and Bowe, R. (1992) Subject Departments and the 'Implementation' of National Curriculum Policy: An Overview of the Issues. *Journal of Curriculum Studies*, 24(2) pp. 97–115.

Barber, M. (1997) *The Learning Game: Arguments for an Education Revolution*. London: Indigo.

Barber, M. (2009) We are the People We've been Waiting For, online content http://wearethepeoplemovie.com (last accessed 30 November 2010).

Barnett, R. (2011) Learning About Learning: A Conundrum and a Possible Resolution. *London Review of Education*, 9(1), pp. 5–13.

Barth, R.S. (1972) *Open Education and the American School*. Berlin, Germany: Schocken Books.

Barthes, R. and Balzac, H. (1974) *S/Z*. New York: Farrar, Straus & Giroux.

Baudrillard, J. (1994) *Simulation and Simulcara*. Ann Arbor, MI: University of Michigan Press.

Bauman, Z. (2001) *Liquid Modernity*. Cambridge, UK: Polity.

Bauman, Z. (2005) *Liquid Life*. Cambridge, UK: Polity.

Beare, H. (2001) *Creating the Future School*. London: RoutledgeFalmer.

Beck, U. (1992) *Risk Society: Towards a New Modernity*. London: Sage.

Bernstein, B. (1990) *Class, Codes and Control: Volume IV. The Structuring of Pedagogic Discourse*. London: Routledge.

Bernstein, B. (2000) *Pedagogy, Symbolic Control and Identity: Theory, Research, Critique*. Boston, MA: Rowman & Littlefield.

Biddulph, M. (2012) Young People's Geographies and the School Curriculum. *Geography*. 97(3), pp. 155–162.

Biddulph, M. (2013) Where is the curriculum created? In Lambert, D. and Jones, M. (eds) *Debates in Geography Education*. London: Routledge. pp. 129–142.

Biddulph, M., Lambert, D. and Balderstone, D. (2015) *Learning to Teach Geography in the Secondary School*, 3rd Edition. Abingdon, UK: Routledge.

Biesta, G. (1995) Postmodernism and the Repoliticization of Education. *Interchange*, 26(2), p. 161.

Biesta, G. (2013) *The Beautiful Risk of Education*. London: Paradigm.

Blishen, E. (1955) *Roaring Boys: A Schoolmaster's Agony*. London: Thames & Hudson.

Bloom, B.S. (1956) *Taxonomy of Educational Objectives, The Classification of Educational Goals – Handbook I: Cognitive Domain*. New York: McKay.

Bobbitt, F. (1916) *What the Schools Teach and Might Teach*. Ohio, OH: Cleveland Foundation.

Bourdieu, P. (1984) *Distinction: A Social Critique of the Judgement of Taste*. Abingdon, UK: Routledge.

Bourdieu, P. and Passeron, J. (1977) *Reproduction in Education, Society and Culture*. London: Sage.

Breslin, A. (2005) Chapter 20 Curriculum, schooling and the purpose of learning. In Alexander, T. and Potter, J. (2005) *Education for Change*. Abingdon, UK: RoutledgeFalmer.

Bridle, J. (2018) *New Dark Age: Technology and End of the Future*. London: Verso.

Brighouse, T. (1994) The Magicians of the Inner City. *Times Educational Supplement*, 22 April 1994, pp. 29–30.

Brooks, C. (2006) Geographical Knowledge and Teaching Geography. *International Research in Geographical and Environmental Education*, 15(4), pp. 353–368.

Brooks, C. (2011) Why Geography Teachers' Subject Knowledge Matters. *Geography*, 95(3), pp. 143–147.

Brooks, C. (2012) Changing Times in England: The Influence on Geography Teachers' Professional Practice. *International Research in Geographical and Environmental Education*, 21(4), pp. 297–308.

Brooks, C. (2016) *Teacher Subject Identity in Professional Practice: Teaching with a Professional Compass*. Abingdon, UK: Routledge.

Brooks, C. (2017) Pedagogy and Identity in Initial Teacher Education: Developing a Professional Compass. *Geography*, 102(1), pp. 44–50.

Bruner, J. (1966) *Toward a Theory of Instruction*. New York: W.W. Norton.

Butler, J. (2010) Performative Agency. *Journal of Cultural Economy*, 3(2), pp. 147–161.

Butt, G. (2008) Is the Future Secure for Geography Education? *Geography*, 93(3), pp. 158–165.

Butt, G. (2011) Globalisation, Geography Education and the Curriculum: What are the Challenges for Curriculum Makers in Geography? *The Curriculum Journal*, 22(3), pp. 423–437.

Butt, G. (2017) Globalisation: A Brief Exploration of its Challenging, Contested and Competing Concepts. *Geography*, 104(1), pp. 10–16.

Carr, D. (2003) *Making Sense of Education: An Introduction to the Philosophy and Theory of Education and Teaching*. London: RoutledgeFalmer.

Chorley, R. and Haggett, P. (1967) *Models in Geography*. London: Methuen.

Claxton, G.L. (1999) *Wise Up: The Challenge of Lifelong Learning*. London: Bloomsbury.

Connell, R. (2009) Good Teachers on Dangerous Ground: Towards a New View of Teacher Quality and Professionalism. *Critical Studies in Education*, 50(3) pp. 213–228.

Connelly, F.M. and Clandinin, D.J. (1988) *Teachers as Curriculum Planners*. New York: Teachers College Press.

Cordingley, P., Bell, M. and Thomason, S. (2004) The Impact of Collaborative CPD on Classroom Teaching and Learning, University of London, Social Science Research Unit. Evidence for Policy and Practice Information and Co-ordinating Centre. Institute of Education, University of London, online content http://eppi.ioe.ac.uk/EPPIWebContent/reel/review_groups/CPD/cpd_protocol2.pdf (last accessed 14 August 2010).

Crombie White, R. (1997) *Curriculum Innovation: A Celebration of Classroom Practice*. Oxford: Oxford University Press.

Curtis, A. (2016) Hyper Normalisation. London: BBC, online content www.bbc.co.uk/p rogrammes/p04b183c (last accessed July 2019).

Davies, I. (1969) Education and Social Science. *New Society*, 13(345), pp. 710–711.

Department for Education (2010) The Importance of Teaching. The Schools' White Paper, online content http://education.gov.uk/publications (last accessed 3 December 2012).

Department for Education (2011) The Framework for the National Curriculum. A Report by the Expert Panel for the National Curriculum Review. London: Department for Education.

Department for Education (2016) Educational Excellence Everywhere. The Schools and Teaching White Paper, online content https://gov.uk/government/publications/educa tional-excellence-everywhere (last accessed 23 May 2016).

Dewey, J. (1916) *Democracy and Education: An Introduction to the Philosophy of Education*. New York: Macmillan.

Dweck, C. (2006) *Mindset: The New Psychology of Success*. New York: Ballantine Books.

Ecclestone, K. and Hayes, D. (2009) *The Dangerous Rise of Therapeutic Education*. Abingdon, UK: Routledge.

Eisner, E.W. (1979) *The Educational Imagination: On the Design and Evaluation of School Programs*. New York: MacMillan Publishing.

Eisner, E.W. (1982) *Cognition and Curriculum: A Basis for Deciding What to Teach*. New York: Longman.

Eisner, E.W. (1998a) *The Kind of Schools We Need*. Portsmouth, NH: Heinemann.

Eisner, E.W. (1998b) *The Enlightened Eye – Qualitative Inquiry and the Enhancement of Practice*. New Jersey, NJ: Prentice Hall.

Eisner, E.W. (2002) *The Educational Imagination – On the Design and Evaluation of School Programs*, 4th Edition. New Jersey, NJ: Prentice Hall.

Elliott, A. (2009) *Contemporary Social Theory – An Introduction*. Abingdon, UK: Routledge.

Fielding, M. and Moss, P. (2011) *Radical Education and the Common School: A Democratic Alternative*. Abingdon, UK: Routledge.

Fien, J. (1999) Towards a Map of Commitment: A Socially Critical Approach to Geographical Education. *International Research in Geographical and Environmental Education*, 8(2), pp. 140–157.

Firth, R. (2011a) Debates about knowledge and the curriculum: some implications for geography education. In Butt, G. (ed.) *Geography, Education and the Future*. London: Continuum, pp. 141–164.

Firth, R. (2011b) Making Geography Visible as an Object of Study in the Secondary School Curriculum. *Curriculum Journal*, 22(3) pp. 289–315.

Firth, R. (2013) What constitutes knowledge in geography? In Lambert, D. and Jones, M. (eds) *Debates in Geography Education*. Abingdon, UK: Routledge, pp. 59–74.

Foucault, M. (1977) *Discipline and Punish: The Birth of the Prison*. New York: Pantheon.

Friedman, T. (2016) *Thank You for Being Late: An Optimist's Guide to Thriving in the Age of Accelerations*. New York City: Farrar, Straus & Giroux.

Furedi, F. (2009) *Wasted: Why Education Isn't Educating*. London: Continuum Press.

Ganti, T. (2014) Neoliberalism. *Annual Review of Anthropology*, 43, pp. 89–104.

Gardner, H. (1983) *Frames of Mind: The Theory of Multiple Intelligences*. New York: Basic Books.

Geographical Association (2009) A Different View – A Manifesto from the Geographical Association Manifesto, online content www.geography.org.uk/GA-Manifesto-for-geo graphy (last accessed 10 June 2019).

Geographical Association (2011) GA Curriculum Proposals and Rationale, online content http://geography.org.uk/getinvolved/geographycurriculumconsultation (last accessed 7 October 2011).

Giddens, A. (2000) *The Third Way and its Critics*. Cambridge, UK: Polity.

Giroux, H.A. (2005) *On Critical Pedagogy*. New York: Continuum.

Giroux, H.A. (2005a) *Border Crossings: Cultural Workers and the Politics of Education*. New York: Routledge.

Goepel, J. (2013) Upholding Public Trust: An Examination of Teacher Professionalism and the Use of Teachers' Standards in England. *Teacher Development*, 16(4) pp. 489–505.

Goodson, I.F. (1998) Becoming a school subject. In Goodson, I.F., Anstead, C.J. and Mangam, J.M. (eds) *Subject Knowledge: Readings for the Study of School Subjects*. London: Falmer Press.

Goudie, A. and Spooner, D. (1993) Schools and Universities – the Great Divide. *Geography*, 78(4) pp. 338–338.

Gramsci, A. (1971) *Selections from the Prison Notebooks of Antonio Gramsci*. London: Lawrence & Wishart.

Graves, N. (1975) *Geography in Education*. London: Heinemann Educational Books.

Graves, N. (1979) *Curriculum Planning in Geography*. London: Heinemann Educational.

Harari, Y.N. (2017) *Homo Deus: A Brief History of Tomorrow*. London: Vintage.

Hartley, D. (1997) *Re-Schooling Society*. London: Falmer Press.

Harvey, D. (1990) *The Condition of Postmodernity: An Enquiry into the Origins of Cultural Change*. Oxford: Blackwell.

Heafford, M. (1967) *Pestalozzi: His Thought and its Relevance Today*. London: Methuen.

Herod, A. (2011) *Scale*. Abingdon, UK: Routledge.

Hicks, D. (1995) *Visions of the Future – Why We Need to Teach for Tomorrow*. Stoke-on-Trent, UK: Trentham Books.

Hicks, D. (2008) A futures perspective: lessons from the school room. In Bussey, M.. Inayatullah, S. and Milojevic, I. (eds) *Alternative Educational Futures: Pedagogies for Emergent Worlds*. Rotterdam, Netherlands: Sense Publishers.

Hicks, D. (2011) A Sustainable Future: Four Challenges for Geographers. *Geography*, 36(1) pp. 9–11.

Hicks, D. (2013) A Post-Carbon Geography. *Geography*, 38(3) pp. 94–96.

Hicks, D. and Holden, C. (2007) *Teaching the Global Dimension, Key Principles and Effective Practice*. London: Routledge.

Hidi, S. and Ainley, M. (2002) Interest and adolescence. In Pajares, F. and Urdan, T. *Academic Motivation of Adolescents*. Charlotte, NC: Information Age Publishing.

House of Commons Select Committee (n.d.) online content http://publications.parliament. uk/pa/cm200607/cmselect/cmeduski/249/24902.htm (last accessed 5 May 2012).

Hirsch, E.D. (1987) *Cultural Literacy*. New York: Houghton Mifflen.

Hirsch, E.D. (2011) Core Knowledge Sequence, online content www.coreknowledge.org (last accessed 15 March 2011).

Hirst, P.H. (1974) *Knowledge and the Curriculum*. London: Routledge.

House of Commons (2017) Multi-Academy Trusts Seventh Report of Session of Education Committee 2016–17, online content https://publications.parliament.uk/pa/cm201617/cmselect/cmeduc/204/204.pdf (last accessed July 2019).

Huckle, J. (1985) The future of school geography. In Johnston, R. (ed.) *The Future of Geography*. London: Methuen.

Huckle, J. (1988) Geography and world citizenship. In Fien, J. and Gerber, R. (eds.), *Teaching Geography for a Better World*. Edinburgh, UK: Oliver & Boyd.

Huckle, J. and Sterling, S. (1996) *Education for Sustainability*. London: Earthscan.

Jameson, F. (1992) *Postmodernism: Or, the Cultural Logic of Late Capitalism (Poetics of Social Forms)*. Durham, NC: Duke University Press.

Jones, K. (2003) *Education in Britain: 1944 to the Present*. Cambridge, UK: Polity.

Kelly, V. (2008) *The Curriculum: Theory and Practice*, 6th Edition. London: Sage.

Kent, W.A. (1996) Process and Pattern of a Curriculum Innovation, unpublished PhD thesis. Institute of Education, University of London.

Kent, W.A. (2000) *Reflective Practice in Geography Teaching*. London: Sage.

Kohn, A. (1999) *The Schools Our Children Deserve: Moving Beyond Traditional Classrooms*. New York: Houghton Mifflin Harcourt.

Kress, G. (2006) Learning and curriculum: Agency, ethics and aesthetics in an age of instability. In Moore, A. (ed.) *School, Society and Curriculum*. Abingdon, UK: Routledge.

Kropotkin, P. (1885) What Geography Ought to Be. *The Nineteenth Century*, 18, pp. 940–955.

Lambert, D. (1999) Geography and Moral Education in a Super Complex World: The Significance of Values Education and Some Remaining Dilemmas. *Philosophy and Geography*, 2(1), pp. 5–17.

Lambert, D. (2009a) A Different View. *Geography*, 94(2) pp. 119–125.

Lambert, D. (2010b) Reflecting on geography teaching in practice. In Brooks, C. (ed.) *Studying PGCE Geography at M Level*. London: Routledge.

Lambert, D. (2011) Reviewing the Case for Geography, and the "Knowledge Turn" in the English National Curriculum. *Curriculum Journal*, 22(2), pp. 243–264.

Lambert, D. (2015a) Curriculum Thinking, 'Capabilities' and the Place of Geographical Knowledge in Schools. *Journal of Educational Research on Social Studies*, 81, pp. 1–11.

Lambert, D.M. (2015b) Geography. In Wyse, D. and Hayward, L. (eds) *The SAGE Handbook of Curriculum, Pedagogy and Assessment*. London: Sage.

Lambert, D. and Biddulph, M. (2015) The Dialogic Space Offered by Curriculum Making in the Process of Learning to Teach, and the Creation of a Progressive Knowledge-Led Curriculum. *Asia-Pacific Journal of Teacher Education*, 43(3), pp. 210–224.

Lambert, D. and Hopkin, J. (2014) A Possibilist Analysis of the Geography National Curriculum in England. *International Research in Geographical and Environmental Education*, 23(1), pp. 64–77.

Lambert, D. and Morgan, J. (2010) *Teaching Geography 11–18 – A Conceptual Approach*. Maidenhead, UK: Open University Press.

Lambert, D., Solem, M. and Tani, S. (2015) Achieving Human Potential Through Geography Education: A Capabilities Approach to Curriculum-making in Schools. *Annals of the Association of American Geographers*, 105(4), pp. 723–735.

Lambert, D. and Widdowson, J. (2006) Using geography textbooks. In Lambert, D. and Young, M. (2014) *Knowledge and the Future School – Curriculum and Social Justice*. London: Bloomsbury.

Lash, S. and Urry, J. (1987) *The End of Organised Capitalism*. Cambridge, UK: Polity Press.

Lave, J. and Wenger, E. (1991) *Situated Learning: Legitimate Peripheral Participation*. Cambridge, UK: Cambridge University Press.

Lawton, D. (1980) *The Politics of School Curriculum*. Abingdon, UK: Routledge.

Lowe, R. (2007) *The Death of Progressive Education: How Teachers Lost Control of the Classroom*. Abingdon, UK: Routledge.

Lyotard, J.F. (1984) *The Postmodern Condition: A Report on Knowledge*. Kings Lyn, UK: Biddles.

Mandel, E. (1998) *Late Capitalism*. London: Verso.

Marsden, W.E. (1976) *Evaluating the Geography Curriculum*. Edinburgh, UK: Oliver & Boyd.

Marsden, W.E. (1997) On Taking the Geography Out of Geographical Education: Some Historical Pointers. *Geography*, 82(3), pp. 241–252.

Maude, A. (2016) What Might Powerful Geographical Knowledge Look Like? *Geography*, 101, pp. 70–76.

McCormick, R. and Murphy, P. (2000) Curriculum – The case for a focus on learning. In Ben-Peretz, M., Brown, S. and Moon, B. (eds), *The Routledge International Companion to Education*. London: Routledge, pp. 130–141.

McCulloch, G., Helsby, G. and Knight, P. (2000) *The Politics of Professionalism: Teachers and the Curriculum*. London: Continuum.

McElroy, B. (1980) School Based Curriculum Development: An Investigation into Teachers Perceptions of Their Role, unpublished dissertation for MA Geography in Education: Institute of Education, University of London.

McKernan, J. (1996) *Curriculum Action Research: A Handbook of Methods and Resources for the Reflective Practitioner*, 2nd Edition. London: Kogan Page.

Mirowski, P. (2008) Defining neoliberalism. In Mirowski, P. and Plehwe, D. (2009) (eds) *The Road from Mont Pelerin*. Cambridge, MA: Harvard University Press, pp. 417–415.

Mitchell, D. (2006) Local Solutions: An Approach to Curriculum Development in Geography, *Geography*, 91(2), pp. 150–157.

Mitchell, D. (2013a) What Controls the 'Real' Curriculum? *Teaching Geography*, 38(2), pp. 60–62.

Mitchell, D. (2013b) How do we deal with controversial issues in a 'relevant' school geography? In Lambert, D. and Jones, M. (eds) *Debates in Geography Education*. Abingdon, UK: Routledge.

Mitchell, D. (2016) Geography Teachers and Curriculum Making in Changing Times. *International Research in Geographical and Environmental Education*, 25(2), pp. 121–133.

Mitchell, D. (2017) Geography Curriculum Making in Changing Times. Unpublished thesis submitted as part fulfilment of the requirements for the degree of Doctor of Philosophy at University College London.

Mitchell, D. and Lambert, D. (2015) Subject Knowledge and Teacher Preparation in English Secondary Schools: The Case of Geography. *Teacher Development: An international journal of teachers' professional development*, 19(3), pp. 365–380.

Moore, A. (2004) *The Good Teacher*. London: RoutledgeFalmer.

Moore, A. (2015) *Understanding the School Curriculum*. Abingdon, UK: Routledge.

Moore, R. and Young, M. (2001) Knowledge and the Curriculum in the Sociology of Education: Towards a Reconceptualisation. *British Journal of Sociology of Education*, 22(4), pp. 445–461.

Morgan, J. (2002) Teaching Geography for a Better World? The Postmodern Challenge and Geography Education. *International Research in Geographical and Environmental Education*, 11(1), pp. 15–29.

Morgan, J. (2003) Imagined Country: National Environmental Ideologies in School Geography Textbooks. *Antipode: a radical journal of geography*, 35(3), pp. 444–462.

Morgan, A. (2006) Argumentation, Geography, Education and ICT. *Geography*, 91(2), pp. 126–140.

Morgan, J. (2009) Challenging Assumptions. *Geography*, 94(2), pp. 115–117.

Morgan, J. (2010) What makes a 'good' geography teacher? In Brooks, C. (ed.) *Studying PGCE Geography at M Level*. Abingdon, UK: Routledge.

Morgan, J. (2011) What is Radical School Geography Today? *Forum*, 53(1), pp. 116–127.

Morgan, J. (2012) *Teaching Secondary Geography as if the Planet Mattered*. London: Routledge.

Morgan, J. (2014a) Foreword in Lambert, D. and Young, M. (2014) *Knowledge and the Future School – Curriculum and Social Justice*. London: Bloomsbury, pp. ix–xii.

Morgan, J. (2014b) 21st Century Learning – Again, Schooling Capitalism, wordpress blog, online content https://schoolingcapitalism.wordpress.com/2014/03/25/21st-century-lea rning-again/ (last accessed 24 March 2016).

Morgan, J. and Lambert, D. (2005) *Geography: Teaching School Subjects 11–18*. London: Routledge.

Naidoo, R., Shankar, A. and Veer, E. (2011) The Consumerist Turn in Higher Education: Policy Aspirations and Outcomes. *Journal of Marketing Management*, 27(11–12), pp. 1142–1162.

Nussbaum, M. (2013) *Creating Capabilities: The Human Development Approach*. Cambridge, MA: Harvard University Press.

Oates, T. (2011) Could Do Better: Using International Comparisons to Refine the National Curriculum in England. *Curriculum Journal*, 22(2) pp. 121–150.

Ofsted (2004) The Annual Report of Her Majesty's Chief Inspector of Schools 2003/04. https://gov.uk/government/uploads/system/uploads/attachment_data/file/235467/0195.pdf (last accessed 5 May 2016).

Ofsted (2011) Geography – Learning to make a world of difference. Department of Education, online content, http://ofsted.gov.uk/Ofsted-home/Publications-and-research/Browse-all- by/Documents-by-type/Thematic-reports/Geography-Learning-to-make-a-world-of-difference (last accessed 13 April 2011).

Oram, R. (1973) An Action Frame of Reference as a Register for Curriculum Discourse. *Journal of Curriculum Studies*, 10(2), pp.135–148.

Pepper, D. (1989) *The Roots of Modern Environmentalism*. Abingdon, UK: Routledge.

Peters, R.S. (1965) Education as Initiation. Inaugural lecture. University of London Institute of Education.

Piaget, J. (1964) *The Early Growth of Logic in the Child*. London: Routledge.

Plant, R. (2012) *The Neoliberal State*. Oxford: Oxford University Press.

Postman, N. (1996) *The End of Education: Redefining the Value of School*. New York: Vintage Books.

Prasad, M. (2006) *The Politics of Free Markets: The Rise of Neoliberal Economic Policies in Britain, France, Germany, and the United States*. Chicago, IL: University of Chicago Press.

Pring, R. (2013) *The Life and Death of Secondary Education for All*. Abingdon, UK: Routledge.

Puttick, S. (2015a) Recontextualising Knowledge for Lessons. *Teaching Geography*, 40(1), pp. 29–31.

Puttick, S. (2015b) Geography Teachers' Subject Knowledge: An Ethnographic Study of Three Secondary School Geography Departments. Unpublished PhD thesis.

Puttick, S. (2016) An Analysis of Individual and Departmental Geographical Stories, and their Role in Sustaining Teachers. *International Research in Geographical and Environmental Education*, published online, pp. 1–16.

Rawling, E.M. (1996) The impact of the national curriculum on school-based curriculum development in secondary geography. In Kent, A., Lambert, D., Naish, M. and SlaterF. (eds) *Geography in Education: Viewpoints on Teaching and Learning*. Cambridge: Cambridge University Press.

Rawling, E.M. (2001) *Changing the Subject: The Impact of National Policy on School Geography 1980–2000*. Sheffield, UK: Geographical Association.

Rawling, E. (2015) Spotlight on: Curriculum Change and Examination Reform for Geography 14–19. *Geography*, 100(3), pp 164–167.

Rawling, E. (2016) The Geography Curriculum 5–19: What Does it All Mean? *Teaching Geography*, 41(1), pp. 6–9.

Roberts, M. (1996) Interpretations of The Geography National Curriculum: A Common Curriculum for All? *Journal of Curriculum Studies*, 27(2), pp. 187–205.

Roberts, M. (2003) *Learning through Enquiry: Making Sense of the Key Stage 3 Geography Curriculum*. Sheffield, UK: Geographical Association.

Roberts, M. (2010) Where's the Geography? Reflections on Being an External Examiner. *Teaching Geography*, 35(3), pp. 112–113.

Roberts, M. (2011) Conclusion. In Butt, G. (ed.) *Geography, Education and the Future*. New York: Continuum, pp. 244–253.

Roberts, M. (2015) Discussion to Part I. In Butt, G. (ed.) *MasterClass in Geography Education: Transforming Teaching and Learning*. London: Bloomsbury, pp. 45–50.

Robins, K. and Webster, F. (1989) *The Technical Fix: Education, Computers and Industry*. London: Macmillan.

Ross, A. (2000) *Curriculum: Construction and Critique*. London: Falmer Press.

Rousseau, J. (1762a) *Emile*. Amsterdam, NL: J. Néaulme.

Rousseau, J. (1762b) *The Social Contract*. Amsterdam, NL: J. Néaulme.

Ryan, R.M. and Deci, E.L. (2000) Self-Determination Theory and the Facilitation of Intrinsic Motivation, Social Development and Well-Being. *American Psychologist*, 55(1), pp. 68–77.

Saussure, F. (1916) *Course in General Linguistics*. London: Fontana.

Sachs, J. (2003) *The Activist Teaching Profession*. Maidenhead, UK: Open University Press.

Schiro, M. (2008) *Curriculum Theory: Conflicting Visions and Enduring Concerns*. London: Sage.

Schiro, M. (2013) *Curriculum Theory: Conflicting Visions and Enduring Concerns*, 2nd Edition. London: Sage.

Schumpeter, J.A. (1994) *Capitalism, Socialism and Democracy*. London: George Allen & Unwin.

Scrimshaw, P. (1983) *Educational Ideologies: Purpose and Planning in the Curriculum*. Milton Keynes, UK: Open University.

Sen, A. (1995) *Inequality Reexamined*. Oxford: Oxford University Press.

Skilbeck, M. (ed.) (1990) *School Based Curriculum Development*. London: Paul Chapman.

Slater, F. (1982) *Learning Through Geography: An Introduction to Activity Planning*. London: Heinemann.

Slater, F. (1993) *Learning through Geography*. Indiana, PA: Indiana University of Pennsylvania: National Council for Geographic Education.

Smith, A. (1993) *An Inquiry into the Nature and Causes of the Wealth of Nations*. Oxford: Oxford University Press.

Somekh, B. (2006) New ways of teaching and learning in the digital age. In Moore, A. (ed.) *School, Society and Curriculum*. Abingdon, UK: Routledge.

Standish, A. (2003) Constructing a Value Map. *Geography*, 88(2), pp. 149–151.

Standish, A. (2004) Valuing (Adult) Geographic Knowledge. *Geography*, 89(1), pp. 89–91.

Standish, A. (2012) *The False Promise of Global Learning – Why Education Needs Boundaries*. London: Continuum.

Standish, A. (2009) *Global Perspectives in the Geography Curriculum*. London: Routledge.

Stannard, K. (2003) Earth to Academia: On the Need to Reconnect University and School Geography. *Area*, 35(3), pp. 316–332.

Steger, M. and Roy, R. (2010) *Neoliberalism: A Very Short Introduction*. Oxford: Oxford University Press.

Stenhouse, L. (1975) *An Introduction to Curriculum Research and Development*. London: Heinemann Educational.

Sterling, S. and Huckle, J. (eds) (1996) *Education for Sustainability*. Abingdon, UK: Earthscan.

Sterling, S. (2010) Living 'In' The Earth – Towards an Education for Our Times. *The Journal of Education for Sustainable Development*, 4(2), pp. 213–217.

Taylor, P.H. and Richards, C.M. (1985) *An Introduction to Curriculum Studies*, 2nd Edition. Windsor, UK: NFER-Nelson.

The Guardian (2017) The Secret Teacher MATs Want Machines Not Mentors, online content www.theguardian.com/teacher-network/2017/aug/12/secret-teacher-multi-academy-trusts-want-machines-not-mentors

Turner, G. (2010) *Ordinary People and the Media: The Demotic Turn*. London: Sage.

Tyler, R. (1949) *Basic Principles of Curriculum and Instruction*. Chicago, IL: University of Chicago Press.

United Nations Convention on the Rights of the Child (2014) www.unicef.org.uk/what-we-do/un-convention-child-rights/ (last accessed July 2019).

Unwin, A. (1992) *The Place of Geography*. London: Longman.

Vygotsky, L.S. (1962) *Thought and Language*. Cambridge, MA: Massachusetts Institute of Technology Press.

Walford, R. (1981) Language, ideologies and geography teaching. In Walford, R. (ed.) *Signposts for Geography Teaching*. London: Longman, pp. 215–222.

Walford, R. (2001) *Geography in British Schools, 1850–2000: Making a World of Difference*. Abingdon, UK: Routledge.

Weber, E. (2007) Globalization, 'Local' Development, and Teachers' Work: A Research Agenda. *Review of Educational Research*, 77(3), pp. 279–308.

Wheelahan, L. (2010) *Why Knowledge Matters in Curriculum: A Social Realist Argument*. Abingdon, UK: Routledge.

White, J. (2006) The Myth of Multiple Intelligences. *Teaching Geography*, 31(2), pp. 82–83.

Wilkins, A. (2017) Rescaling the Local: Multi-Academy Trusts, Private Monopoly and Statecraft in England. *Journal of Educational Administration and History*, 49(2), pp. 171–185.

Winter, C. and Firth, R. (2007) Knowledge About Education for Sustainable Development: Four Case Studies ff Student Teachers in English Secondary Schools. *Journal of Education for Teaching*, 33(3) pp. 341–357.

Young, M. (1971) *Knowledge and Control: New Directions for the Sociology of Education*. London: Collier-Macmillan.

Young, M. (2009) The school curriculum, theories of reproduction and necessary knowledge. In Daniels, H., Lauder, H. and Porter, J. (eds.) *Knowledge, Values and Educational Policy: A Critical Perspective*, 2nd Edition. London: Routledge, pp. 10–17.

Young, M. and Lambert, D. (2014) *Knowledge and the Future School – Curriculum and Social Justice*. London: Bloomsbury.

Young, M. and Muller, J. (2010) Three Educational Scenarios for the Future: Lessons from the Sociology of Knowledge. *European Journal of Education*, 45(1), pp. 11–26.

INDEX

Locators in *italics* refer to figures and those in **bold** to tables.

Printed in Great Britain
by Amazon

80546067R00118